ONE MINUTE CRYING TIME

ONE MINUTE CRYING TIME

BARBARA EWING

MASSEY UNIVERSITY PRESS

IN NEW ZEALAND IN THE 1950S it was very expensive to make a telephone call from one part of the country to another. Toll calls, we called them. And the price of making a telephone call to another country in those years was prohibitive. It cost *£1 per minute* when I first arrived in London to telephone, or to be telephoned from, New Zealand, and I was living on about £5 per week. I was a student at the Royal Academy of Dramatic Art and my £5 per week had to cover rent and board and tube fares and tomato soup for lunch. So I kept in touch with friends and family by letter (and got into the habit of sticking their photographs on the walls of wherever I was living).

But one of the New Zealand telephone operators I had got to know earlier when I was 'sent away to the South Island' — a euphemism in those days for pregnant unmarried girls being dealt with, although in this case I was simply being sent away to the South Island — told me that the overseas operators (who connected calls manually in those long-ago days) had to stay on the line to make sure the connection was not lost. An agreement had to be made with the operator beforehand as to how long the call would be: it was conventionally three minutes. And as these expensive phone calls were almost always made only when it was a matter of life, or death, or heartbreak, the listening New Zealand operators — who had to interrupt to say, 'I'm sorry but your time is up' — were informally permitted to allow, as well as the three minutes, one minute crying time.

Today, with certain twenty-first-century technological and financial arrangements, I can phone for as long as I like from or to either country, and am permitted to cry — or laugh (hopefully without anyone listening in, though who knows) — for free.

MONDAY 1 JANUARY 1951

Stayed up on New Year's Eve to sing Auld Lang Syne at midnight. Drank ginger ale with Mum and Dad and Andrew. Ross was asleep. Tonight we left Wellington for Timaru. A calm night. We are sailing across Cook's Strait on the "Rangatira".

TUESDAY 2 JANUARY 1951

Landed at Lyttleton at 7am. Caught train to Christchurch. It was cold. Caught train to Timaru. We have got a house for us to stay in near where Nana and Granny live. It is very old-fashioned but nice. It has a poem over the lavatory. We saw Sound Shell concert at Caroline Bay. A fireworks display was very beautiful. Rockets were let off.

SATURDAY 6 JANUARY 1951

Saw Nana and Granny. Andrew and Ross and I gave them a concert with our gazoos. Then went on merry-go-round, Big Wheel and chair-o-plane. Went for two swims. Saw Sound

Shell concert. There were 2 Lady singers, 2 Men singers, 1 Guitar player, 1 Accordian player, 1 Tap Dancer and 2 Irish Dancers. And a Clown. There was a Nigger Minstrel Show before we came. Miss Caroline Bay was picked. It was Miss Catherine Jones, Balclutha. She intends to spend the £50 prize on an electric sewing machine.

SUNDAY 14 JANUARY 1951

My twelfth birthday! Dad and the boys gave me a Royal Family book and a cake of choc. Mummy gave me a brooch. Nana gave me a card and soap and powder and a bowl. I also got a writing pad, rubber, envelopes and Minties. And choc and lollies from Cousin Jack. We had a party tea. Then played paper games after tea with Dad.

FRIDAY 19 JANUARY 1951. BEST DAY

Went to Temuka in Rental Car to Uncle John's farm. Was on Betty the pony most of the time, trying to ride, also Uncle John milked the cows. He showed us how to put hens to sleep. He twirled them round with their heads under their wings. Then he put them on the ground and they were asleep. When they woke up they looked very surprised and sqwarked. Had a sing song before we went home.

SUNDAY 21 JANUARY 1951

Went to the Timaru Botanical Gardens in the afternoon while Dad and Mum took Nana and Granny for a ride. Met them at the Gardens and had an ice-cream. Granny is Dad's grandmother. Granny is nearly 100. She is deaf and so we shout to her. She talks funny. It is Scotland. Played Paper

Games after tea. Tomorrow before we go home will change my birthday Royal Family book to "Princess Margaret in Italy".

That poem over the lavatory in that rented house: I still remember it. We three kids thought it was very funny and rude (over a *lavatory*!) and we laughed and recited it to one another when no one was listening:

IF YOU'VE GOT A JOB TO DO, DO IT WELL.
IF IT'S ONE YOU WISH WAS THROUGH, DO IT WELL.

Once upon a time, so long ago and (some would say) so far away, as we set off to visit my father's family, including his sisters, his mother and his grandmother in the South Island of New Zealand, I — about to turn twelve and about to start my last year at primary school — started to keep a daily diary. Millions — trillions — of people keep diaries and journals recording their lives; who knows how many may have started before they were twelve and not missed one single day for 2400 days, but I was one of them. On the 2401st day I stopped, unable to write. I was then eighteen years old.

After that it became a journal, which I have never stopped writing. Until now.

❀

THERE IS A MĀORI EXPRESSION, *karanga mate*, which means to call death. And there is an old Māori belief: if you wrote a will, like the white men wrote wills: karanga mate.

When my husband, a New Zealand Māori, died and — like his parents before him — died without leaving a will (I know he too — a lecturer in Māori tertiary education — somewhere deep inside still believed in karanga mate), he left incalculable emotional, as well as legal, difficulties behind him.

After the long, sad, turmoiled days, I was finally on a twenty-seven hour flight back to London, crossing the world for what seemed like the thousandth time (but was perhaps about the 107th, and yes I do now worry about my carbon-dioxide footprint). Somewhere past Australia I was suddenly consumed with terror that the plane would crash, and my terror was not that I would die but that I would leave behind similar problems — I had no up-to-date will. High, high up in the sky, clouds often turn bright red at dusk, red like fire. In the olden days fires used to be lit along the New Zealand coastline between villages, as warnings. I stared out at the fire and felt my heart beating fast as the plane sped on and into the interminable dark night.

In London I immediately set about the task of, as they say, putting my affairs in order. And among my goods and chattels I had drawers and drawers of those old fading diaries and journals, and the only sensible thing to do with them was to burn them. I live in a London attic but some friends offered to make a bonfire at the bottom of their large garden.

As I was packing the diaries into cardboard boxes to take away for burning, I glanced at one or two of the very early ones . . .

. . . Terrible forms of torture in my Wellington suburban street in 1951 (apart from hard pinching) were horse bites and Chinese burns. Re-reading some of the old, very first, diaries has sometimes been like having a horse bite or a Chinese burn inside my head. Who in their right mind could bear to read, let alone enable anyone else to read, any of their adolescent, sentimental, excessive, self-obsessed writing? — don't be ridiculous.

But: one of my professions, in one of my countries, is Writer of Historical Novels. I therefore am slightly obsessive about finding old papers and letters and records concerning the people I am writing about: they are so often very revealing and occasionally genuinely exciting. (I stood up with a red face shouting 'WHAT?' in the British Library when I was researching for a novel that became *The Petticoat Men,* because by pure chance I had found *undiscovered information* that might solve a puzzling 1870s court trial I knew about — and I had to leave the Reading Room to compose myself.)

Considering my ignominious record in the History Department at Victoria University of Wellington, it is odd to record not only that I write historical novels but that I also have a strange fascination with 'touching history': other times, other countries, other lives. Somehow to actually — as well as learn — *connect.*

For instance. At the end of the eighteenth century one of Napoleon's scholar-soldiers in Egypt recognised that one of the huge old stones holding up other old stones used to make one of the coastal forts had Greek writing carved into it — alongside some of the mysterious, untranslatable Egyptian hieroglyphs. This ancient stone, which the soldier had carefully had removed, became known as the Rosetta Stone; it was the key, finally, to *unlocking* those unfathomable hieroglyphs and the culture that made them. Two centuries later I had gone to Egypt to research my novel *Rosetta.* And I stood there, on the site of that old fort: an odd, eerie, 'connecting' moment for me. Because (as unlikely as this may sound) inside the closed British Museum in London some years earlier, in the middle of the night, I had — for some instinctive, unexplainable reason — put my arms around that *actual* Rosetta Stone from Egypt, *the very stone* that French soldier had found, and I had hugged it, possibly a prosecutable offence. There, in the empty, dimly lit, silent exhibition room in a museum: carved figures, and tombs of pharaohs, and an old Egyptian stone. (These days the Rosetta Stone is safely locked in a glass case, out of the reach of vandals like me.)

Perhaps my weirdest experience of 'touching history' was when I was invited to take my one-woman play about Alexandra Kollontai, the only woman in Lenin's first Cabinet after the Russian Revolution, to the Soviet Union during the last years of Gorbachev's leadership, the time of *perestroika*. In Moscow I met Alexandra's grandson, Vladimir Kollontai, and his wife Ritta. They were an elderly couple but we became friendly, talked much of his grandmother, and eventually they asked if they could come to stay with me in London. I gave them my bed, and in the night I suddenly thought in stunned, somehow incredulous amazement: *Alexandra Kollontai's grandson is sleeping in my bed.*

However.

Heightened blood pressure and palpitations, nightmares and dreams have been my reactions to opening old diaries that have inside them a daily, factual, emotional record that touches the history of my *own* life. It's all very well, in later years, to have — in your head — some version of your life (in this case, crossed countries, crossed cultures, crossed careers) as you remember it. But how can you hold on to that securely if you open a notebook and it is all written down there, in your own handwriting, every day — day by day by day by day by day — and *not* always as you remember?

Some of these early diary entries record events that I can still easily recall: a school friend's pretty mother, when we were twelve, playing the piano and singing 'Paper Doll', and her drunk husband coming home, and no carpet on the floor. But also: some entries are *different* from what I thought I knew still so clearly. Not just feelings but sometimes checkable facts — and when I have been able to check what I wrote then, different from my memory now, it is the diary, not my memory, that is correct. And sometimes an entry is about something really important: yet I had completely forgotten it. I have also found among the pages one photograph about which I want to say: 'No. This isn't true.' But there it is. Well, of course we forget many things in our lives — our heads would burst otherwise — and there are details in the day-by-day diaries that I don't remember at all. It is also well known that people can remember the same event differently.

And yet . . . and yet. Some entries are *so exactly as I remember*, right down to the moment, and the room, and the song, and the light, and the air . . . the old song 'Night and Day' drifting in the dusk through the windows of an autumn hotel room in Christchurch, and the New Zealand poetry books on the bed . . . so that my heart beats oddly at the thought of how clear memory can be, so long afterwards.

Then, right at this very confusing time, I read the Nobel Prize acceptance speech by one of my favourite writers, Kazuo Ishiguro, in which he described a turning point in his writing life when he could suddenly see a way of writing that could properly suggest *the many layers of self-deception and denial that shrouded any person's view of their own self and past.*

Self-deception and denial? All of us?

'Know thyself,' said Socrates in Ancient Greece.

All these layers of discovery have thrown me and muddled me — and distressed me — and have led to the emotional Chinese burns and the horse bites. And, finally, unwrapping memory, I can only conclude, as I now find philosophers and psychiatrists and poets have concluded long before me: sometimes memories change and rewrite themselves in our heads. And perhaps we also have to face the idea that until we realise that to some extent memory is *selective*, we can't really know ourselves (if we want to know ourselves). We perhaps sometimes instinctively choose to have a version of memory that suits us — our view of ourselves, the view we *want* to be true.

And even the very oldest diaries were there, waiting . . .

Because even though I went as far away from my homeland as it is possible to go without starting to come back again, I kept even the very early (sometimes funny, sometimes devastating, but often really boring and deeply, deeply embarrassing) diaries: I packed them in a big wooden tea-chest with my poetry books and my photo albums and my LPs — and even my 45rpm records ('Rock Around the Clock', 'Crazy', 'Sad Movies (Make Me Cry)') — and they crossed the 12,000 miles with me, on a big ship, to my new life. As if I was making sure to bring myself with me.

My favourite phrase about the people who made, the other way, that long and dangerous sea-journey from Great Britain in the nineteenth century was written by a New Zealand historian:

'The drones, of course, did not go.' And my brothers and I knew our great-grandmother who had actually made that perilous journey. A very un-dronish person: a straight-backed, austere woman, rather alarming to us, dressed in long black dresses and buttoned boots. (Granny is nearly 100 . . . She talks funny. It is Scotland . . .) Yet how un-curious we were then, in Timaru in 1951, eating our ice creams and giving concerts on our gazoos, about the woman with us to whom we were related, who had been born nearly a hundred years ago on the other side of the world.

There is a poem by Ruth Dallas about photographs of pioneer women which starts:

> You can see from their faces
> Life was not funny . . .

You could see that, from our great-grandmother's face.

And (though I didn't think of it in this way in the least) when I left New Zealand on a ship for Great Britain, I was tracing back, with my tea-chest and my poetry books and my pop records and these diaries, the route my own great-grandparents had taken. And to a foreign place also: to such different people who said (sternly at the Royal Academy of Dramatic Art in London) what I had said about my great-grandmother: that *I* spoke funny; to a different, paler light, and to trees that were a different green, and where our word 'football' didn't mean rugby. And where people treated one another differently, depending.

A foreign place, despite all the games of Monopoly I'd played and all the books I'd read.

When I was growing up reading *The Lark in the Morn*, *The Adventures of Sherlock Holmes*, *Jane Eyre*, New Zealand was still perhaps something like a rather prim British country, except with — for this was many (though not all) of the early settlers' ambition, having made that long and dangerous journey — equality instead of a class system (or so we told ourselves), and with sheep, and little rural Māori villages. And how very proud we were of our country — and we had much to be proud of: we were the first country to give votes to women and we were a 'welfare' state with universal healthcare and free education. Still a huge British influence, though: *our* King George VI, and the BBC World Service on our wireless, and always newsreels about Great Britain at the pictures, before the main film. And a few private schools, and 'china cabinets', and gloves and hats to go to town on the tramcar — but in our country *everyone* should be free to have china cabinets. And we looked after war-damaged, dear Great Britain with our lamb and our butter. Great Britain, we were told, was 'Home'. And although, by 1951, writers and poets and artists and critics had — I later realised — been fighting for years to break the constricting net, there was still a belief among many intellectuals and others that *England* was the place to escape to as soon as possible: it was *there* that the most valued Art, and Poetry, and Writing, and Theatre was created and appreciated.

However when dear, Great, Britain somewhat abruptly discarded Commonwealth trade and joined the European Common Market, of course those old ties changed forever. New Zealand had to find other markets (and learned to make wonderful wine). And began to really understand and be proud of its *own* artistic heritage. Now it seems to me (as I come and go like a yo-yo) almost nothing like a British country at all, no matter that little pockets of it try still to recapture that past, and people still love Royal visits.

The world turns.

As I write, the United Kingdom is still trying to deal with the chaos Brexit has thrown up, and Britain is suddenly looking *back* somewhat keenly for trading deals with those very Commonwealth countries which it left. Like, said a nephew of mine, contacting an old girlfriend again: *'Hello! How* ***are*** *you? You know, after all this time, I realise — I've* ***missed*** *you — I know, I know, I behaved badly but — oh,* ***of course*** *I always thought of you. Let's meet up again?'*

Perhaps we will. New Zealand will know that in this present, alerted, time of climate change there is much talk of food miles as well as air miles. But now New Zealand has other markets too. And its *own* artists, and writers and poets and philosophers and historians and creative spirits.

It is: itself. Aotearoa. New Zealand. And now sometimes even 新西兰.

Yet — other changes too. In a country that so, *so* prided itself on being 'class-less' and *fair*, I see that money has some other, different power now, and it is *not* fair sometimes, and it is somehow shocking (to me) to hear Auckland buses being casually described (by a family of two with two cars) as 'loser-cruisers'.

No television. No computers. No internet. No mobile phones. No email, no texting, no googling, no Facebook, no WhatsApping, no FaceTiming, no Snapchatting, no streaming, no podcasts, no blogging, no Twittering. I am so very aware of how immature and naïve I sound in my diaries — and absolutely was — especially compared to young people today. We did twitter of course, but to each other in person, like birds. We listened to the wireless. We went to the pictures. We also wrote lots of letters with pencils and pens, and posted them in the red box (just like Great Britain's red boxes) at the end of the street; the postman passing your house in the early morning would blow his whistle if he put something in your letterbox. Occasionally a man in uniform arrived with a telegram: a folded yellow form in a brown envelope with capital letters typed on strips of white sticky paper: HARRY ASHBY ARRIVING RAILWAY STATION 9.30AM SUNDAY.

Also: I often didn't see things that were there in front of me, even though I wrote about them. The lack of carpet in that school friend's house was to me just perfect for dancing young girls' dances, not a sign of poverty, because *of course* we didn't have poverty in our country; we were all equal, all of us; my friends and I lived together — state houses, owned houses — and went to local primary schools together, and most of our mothers, the Happy Homemakers, made Happy Homes. And (even though there was a Māori in our class) Māori people lived in their far-away villages with their 'Native' schools, and were very happy there — we'd seen them, laughing — and sometimes we did Māori stick games at school and learnt a little Māori song. And all fathers had jobs, of course.

None of this, my diaries slowly reveal, was entirely true.

The diaries also reveal my — and many people's — huge ignorance of many things in the 1950s, but I haven't cut the ignorance out, or changed the basic facts, as I could have done to make this story more acceptable. I have left them in to show how far (and yet, sometimes, how un-far) our country has travelled in all these years. We simply did not know, as so many — most — people all over the world did not know then, of concepts like 'feminism', 'emotional intelligence', 'cultural appropriation', 'patriarchy', 'environmental degradation' or 'political correctness'.

I may come — and go — often (perhaps it *is* 107 times) but I am so aware as I read the 1950s diary entries that since the 1970s and 1980s and the new Māori renaissance that has changed so many things — and many people — it has not been considered appropriate for Pākehā to try to write personally about Māori matters. This is part of a strong, worldwide movement by indigenous peoples who have had, for so long, their histories and their stories told *for* them, *about* them, not *by* them, as if they could not tell their own story. Māori have excellent writers of their own who now tell their own story in their own way, and write their own histories from their own knowledge and their own point of view. In telling *my* own story, I have to recognise that it comes entwined with that earlier, boundaried history. And if, by chance, you break through a boundary you learn so much, but sharp splinters of that broken boundary fall — on both sides.

This story was our particular growing-up, and our young lives, in our country, then.

II

HOME (OUR *REAL* HOME) WAS WELLINGTON. The Capital City, we said proudly. Mum and Dad and me and my two younger brothers, Andrew and Ross.

My Auntie Ellie, 'the most beautiful girl in Wellington', reminded me that I was actually born in and spent the first three weeks of my life in a small town over the hills. Carterton: many years later the first place in the world, I am always glad to tell, to vote for an openly transsexual mayor. First, as New Zealand has been so often. But when I was three weeks old Mum and I came over the hills from Carterton into Wellington where Dad was just beginning a new teaching job. So: Wellington is my place. My first memory is an earthquake: holding on to the sides of a cot and seeing in fascination — not fear — things falling over, and off the walls, and a rumbling sound. Recent research suggests that children can't remember things before they are two years old, that our early memories are perhaps things people have told us. Who knows? But I *think* I remember an earthquake. My next memory — definitely three years old now, because my mother was in hospital giving birth to my brother Andrew — is of staying with that same beautiful aunt in a (luckily) ground-floor flat and feeling for the glass in the window — leaning towards it, nearer and nearer, I wanted to touch the glass — but the window was open and I fell out and got a black eye. Which I no doubt presented to the Maternity Hospital with great self-importance.

Wellington.

Still partly the same: that wind-buffeted, earthquake-prone city of hills and sea and gales; so, so beautiful on a fine, still day. In all the bays around the harbour and on those hills the native bush and the pine trees, the wild flowers and the yellow-flowering gorse. Pōhutukawa trees with gnarled roots flowered red at Christmas, and there were bushes of native karaka with their bright green, thick, moisture-holding leaves. Reaching out to the horizon, the hills seemed to rumple in the wild wind, change their colour with shadows; New Zealand painters capture it. We went to places called Karaka Bay or Ngauranga Gorge or Titahi Bay: evidence of other times (though then the names were mangled, anglicised). The houses almost all wooden because of those earthquakes; roofs of corrugated iron, red and green and orange — I loved the sound of rain on our corrugated-iron roof while we were safe and warm inside. The nineteenth-century monastery with its tolling bell overlooked the enclosed harbour, ships steaming out with butter and cheese and wool and lamb for those poor war-torn people who lived in Great Britain, who we were looking after.

And the plangent, mournful sound of a lone foghorn echoed there sometimes, across the water.

I loved that city.

But in 1951 there were still very many Victorian buildings

made of concrete and bricks in the main Wellington streets. Some remain — defiant, often attractively shabby, louche even; Wellington hasn't altogether smashed its past to pieces with a big wrecking ball. Even right in the middle of the city some old buildings stand there still (earthquake-proofed). But now, of course, tall metal-and-glass (earthquake-proofed) global businesses, and banks, dominate parts of the city centre; New Zealand on the Pacific Rim is well positioned to do global business. Partly because of its long and friendly past with China (which I remember even as a child; I knew people who visited there regularly, they told us strange stories of a different place). And partly because of its membership of not only the Commonwealth but also of that shadowy little group of security sharers and tax-haven arrangers that people like Edward Snowden, and documents like the Panama Papers and the Paradise Papers, have revealed. And we are, we now find, a part of some shadowy Global Phone-Listeners (not, presumably, interested in crying time).

But Politics was never discussed in our house. When I asked Mum and Dad what they voted, Dad said very solemnly: 'I work as a civil servant for the New Zealand Government and I must serve whichever Government is elected so we must never talk about politics', and this seemed to include Mum as well. And so it seemed, but it is not true (as later diary entries show) that 'politics' did not affect our lives.

I believe 'the personal is political' was first said by the aforementioned Alexandra Kollontai. The personal and the 'political' (if that is even the right word) in our house came together a few years later, and many things changed forever. But in 1951 I doubt any of us three children knowingly knew anything about politics, either formal or informal. There was a bitter and violent and divisive 'wharfies' strike that year to which the government sent soldiers. This strike impinges on my diary entries: an entry about a girl whose father was a wharfie. In 1951, at what I always spelled in my diaries as 'Manuel Training', there was sometimes no butter, no sugar, no eggs, which I note: I don't know whether that was the strike or not. The strike was said to be organised by 'communists' but at our school we didn't know what communists were. But I did recognise that another girl whose father was also a wharfie and whose mother, in an election, stood for the Communist Party (whatever that was), was bullied by one of the male teachers and often strapped — hard. I only remember one 'political' thing as I understood the word then. There had been an election, and a new government had got in. At the local dairy — on the same day as the election — sherbet cost one penny less! I excitedly reported this to my parents and asked them, 'Is this the result of the election? It must be, mustn't it?' — and I decided I was all for elections.

In those long-ago days of my first diary — and for a long time afterwards — New Zealand was open Monday to Friday only. I worked once in London on a TV series called *Within These Walls* with the Australian actress Googie Withers: she was the governor of a prison, I was a bulimic prisoner and kept having to put yellow things like mashed banana in my mouth and then vomit it all into the prison toilet. She said to me, 'I went to New Zealand once, Barbara, but it was closed.' Indeed, 1950s New Zealand was closed not just in the weekends but often in the evenings too. Only Friday had 'late-night shopping'. Restaurants were almost non-existent, except in hotels, though in 1951 we children — perhaps even our parents — had never been to one. There were no pubs in our respectable suburb. Elsewhere, pubs were allowed to open on Saturdays (*certainly* not Sundays) — but they closed at 6 p.m., as they did every night, and women might have the vote but if, most unusually (and necessarily over twenty-one), a woman went anywhere near a pub, she could only go into one of the little private bars at the back — and had to be be accompanied by a male. So if you didn't go to the pictures, which was pretty exciting, or visit relations or neighbours, there wasn't much to do on a Saturday night when I first started writing; usually we kids walked to that local, sherbet-price-reducing dairy which did open for a short time in the early evening on Saturdays to sell the hastily printed *Sports Post*, which arrived in the suburbs from the city centre in bundles tied with string, on tramcars. So the men could have all the up-to-date sports results on a Saturday night. But the *Sports Post* also contained 'Blondie' and 'Popeye' comic strips, Ripley's 'Believe It or Not', and an Agony Uncle, 'Dear George'. My brother Andrew and I would read out the agony problems to each other as our entertainment on a Saturday night, and roll about on the carpet giggling at people's funny lives until my mother said sharply, 'That's enough', and told us both we were 'silly-tired'.

My parents were John Ewing, a school teacher, originally from the South Island where all his family still lived, and Jean Ashby, a typist from Wellington, and they got married in Wellington on my mother's twenty-fifth birthday in 1935; the autumn wind was probably blowing as usual around the Hataitai church that April day. In 1935 the world was still suffering from the Great

Depression, and when we had to write an essay about that at school my dad told me about men walking the Wellington streets and rattling stones in their pockets to give themselves the feeling they had coins there. 'Poor beggars. I was just lucky', were my father's words that I remember. And he didn't mean street beggars: I wonder if, in the 1950s, the word *beggar*, often used, might have been a transmutation of the word *bugger*, which polite, conventional people like us didn't of course say out loud, though it was, oddly, very commonly used. A term almost of endearment (but perhaps only among an older generation than us, perhaps from the war?) was still, then, 'you silly old bugger'; even the later, famous and funny Toyota TV advertisement with a dog saying 'Bugger!' possibly would have had a different reaction in England.

My parents were hard-working, honest, thrifty, and — importantly — puritanical and scrupulous. Dad was totally, totally immersed in education; in primary school education, in particular. My friends told me in later years that they were nervous if they were invited to come to tea on Sunday at our place because my extremely mild-mannered and kind father would innocuously ask, 'Six times four, Vivian?' or 'Nine times seven, Pauline?' or 'Eleven times eight, Isabel?' across the dining-room table. He worked as a teacher; as an editor of the *School Journal* that all primary school children received several times a year; and as a school inspector. He finally became Senior Inspector of Primary Schools in New Zealand and worked in 'the Oldest Wooden Building in the Southern Hemisphere' down by the railway station. He often brought home books from the office for Andrew and Ross and me, and I read almost every single one of them, often running up to the tram stop at the end of the day to meet him. I almost *ate* books. On one thrilling occasion he brought home Comics — the Education Department was doing a survey on how reading comics affected children. They affected us anyway with great excitement: we immersed ourselves in 'Captain Marvel' (Shazzaaam!) and 'Film Fun' (Laurel and Hardy); sitting in the warm sun on our wooden back steps with comics (from 'Overseas', like everything else). Captivated.

My mother had been found to have a genius IQ when she was a child and was sent, aged fifteen, to Victoria University in Wellington to study for a science and maths degree. Before her first year ended she had had a breakdown and left. Later she became a typist. Now, with the event of this April wedding, she was to be a 'Homemaker', for she had had to leave her typing job to marry Dad, as was the norm for women in 1935. The wedding certificate says 'Spinster' and shows a blank for her 'Occupation'. As Homemaker my mother strived for a certain gentility in our house that I think she didn't have in her childhood house where her mother had died when Mum was eleven, her sister Ellie was thirteen, and their young brother Harry was two. Our house always had to be immaculate, and I do mean *immaculate* (my bedspread was not allowed to be crooked on my bed: she would stand at the door of my bedroom and instruct me until it hung perfectly). She scrubbed, she dusted, she polished, daily. Mirrors shone, and tables, and china cabinets. She pounded lumps of concrete to make a crazy-paving path through our back garden where Dad grew beans and potatoes and peas. She sewed all my clothes, and her own, from Simplicity sewing patterns. She was a most excellent baker of cakes and biscuits and was famous for her pavlovas. She wasn't very interested in music although she liked listening to Anne

Ziegler and Webster Booth singing 'Only a Rose'. She never read fiction, always saying, 'I have enough problems to think about in my own life without thinking about other people.' She liked good new mahogany furniture (nothing old or second-hand), and we indeed had a china cabinet — and an afternoon-tea trolley — and she liked thin bone-china cups to drink tea from, and criticised me if I bought her a present of 'cheap pottery'. Our front room was called 'the lounge' and we also had a dining room and a front and back garden, as did everyone in our neat suburban Wellington street. (The neat streets in the suburb of Strathmore were named Bentinck, or Glamis, or Cavendish.)

My parents' social life in the 1950s revolved around a group of local friends, many of the men school teachers, almost all of the women homemakers. (I remember only one single woman, but she finally got married to a short widower with children, and everyone was so, so pleased that she was 'married at last'.) Perhaps once a month this group used to do rehearsed play-readings in each other's houses, with tea and sandwiches and home-made cakes afterwards. I don't remember any drinking of alcohol at the play-readings, but they had very jolly and noisy occasional parties, and one year my father got a home-brew beer kit and kept it in my wardrobe, so there was often a slight, not unpleasant smell of yeast emanating that year from my frocks and cardigans. There was no home-grown professional theatre in New Zealand (but British actors like Dame Sybil Thorndike and Sir Ralph Richardson sometimes 'fitted in a little tour' after visiting Australia). There was an amateur Wellington Repertory Company and some smaller amateur companies, like Unity Theatre. And every year a country-wide drama competition for one-act plays was held in the Wellington Concert Chamber, and groups like my parents and their friends would enter. At least once my parents' group, The Strathmore Players, won.

Whatever my parents' difficulties, all our lives they never argued in front of us about money. My father had a secure job and we were secure as a family, although sometimes we didn't have *actual* money — once Mum already had her gloves and hat and lipstick on, to take us into town on the tramcar, when she realised she didn't have enough in her purse for fares for all of us. So she removed her hat: we couldn't go. We didn't have a car, or a washing machine, or a refrigerator. Most people didn't have these things in New Zealand when we were children; they were mostly imported, and expensive, and I always thought the washing machine/dishwasher combined that I report in my diary that we were saving up for had never been invented. (But a friend assured me recently that her family had acquired one, which had to be held down by physical force when it started drying things.) We lit a little fire with kindling under the copper in the wash-house to boil the water to do the washing; rinsed everything, wrung them through a wringer and hung them on the clothes-line outside to dry in the Wellington wind. (When I say 'we' it was mostly Mum the Homemaker, helped occasionally, usually unwilling, by the Putative Homemaker-to-Be.) And we kept food cool outside in a kitchen safe on the dark side of the house. But: we had a house, we cycled safe streets to school where we had free education, we were healthy, we played in the safe streets until night fell on our safe country. Our parents gave us the great gift and privilege of basic material security, which seems to me to somehow stay with you — even if you haven't actually got much money. And very many of our friends were given that same material security also.

And guilt.

If your heritage is puritanical, you also inherit guilt. Puritanical guilt affected many of the New Zealand children of my generation strongly, always. And still.

And the absolute importance of honesty.

Or — as we three children understood in some surprise much later — what our parents saw as the best honesty that could be presented in the circumstances.

In particular: Dad's father had, we knew, been a most upright man, a solicitor and the Master of the Masonic Lodge: there were old sepia photographs of him in his Masonic regalia — I have one still. And he was the Mayor of St Kilda, near Dunedin. And we knew and were fond of his 'widow', our Nana, although we didn't see her very much because she lived down in the South Island. We were told that, like both of Mum's parents, Dad's father the Mayor of St Kilda had 'died before you were born'. Which was not true. He had been assisted by his Masonic brothers to escape arrest (for financial chicancry); they got him away — without his family — to England, and he was still alive long after we three children were born. This furtive flight, we later realised, devastated and formed my (then fifteen-year-old) honest and conflict-avoiding father. And his younger sisters — and of course their mother, my Nana (and no doubt that austere Scottish mother-in-law, who talked funny) — who were all left behind to face the shame. The Masonic brothers apparently presented my grandmother with a grocery shop in lieu of a husband, and this, I gather, failed dismally; perhaps people passed by a shop that was run by the disgraced wife of a criminal. She finally took in boarders to survive. In later years, among our cousins, the story grew in the telling: that our grandfather had 'taken his secretary with him', that he had had 'another family in England'.

But my grandmother never spoke of her own past and only ever gave me one piece of advice: *Don't get married yet, see the world* — fairly unusual advice, I would guess, from a seventy-nine-year-old grandmother in the 1950s. When I was living in the South Island my Nana and I would go for long walks in the freezing cold winter streets of Timaru, the town where she had grown up and trained as a 'tailoress'; and then we would sit together in her kitchen and put our feet into the warm old coal oven and talk and laugh. And run to the outside lavatory (with a potty under the bed for night-time). But my Nana never told me she had once been the wife of the Mayor of St Kilda.

Nevertheless my mother was such a believer in the importance of honesty that once, in the night, when I woke terrified from a nightmare and begged her to tell me that the house wouldn't catch fire while I was asleep, her answer was: 'Well dear, no, I can't *promise*, that would be wrong. But I am almost sure there won't be a fire.'

My mother also had what might be described as some interesting theories. When I was smaller and had my hair in two plaits she would pick me up just off the ground by those plaits — not in any cruel way but because she firmly believed the roots of my hair would be strengthened if she did that. (I still have my hair.) When we came home from school, before we were allowed to go out into the street to play cricket or rounders or tennis, we had to do something called Floppy Fish. We had to lie down on the floor of the lounge and be floppy fish — i.e. *relax*. We could hear the voices of all the other children playing outside, and often lay there in a paroxysm of tension because we wanted to be out there playing too. Here the results were less successful: whatever the other reasons, Andrew and I both developed life-long insomnia, and all his life Ross got up in the middle of the night and worked, and then — lucky him — went straight back to sleep again.

There were also distinct house rules for being ill. If we couldn't — or wouldn't — go to school, the first thing we had to do was get into a bath full of cold water and turn over and over six times. (Sometimes the thought of this sent us to school anyway.) If we survived the bath we put our pyjamas back on, and could get into Mum and Dad's bed and listen to the wireless: *Aunt Daisy's Household Hints*, followed by several fifteen-minute serials that went on for years and years, like *Doctor Paul* and *Portia Faces Life* ('The Story of Any Woman Who Has Ever Dared To Love — Completely'). All made in Australia with soap adverts in between.

And all bodily functions were distasteful and never discussed: when Mum went to the lavatory she turned the cold tap in the bathroom basin on full and left it running loudly until she had pulled the chain.

In exasperation or anger she slapped or hit all three of us (though not Andrew much, because he was the favourite, and not Ross much because he was the youngest), but it was not until I was older that I started mentioning it in diaries. Hitting children is now illegal in New Zealand but it was common then, and accepted. I'd certainly seen kind Mrs Burley down the road hit her daughter, my friend Pauline — her anger not helped by her younger son commenting laconically, 'Mum's arm flashes out.' We were strapped at primary school — boys and girls — and fathers (almost never ours) occasionally strapped children with their trouser belt when they came home from work, if required. But once I got to secondary school we received not the strap, but — oh the shame — black marks against our House if we behaved badly: there was no more corporal punishment. That is, at school.

Someone once said, 'I never knew anyone so *driven* as the Ewing children.'

It was of course our mother's drive we had inherited, and maybe very lucky we were, Andrew and Ross and I. But Mum funnelled all that unused, un-honoured, scientific intelligence and mental energy into us, the family, whether we liked it or not, and in later years she wrought some havoc behind our suburban door.

However: she also, when she was forty-three, returned at last to Victoria University for a year, enrolling in Zoology I: she came top of the class and won a prestigious prize for the best student.

When she had to cut up a foul-smelling dead dogfish, she pinned a posy of violets on her lapel so she could breathe in their scent. That year, when we did the dishes at night — often, my diaries inform me, after very mediocre meals cooked by sulky, fourteen-year-old, horrible me — she would be sitting on the double bed with the green bedspread, surrounded by zoology books.

❀

ALL THESE THINGS MADE US, of course.

But in my 1951 the two things that would echo and wind themselves deeply round and through the rest of my life had already happened. Often we don't understand when life-changing events occur: only later does it become clear how important they were. And I have only my own memory (whatever that is, however reliable that is), official records, old newspapers and a couple of childhood friends to consult about the unrecorded-by-me earlier years. Because not just my mother and my father but — life not being fair — also my two beloved younger brothers. Are dead.

Two echoing, winding things.

My Uncle Harry.

And Maungatapu.

My Uncle Harry. Any references to him in the early diaries are oblique — but there.

I was born in January 1939, so I was the only small person in his small family that Harry Ashby — my mother's and my Auntie Ellie's much younger brother — knew before he went away to serve King and Country. We kept for a long time a 'soldiers' postcard' sent from Egypt during the war, of the Alexandrian coast, with a small oval photo of my Uncle Harry in one corner, and a small oval photo of me aged perhaps two that they must have sent to him, in the other. (That same Alexandrian coast I was — so many years later — driven along, to see that old fort where, although many Egyptians couldn't have been more welcoming and I liked being in Egypt, an armed police escort waited for us: it was soon after 11 September 2001.)

When my mum's mother died, her father, a printer, didn't (unusually for the time) quickly find another wife but cared for his children himself, with the help of neighbours, and with the huge help of his eleven- and thirteen-year-old daughters in looking after his two-year-old son. We did believe that my laughing Auntie Ellie was 'the most beautiful girl in Wellington' and my mother was 'the cleverest girl in Wellington'. These may well be apocryphal stories but they definitely each believed it absolutely of the other, and they were each other's best friends for all their lives, and together they had brought up, and loved, and — importantly — felt responsible for, their much younger brother, my Uncle Harry.

Now the war was over. Uncle Harry had finally come safely home again. And somehow he was staying with our family. Not at first, because he was a fireman and we visited him at the Newtown fire station, and we saw how they slid down the pole from their living quarters and straight on to the exciting red fire engines, sirening out into the windy city to douse the flames. And then he'd gone to Auckland. But now, six months before I began writing my first diary, he was staying with us in our suburban wooden house. Uncle Harry was ill, they said to my brothers and me, 'from the war'. He slept in the boys' bedroom, just a glass of water by the bed, and I clearly remember thinking it was sad to be lying in bed in the middle of the day with just a glass of water beside you. Andrew and Ross and I didn't know a lot of things about our family then, and we didn't know what 'shell shock' was. We didn't know until years afterwards that he had sat with a soldier mate in the Egyptian darkness smoking, and — the glow of the cigarettes perhaps — the mate was shot dead and his body and his face and his brains splattered all over Uncle Harry. We didn't know then that our uncle had developed a drinking problem. And we never knew (I have only recently retrieved the records) that in Auckland our uncle had been living in a mental hospital, and that Dad had signed papers (women of course couldn't sign for such important things) to take responsibility for him, and that's why he was staying with us in 1950.

All they said was: 'He is ill, from the war.'

It was Sunday lunch: roast mutton and mint sauce almost always. New Zealand was so lucky: everyone knew how dear, great, Britain was still suffering after the war but we were God's Own Country where everyone knew there were many more sheep than people and we loved our Sunday roast and Dad and I had picked the green beans from our garden that morning.

Dad was standing carving the meat, at the Head of the Table as if he was the boss of the house, which he wasn't. The knife and the meat and us.

Suddenly Uncle Harry in striped pyjamas burst into the room and hurled a book onto the dining table: plates and mutton and gravy and potatoes and the beans, and a book, all over the table. The book was *The Egg and I* by Betty MacDonald.

'You can keep your dirty, stinking book!' he yelled at Mum.

She tried to stand. 'Harry!' she tried to say. 'Harry.' Shocked, frightened. He went on shouting and shouting, getting louder and louder and angrier; perhaps Dad put the carving knife down; Uncle Harry suddenly had the knife and was shouting at Mum: terrible shouting noise, voices, mutton, *The Egg and I* with its paper cover torn, and a carving knife in the air, and Andrew and Ross and I paralysed. Somehow Mum and Dad must have got him away, back to the bed and the glass of water. The next thing I remember is Mum telling me to take the boys to Mrs Burley, the neighbour down the road whose children we played with, and just say that we had come to be with her for a while.

Mrs Burley opened the back door. She was smoking a cigarette, as she always was. We must have looked somehow peculiar: I clearly understood that she was somewhat surprised to see these three pale children appear suddenly at her door.

'Mum said we have to come and be with you for a while. Uncle Harry is shouting.' Without further questions the admirable Mrs Burley took us inside and I suppose we played with Pauline and Wayne and ate lamington cakes. It was dark when Mum came to get us.

'But what about Uncle Harry?'

'He is asleep. Everything is fine.' As my mother never, ever, told lies, everything must be fine and Uncle Harry was indeed asleep. But I lay wide, wide awake under my pink bedspread all night long, listening to our house and the people it held.

In that tense house next morning presumably a plan had been made. Dad must have gone to work, Andrew and Ross must have gone to school, but there was a small shocked eleven-year-old who had been listening all night for more shouting. So Mum put me in her and Dad's bed with the green bedspread and turned on the wireless so I could listen to *Aunt*

Daisy's Household Tips and *Portia Faces Life*. And then — she disappeared. We never talked of that morning ever, but thinking about it later I guessed she perhaps had gone to use somebody else's telephone because ours was in the hall, and everybody in the house could hear any phone conversation. And then the man in the striped pyjamas lumbered in to Mum and Dad's bedroom. He just looked at me. He looked so terrible.

'Please don't shout any more, Uncle Harry,' I whispered.

'*I can't help it.*' Such terrifying despair in the voice. I had probably not yet known the depths of the word 'despair', aged eleven. But I knew it then.

'But you make us so frightened.'

And the man threw himself down beside me on the bed. Not on me, not attacking me; lying face down beside me, his head in his arms and crying, great, heaving, terrible cries. I had never seen, or heard, a man crying before — or anybody crying like that. A minute or five minutes. I so much want to write now that I comforted him somehow. But I was too frightened. My mother returned. She must have led him back to his room and soon there was a black car and men, and most of all I remember they had heavy black boots and the bottoms of their black trousers were different from Dad's.

I had a favourite place in the whole world. It was called Maungatapu, and Maungatapu was the second echoing thing.

Our family — my parents and my two brothers and I (and sometimes one or other of my friends would come too) — often had our Christmas holidays in Tauranga, where that favourite place is. In those years (it is indeed very different now, named in 2019 as the world's 'eighth most unaffordable city'), Tauranga was a country-and-western port town where that beautiful aunt, my mother's sister Ellie, now lived with her Norwegian husband who worked for a fruit grower near the small Māori settlement on a small peninsula called Maungatapu. They had young twin sons, and rented a little brown cottage on the land my uncle worked on; below the land was the sea. Our family

camped in a tent at the back of the cottage and heard the sound of the sea in the night. Later my uncle built his own house there. The white people who lived in Maungatapu were all prosperous; they had somehow acquired the land from the Māori tribe who mostly lived at the tip of the peninsula — 'the Maori pa', the Pakehas called it — at the end of the unpaved road. The Pakehas cultivated the land, grew fruit; in one fascinating case began a vineyard, employing Maoris to tread the grapes. (I have used the 's' plural deliberately for a moment, as both Pākehā and Māori did in those days — and often still do — although there is no 's' in the Māori language. Also: the macron was not used in written Māori in the days I write of: I mostly use it in the narration of this story, but not in the diaries.)

Our very first visit to Maungatapu was in 1946, and I had just turned seven. As editor then of the *School Journal* Dad was only able to take a holiday when schools had started again in February, having spent all of January getting the first journal of the year ready. So that year our summer holiday was taken, in wonderful Maungatapu, in February. And so I spent several weeks as one of the few white pupils at the Maungatapu Native School where the Natives — I knew this only years later — were supposed to get strapped if they spoke Māori at school, but who seemed to me to be so free and happy and lucky because they often came to school along the unpaved road on a horse, dust rising about them in the sunshine, and they tethered the horses on fence posts, and old sacks hung all along the fence: their saddles. And they usually had bare feet, while I and another white pupil, Anthony (who was soon to be sent away to a private school, and whose English father had started the Maungatapu vineyard), had to wear sunhats and shoes. And there was always laughter and singing, often a guitar playing somewhere, and the sound of this soft and beautiful strange language. And the heavy, hot, summer scent of macrocarpa trees all along the dusty road to school and the cicadas singing.

The pupils came from all the surrounding Māori settlements — I can't remember how many children, maybe fifty or sixty, aged from five to maybe thirteen or fourteen — and they spoke a mixture of Māori and English to each other, presumably quickly reverting to English if there was a teacher in sight. The headmaster and his wife were white and there was another white teacher also. One hot February day I was standing, a bit shyly at playtime, in the shade of the corrugated iron of the outdoor school toilets and one of the boys came running towards me — and then kissed the corrugated iron with a big sloppy kiss and said 'Ooooops, missed', and everyone laughed and the laughter was so infectious that I laughed too, all of us laughing together in the school playground in the hot sunshine as the horses pulled at the grass by the fence and the cicadas sang so loud.

Whenever we went back to Maungatapu after that I would often see the pupils from the school along the road and we all waved. I knew and loved so much this place where we could just climb down from the house to the sea below. If, very occasionally, it rained on those summer days, we might go to the pictures — one year my mother took me and my friend Vivian to *The Red Shoes*, starring Moira Shearer, that tale of ballet and show business and love and jealousy and art and death: perfect entertainment for ten-year-olds. The sun shone again next day of course and we went swimming as usual at the bottom of the little cliff at the end of the garden. But in the sea, ignoring my two younger brothers and the twins who we were supposed to be looking after, Viv and I went over and over *The Red Shoes* — and decided to give a performance of it to the family. We rehearsed in the sea, in our bathing togs; the water helped us dance and leap so gracefully, we knew how enchanting we were — but we both absolutely *insisted* on playing Moira Shearer (aged ten). So we performed it twice over, to an enforced family audience, so that we *both* had the chance to say in arm-waving anguish, pretend tears pouring down our cheeks (still in our bathing togs): 'Take . . . off . . . the Red Shoes.' (There were probably tears of suppressed mirth running down the cheeks of our audience also, but we were too involved in our anguish to notice.)

One year one of the Māori boys from the school took me

for a ride on his horse with a sack for a saddle, galloping along the hard sand when the tide was out at the bottom of the dusty road by the Māori settlement — an adventure that would have absolutely horrified my parents if they had known. Once I was walking down the road by myself and met some Māori girls I had known at the school — they were singing. We all stopped and sat on the road, and talked. They taught me a few Māori words. They told me they lived beside a mountain — to me it was a small hill — but they explained to me carefully and slowly that it was called Maunga-tapu, which meant 'sacred mountain', and they taught me how to say the word properly. Then they pointed to the little holiday island just out at sea that you could get to by boat, where people including me and my family ate candyfloss and screamed in the big breaking waves. The girls said that the island out at sea was called Maunga-nui, which meant 'big mountain' — 'But it's not sacred, like ours; we live with our ancestors and their wairua.' I asked what wairua was and they looked at each other and shrugged and said, 'Wairua is — wairua.' And over the years the Maungatapu girls taught me old party songs; cicadas sang and we sang — 'Slowly I'm Falling More In Love With You' and 'Tahi Nei Taru Kino' and 'You'll Never Find Another Wahine Like Me' — songs that stood me in good stead when, later, I became a party girl myself.

Going to that remote 'Native' school, hearing the sea at the bottom of the garden in the night, sitting on the dusty Maungatapu road with other children while cicadas sang: this was the second echoing thing in my life, even before I began writing my diary in 1951.

❀

AFTER THAT HOLIDAY WITH MY father's family in the South Island which I had so meticulously recorded in my first diary entries, my last year at primary school began. I was made Head Prefect and Bell-Ringer. We cycled to school every day and we would speed along trying to beat the bell-clanging tramcars. At school there were wildly important friendships with a particular group of girls ('those girls' or 'those kids', as I sometimes call them): sitting together, playing together, best friends, jealousies, secrets, falling out and then being friends again (all faithfully reported); we pulled each other's hair occasionally. We also pinched each other in quarrels, a habit I didn't grow out of for years.

. . . Mum and Dad went to see Uncle Harry . . . the diary says on some Saturday or Sunday afternoons: nothing more than that is written in 1951 about Uncle Harry. He was now in Porirua Mental Hospital, 'the loony bin' as most people called it. He would escape occasionally and come to our house: we would find his cigarette butts, untipped Navy Cut, in ashtrays, and there would suddenly be urgent phone calls and quiet conversations, but we children never actually saw him.

The 1951 diary shows I had lots of energy — but not much sporting prowess: I was mad on tennis but never got high on the school tennis ladder, despite challenging girls higher than me at 7.30 in the morning all through summer, and I was never chosen for the A or even B1 basketball or cricket team. We were often taken to the beach from school on the tram. I so loved the sea — but I could hardly get my fifty yards swimming certificate, although many of the girls in my class got certificates for half a mile. (I was scared to put my face under the water.) And when I did finally do my completed fifty yards, I definitely remember putting my foot on the bottom as I turned the measured distance to come back. And sure enough, puritanical guilt even then: the diary entry about the fifty yards certificate just says (Private) without saying why, but I remember clearly why: I had cheated. So I was pretty useless at sport but I used all that energy to cycle everywhere, and write stories, and play the best tennis I could. And every Wednesday morning, to train us to be Home-makers while the boys in our class went to Woodwork to train to be Men, we girls went to 'Manuel' Training — mostly cooking, occasional 'horrible sewing' (which I always had to get Mum to help with because I was so bad at it).

I cycled to the library after school, and the books I write of that year are a devoured mish-mash of titles like *The Secret Garden, Carol in Repertory, The Cloister and the Hearth, Carol on Tour, Dear Busybody, Bunkle Baffles Them, The Swish of the Curtain, Ballet Shoes, Sue Barton: District Nurse, Macbeth, Sue Barton: Senior Nurse*... (*Sue Barton: Senior Nurse* and *Macbeth*? Really? Could such an unlikely combination account for the fact that years later at the Liverpool Playhouse I got the worst review I ever received in my entire acting career, the words still seared on my memory: **Barbara Ewing plays Lady Macbeth like an executive's wife who has lost her tranquillizers**.)

Our social life was based round those school friends, and the children in our street: bike rides, birthday parties, and trips with either our parents or our friends to the pictures — I record such films as *Lassie, Annie Get Your Gun, City Lights* and *Harvey* (after which I talked to an imaginary friend for weeks). My friend Pauline and I gave up the Royal Family and started instead collecting photos of our favourite film stars and putting them on our bedroom walls: Gregory Peck, Doris Day, Gene Kelly (who tap danced), Elizabeth Taylor. I liked Betty Grable (whose shapely legs were Insured For A Million Dollars). Pauline liked Esther Williams who would rise up out of an underwater ballet sequence always smiling and thus must have a mouth full of water at the same time: how did she *do* that? I liked James Stewart. Pauline liked Alan Ladd. When the following year the film *Shane* came out, rumours circulated in my film magazines that Alan Ladd was *short*. Pauline absolutely refused to believe such an insult, and stuck by him. But I put Jack Palance who, dressed all in black and very tall, starred with Alan Ladd in *Shane*, up on my wall with the others. Years later I made a film with Jack Palance and he took me out to dinner and I asked him if it was *true* that he had had to walk in a ditch in *Shane* so as to not be taller than Alan Ladd and he said yes, it was true. (I imparted this information to my old friend Pauline across the world by airmail letter immediately.)

'Those girls' and I sometimes met boys from school if we were allowed to go to the pictures to see these stars on Saturday afternoons: very chaste, giggling meetings, except one older boy in our class, Albie, who smoked behind the toilets, sat in the Miramar Kinema with his arm round Noelene and . . . KISSED her . . . written in my diary in seeming disapproval, but without doubt pure jealousy. We also went to the local Presbyterian Sunday School (my first acting appearance ever was as the Virgin Mary with a blue shawl and a girl doll, swaddled). Later I was a keen Bible Class attendee but that seems to have had a great deal to do with seeing, and later dancing with, boys. I was never pressured to go to church: my mother declared herself to be an agnostic and I had to look up the word.

The first mention I make of going to see live theatre was to see The Kiwi Concert Party — soldiers who had been in the Entertainment Corps during the war. There was a confusing disapproval when I came home glowing with astonishment and speaking excitedly about the talents of the female impersonators — and I was immediately forbidden to go again.

I so often mention the weather: loving the days and days of sunshine we took for granted — even though our house was slightly inland we were only about a mile from the nearest beach, and we sunbathed madly and certainly without sunscreen — but I also record, all through the Wellington winter, the wind and the rain and grey wild clouds and the cold and lighting the fire and the comfort of hot-water bottles . . . It thundered and lighteninged and hailed. The hail was heck of a big and didn't melt. We ate it. I didn't feel well . . . And, in the earliest diaries, there is a great deal of writing about chocs or lollies, things I suppose we didn't feel we had enough of still, though the war was well over. I think I must've eaten a lot of them — I started getting a lot of spots, and holes in my teeth . . . Today at 2.15 I left for the Dental Clinic. I hate it. They always find something wrong with my teeth . . . The buzzing drill is so loud and hurts . . . Today I had two fillings with that runny mercury. They let me roll it in my hand . . . I wrote all these things down in a very small Collins diary before I went to sleep every single night. But I didn't have the space to write in detail. I was shocked and horrified and upset when I had the accident with my new kitten . . . April Fools' Day. I accidently trod on Tuppence and killed him . . . I didn't 'tread' on the kitten as I record. I jumped down on it from the kitchen bench in brand-new black shoes (dressed ready for Sunday School) because I had been reaching up into a cupboard above the bench for the cat food. I landed right on the little kitten — I saw its squashed insides, they were yellow, and moving still, and Dad had to get a spade and shovel it up and take it outside and make sure it was properly dead by hitting it. All that detail could not have fitted into the small Collins diary, although the entry on April Fool's day is *so* short that I think I didn't have the heart to write more anyway.

There is only one mention of a boy called P. who smiled at me 'charmingly' in the street before he writes me an actual 'love letter', but he soon disappears with appendicitis. And there was the play my best friend Bev and I wrote, 'Bartholomew'. Bartholomew was a boy who smoked (played by me). All the grown-ups smoked: Players Tipped, de Reszke, Senior Service. The teachers smoked, Mum and Dad smoked then — and schoolboys, like naughty Albie who kissed girls, smoked behind the toilets. I expect that when I lit up in 'Bartholomew' actually in the classroom all the other kids would have laughed and looked at the teachers. But the teachers would have just laughed too — and because smoking was so commonplace there is not a single mention of a cigarette in the whole 1951 diary, not even Bartholomew's. And when smoking does emerge in this story, as indeed it does, it is because it is 'common' and 'cheap', not because it is a health hazard.

And ohhhh . . . the *music.*

The story of the 1950s is also the story of the popular music of those years and the emergence of 'teenagers' — in 1951 the explosion was already on its way. And my brothers and I were already music mad. We listened weekly to the Lever Hit Parade on the wireless and I meticulously wrote down the top hits, almost always American, on a little pink pad. We'd always liked 'cowboy songs' — songs like 'Don't Fence Me In' sung by one of those cowboys: Gene Autry, or Roy Rogers on Trigger the horse. 'Open the Door, Richard', 'Slow Boat to China', 'Baby, It's Cold Outside' (frowned on now), 'Goodnight Irene' — we could sing them all and so many others, word perfect. And Gracie Fields and Bing Crosby had both had a hit with 'Now Is the Hour' which Gracie Fields first heard, we proudly boasted, being sung in Māori in our country: 'Po Atarau'. But some years later my Norwegian aunt heard 'Now Is the Hour' in New Zealand in surprise and told me that the tune was definitely a lullaby she'd heard when she was a child in Norway: German, she thought. Today music can travel all over the world in a split second, but in my youth I slowly understood something else: music always travelled with people, when they moved from place to place. I liked to think of a foreign whaler maybe whistling that lullaby tune in a Māori trading port. What we didn't know in 1951 of course was that — soon — the music would — so thrillingly — change, and then echo through our lives.

My father was known to have a good tenor voice and sometimes we visited my mother's cousin who played the violin while his wife played their piano, and Dad would sing to their accompaniment 'The Fishermen of England' and Mum would sit slightly apart, slightly pursed lips, that look she had. She didn't really sing. But very occasionally, not maternal in the cuddly sense of the word, she would sing to us a bedtime lullaby called 'Little Man You're Crying' telling a little boy to go to sleep and Daddy would buy him some new marbles tomorrow. (I was expected to be a boy too, and was obviously received in some disappointment: they told me they had my name all ready: Christopher.)

❀

MANY PEOPLE SAY THERE IS no narrative to a life although we may try to make one; many people say they don't feel connected to their past (or don't want to feel connected to it) — or they have forgotten it, or feel as if it must have happened to another person. For better or for worse (sometimes very worse — I don't always *like* her), I do feel connected to this young, growing person, although it is so odd and unsettling to meet her so . . . alive . . . after all these years. And of course everyone's life *has* a narrative, often just not a very tidy one. It's the 'plot' that often gets lost. A novelist who is not happy with the way his or her plot has developed goes back and changes it, to pull the threads together more satisfactorily: to clarify. But it's much harder to tidy up a life, because we can't go back and change things, and the connecting threads are often not clear to us as they are happening; are not — at the time — understood.

Or are hidden.

So very many things forgotten, of course. But also: the revelations that are never made, the connections that are never known. The truth that is never spoken. *Truth,* I recently heard a theatre director say about a new play, *is sometimes complicated by responsibilities.*

And so it is, partly, here. Some of the people I write of who are part of this story have asked me to omit certain things, or to not be identified. Because in writing my own early, personal story I write part of their young story also, which they choose not to tell. But they also think that . . . history . . . should be told.

Part of me understands their decision. Twice I have been asked to write an Autobiography or a Memoir — both times I have (quite literally) screamed in horror, as witnesses can confirm, and I will never, *never* write about my life again; this present shock of emotional Chinese burns has been difficult enough. Also forests would be demolished and you (and I) would die of boredom if even 0.01 per cent of my written records were ever to be made public. (I would also die of embarrassment.) The bonfire awaits. Yet, by stealth almost, some of the very early diaries I opened perhaps show more than I at first understood. They trace, like old black-and-white photographs, a picture of my family, and me, and the people I knew so long ago in the 1950s. But perhaps they also tell something of the country we lived in — and the stories we told ourselves about our country, then. Kasuo Ishiguro also wondered in his Nobel Prize lecture: *Does a nation remember and forget in much the same way as an individual does?* Sometimes re-writing itself also?

And just one thing more about the 'bloody diaries', as I have now once actually shouted at them. Even though I have cut hundreds of thousands of words, sometimes as the story told in these pages — the plot — changes, a chapter *is* mostly diary entries. This is *not* because I think I was a talented teenage writer who wasn't as self-obsessed and intense as most teenagers, and always, always I have to stress that the entries were that teenager's point of view. I have 'narrated' very many parts of this particular history, using the diaries as reference: the me of now observing, sometimes commenting. But in parts of the story — often where something important happens — I can't do that. The diary entries just have to tell the story as seen by the 'me' of 'then'. If I cut some of these things, sometimes perhaps to be less controversial now, I cut the truth of 'then'.

I sat in my small bedroom recording our lives every night.

First I wrote in (fading now) pencil, then with a pen dipped in ink (once, in a half-asleep night, I tried to drink ink, thinking it was the glass of water by my bed). Finally I got a *real fountain pen.*

And in defence of narrative, and story, and plot: in the very first writing year this twelve-year-old writes that she wants to be, when she grows up, three things: a hairdresser, an actress, and a writer.

I never was a hairdresser, although in my somewhat wild youth I would chop at my own hair because I thought I was ugly.

WEDNESDAY 14 FEBRUARY 1951

Went to Girls' Manuel Training at 10.30am. Miss Allen is a nice teacher but she is leaving. Preserved greengages . . . hmm, not very good. After school we were skipping as it has come into the Season. Listened to "Much Binding in the Marsh" with Dad.

MONDAY 19 FEBRUARY 1951

Andrew's 9th birthday. I gave him a squeezer beaker. And he got £2, a box of chocs and a pencil with a top. I challenged Valda on the tennis ladder at 7.30am. She won 3-2 but it was juice. We went for a swim on the tram. Went for my 50 yards certificate. I got it but it took all my energy. I'd just about had it when I came out. (Private.)

SATURDAY 24 FEBRUARY 1951

Ross's 7th birthday. Gave him a clicking cowboy. Andy gave him a blowpipe. He got a check and a box of chocs from Mum and Dad. Played hairdressers. I want to be one now. Went fishing on Seatoun wharf about 5pm but it was too rough. We've got a little china rabbit for Miss Allen's leaving present. Mum says it is cheap pottery.

TUESDAY 8 MARCH 1951

Eclipse. After school Noelene and I had to stand under the clock for pinching each other. We couldn't stop laughing. Then I went to Mrs Webb's and got a kitten. A dear little black one. I brought it home in a bird-cage. I'm going to call it Tuppence.

SATURDAY 31 MARCH 1951

Tuppence wet my bed. It has to sleep in the wash-house. Went with the Burleys to Mr Burley's Masonic Lodge picnic. Pauline and I played lots of tennis. I got a free bag of lollies and about six free ice-creams. Then I came second in a running race with two in it for which I got a prize which was another bag of lollies and 1/- . Got the Sports Post.

SUNDAY 1 APRIL 1951

April Fools' Day. I accidently trod on Tuppence and killed him. Was getting cat food. Went to Sunday School. Took the bird cage back to Webbs. They were very sorry and I am getting one of her next kittens.

TUESDAY 24 APRIL 1951

Had our school Anzac Day service. I had to say "We give thanks for the privileges we receive as New Zealanders and members of the British Commonwealth of Nations. We honour the memories of all those who served our country. We will honour our King, obey the laws of his Government and serve our country and fellow men." Raining. Bev and I are writing a play called "Bartholomew". I make it up and she writes it down. It seems quite good so far. Andrew and Ross cooked (wow).

TUESDAY 1 MAY 1951

Dev, Bev, Jennifer, Noelene, Beryl and I decided to have a Concert for the Blind. We asked the teachers. I'm Bartholomew in "Bartholomew". Also I'm singing "A You're Adorable" with Rae, Bev and Noelene. Dev and Beryl sing and tap-dance. It will be 3d to get in, and we practiced after school. We had a fire. I've got a hottie. We're saving up for a washing machine and dishwasher combined. (thank goodness, no dishes).

FRIDAY 4 MAY 1951

Gave first concert in Mr Simmonds's room. I was wearing tap shoes (good) with Rae in "Down among the Sheltering Palms". I've got a real ukulele which I pretend to play and I make a banjo noise with my mouth. After playtime we did Mr Butcher's room. Third concert in our room, altogether we raised £2/17/6 for the Blind. I wish wish I could learn tap dancing properly but Mum doesn't like it. It is common. It's hailing.

SUNDAY 13 MAY 1951

I was allowed to stay the night at Bev's. And did we have fun?!! Well, we pretended we were all sorts of people. Swing Sission and his band. People who lived in the slums. Mannequins, and we did dancing and Bev's Mum played the piano. They haven't got carpet and it's so good for dancing. Her Mum sang "Paper Doll". Her Dad was a bit drunk and stumbly when he came home. I wish wish we had a piano. I'd love to be an actress when I grow up and that's what I'm going to be (I hope). Wind and rain and hail and more wild wind. Bev's Mum gave me a hottie.

TUESDAY 22 MAY 1951

The Headmaster sent me to the cooking teacher with a message. Jeanette couldn't pay 2/6 for cooking ingredients this term as her father is a wharfie. The school paid. Poor thing. At horrible sewing I did one leaf on my Dorothy Bag and yapped. Saw P. in the street. He gave me a charming smile. Listened to Lever Hit Parade. It's cold.

SATURDAY 9 JUNE 1951

Worked round the house in the morning. Went to the Kiwi Concert Party with the others this afternoon. It was super. How, how can John Hunter impersonate a woman so well? I want to go again but Mum says I am not allowed. Tonight I made up a play called "The Ferns". Of course I was the main character. I burnt it on the fire though and didn't let anybody see it. But I want to be an actress, and that's what I'm going to be.

MONDAY 2 JULY 1951

Mr Curran said he'd send me to Miss O'Connor for the strap if I made any more noise so I'll have to be quiet. At cooking we couldn't get any eggs or sugar or butter. So we had to make bread pudding (ugh, awful). Got a love-letter from P.

He asked me to go for a bike ride on Sunday. Mum said if he calls for me she doesn't mind. Dev and Noelene rang up tonight and said they were the Yellow Phantom.

SUNDAY 8 JULY 1951

Went to Sunday School in the morning. Then P. was supposed to take me out but he didn't come. I wonder why. Noelene, Dev, Bev and Rae saw some boys at the Air Raid shelter and they LOVE them. They're just big flirts. But I still like them. Isabel brought knitting so I got a whole lot of wool from the attic and I'm knitting a lot of nothings. I'm not allowed to learn tap dancing. That is final says Mum. It is Common.

FRIDAY 14 SEPTEMBER 1951

Today Noelene told Deveney that she didn't want to sit with her any more. Dev howled and I howled because Noelene is taking Bev away. Anyone can see that. I lost my temper and made Jennifer cry. Now Bev is out of friends with me because I hit Dev for talking awful about Beryl. Let her. I don't care!! Reading "The Cloister and the Hearth". P. is in hospital with appendicitis poor thing but I don't really like him now.

THURSDAY 15 NOVEMBER 1951

At school today we had Essay and Letter exams. I do hope I get Ex. as I want to be a writer. I did it on "Thoughts by the Fireside". Bought two dozen Christmas cards – 2/-. Interview at Wellington East Girls' College. Mum's trying to make me take Latin and I don't want to really. Oh well. Ross keeps being an aeroplane, even in the kitchen.

SATURDAY 24 NOVEMBER 1951

Gosh I have to work hard at housework on Saturdays. Then I went to Webbs and got my new kitten. We've decided to call it Wobbles. It is so sweet and wobbly – but we'll have to be Careful. Went to Jennifer's party which was good. Got a packet of bubble gum for a prize. I've only seen it at the pictures! Jennifer's father gets it from America. He is funny, he squashes the bottom of all the chocolates to find the hard ones.

FRIDAY 30 NOVEMBER 1951

Oh crumbs what's the matter with me . . . My Art exam was pretty awful. And instead of having P.T. we had our Social Studies exam. I only got 31 questions right out of 50. The highest was 39. Janice got it. Rae took my tennis racket off me so I tore her book. Started reading "Macbeth". I got a signed photo from Moira Shearer that I wrote to Hollywood for. Woke up in the middle of the night and shelled peas.

WEDNESDAY 19 DECEMBER 1951

Dear Diary, Well – today was the last day I'll ever be at Primary School. Gave out all my Xmas cards. Bev gave me a present. While I was saying goodbye to the teachers I burst out howling. Nearly everyone cried. Came top. 8 Excellents. So Dad owes me 4/-. Got my uniform for College and new diary – like this one. Had to step over a drunk man. He was sleeping on the footpath in Manners Street with a bottle. Wobbles is so cuddly and purrs loudly. I am very careful of him.

MONDAY 24 DECEMBER 1951

Mum and Dad went to town early to "see a man about a dog". Andy and Ross and I played around all day, singing "The Tennessee Waltz". Andrew got a loan of a trolley and we went whizzing down the hill. I mowed the lawn. I like the smell of the grass when I mow. We decorated the Xmas tree – Wobbles was so sweet and excited.

TUESDAY 25 DECEMBER 1951

Gosh it was good today. I got tennis shoes, two tennis balls, "Knob Hill Mystery", Glass, half pound box of Queen Anne Chocolates, soap in a plastic box, ten handkerchiefs, candy stick, facecloth soap and comb, table covers, Pixie Caramel Bar. Big Xmas dinner! We played bowls in the lounge with neighbours who visited. Hot.

MONDAY 31 DECEMBER 1951

Well today is the last time I'll write in this diary. And I'm proud to say I've kept my diary every day, for a whole year. Today I didn't go to the beach again. I went to town instead and Andy and I saw "Dear Brat" at the Regent. Tonight we're getting up at 11.45pm. Tell you all about that next year. Cheerio 1951.

III

WELLINGTON EAST GIRLS' COLLEGE. Navy-blue school uniform so that, my dad explained carefully to me, everyone could feel equal (that is, some girls might have nicer clothes than others) and always a beret which was emphatically not, in 1950s Wellington, a fashion item. We were perched on top of a hill and a tunnel, overlooking the Basin Reserve Cricket Ground. And overlooking Wellington Boys' College just below, which meant that as we progressed (and got older and more sensible) we could have ballroom-dancing classes with boys for partners, instead of each other or wooden chairs, about whom or which in the meantime we had to place our arms in the lady-like manner we were to emulate with boys later. In 2017 some of the descendants of the boys at that college were boasting on the internet about getting some of the girls at the school above drunk, making 'rape jokes'; some of the girls at Wellington East Girls' College arranged a demonstration to protest about this outside Parliament. Indeed a different world from the one I am describing and I am proud of my school's descendants.

When I became a professional actress I was lucky enough

to come home almost at once in a Royal Shakespeare Company production of *The Comedy of Errors*, and I was asked then, and several times later, to speak to the girls at the college and I always refused (not understanding that, having been described as unrealistic, childish and — above all — selfish because of the dreams I had had and the choices I had made, I might possibly have something of use to say to some of them). One principal said severely: 'You owe it to us.' I answered that my days at that school were the unhappiest of my life. I wasn't being either fair or honest. It wasn't the school's fault, and important and formative things happened to me while I was there. But I could never bear to go back.

In 1952 at my new school I — so suddenly — hardly ever saw 'those girls' whose lives had been so hugely part of mine: my best friend and co-writer Bev; Noelene and Deveney and Rae who were allowed to do tap dancing and flirted so successfully with boys; gentle Jennifer whose father pressed in the bottoms of all chocolates to get the hard ones. And I missed them. Many of us went to the same school and wore the same uniform but we were streamed into different classes and that was like being in different worlds. I was in the Latin class for the 'clever' girls — but I was certainly no longer the cleverest one.

I think of our college teachers then: all women, many affected also by World War II. Very few of them were married; many of them (we heard rumours and drifting talk) had lost boyfriends or fiancés or chances of marriage — New Zealand's ratio of young men killed to population was the highest in the Commonwealth. (That little Anzac speech I had had to give the previous year could perhaps have mentioned the privileges the Empire received, as well as bestowed.) These women got on with their lives; they walked briskly about the school, their black gowns billowed out behind them in the Wellington wind as they crossed the quad to the Assembly Hall or to the pre-fabs where some of us had classes. One teacher went mad in the science lab during a lesson and tried to put iodine into a cat's eyes; one was a Plymouth Brethren who was also our Careers Advisor; one wore very, very bright red lipstick and slacks but she was the Sports Mistress. And one, a short woman with round glasses and a sweet smile which hid a scythe-sharp mind, Miss Gambrill, was a brilliant English teacher who inspired so many of us. I owe her a debt of such gratitude: it was she who encouraged my growing knowledge of, and love of, New Zealand literature, and she also paid great attention to my own writing. Once (I record) she — very carefully — implied that something I wrote was sentimental: that I was sometimes . . . drawn to the pathetic . . . The diaries then follow with entries like . . . I'll show her! . . . and . . . no sentimentality in this story . . . Thank God for Molly Gambrill.

I have long, long become experienced in writing about myself or speaking about myself in public without in any way writing or saying anything *really* personal about my real life. Even now some of my friends complain about my privateness. But, O Irony! (as well as O Irony! about me writing this, now). As I went through college my diaries make quite clear that I was a blabber-mouth — told everybody everything, or nearly everything, especially about the continually changing and ongoing dramas of my relationships with boys. I also, to a certain extent — but not entirely — disloyally blabbed about my growing difficulties at home, especially with my mother, which are recorded in my diaries in such vivid detail day after day. And I believe I wrote the real truth (as I saw it of course) in the diaries. Never under-estimate the lingering power of a puritanical upbringing: at this point the inheritance was in full flower. If I told a lie to anyone, I wrote about it in the diary. If I lied *in* the diary or left something important out, I picked myself up on it and then told the true story. If I flirted with other girls' boyfriends, I guiltily recorded it in the diary. If I over-wept to get my way with my mother, or if I said sorry when I didn't really mean it: all recorded.

But unexpected, unimaginable changes overtake faster and faster anything one might write in this global, digital age — especially about truth. I am writing this at a time when a new concept has arisen (even in the new *Oxford English Dictionary*) — '*post*-truth'. In the Brexit referendum in the United Kingdom actual, factual lies were paraded shamelessly on the side of campaign buses: Brexit was voted for. I then followed the American election closely, and by chance found myself working in Berlin with stunned, disbelieving, angry American actors the week Donald Trump was elected. *'It can't be true!'* they said, checking their mobile phones over and over. *'The result was faked, obviously!'* and famous film stars forgot their lines. After Donald Trump became President 'alternative facts' began to emerge from the White House, accusing the media of purveying 'fake news' (*Collins English Dictionary*'s 'word' of 2017). Who knows what will happen next, and this paragraph may quite soon read like gibberish. But my whole childhood emphasised the absolute importance of truth, which is why I write that way in these early diaries. And if I didn't still feel somehow influenced by that early stricture, the picture that I find of myself as a young person in the diaries would have been presented here in a somewhat more attractive manner. (And — final puritanical admission — I've still cut the worst bits!)

Because of the story of my mother's 'genius' IQ (and presumably because these particular tests were still done in those days), we three Ewing children had our IQ measured with tests that would no doubt be considered totally invalid today. Whatever the IQ attainment for 'genius' was, Andrew — that beloved, beautiful boy-at-last three years after my birth — just attained it: he was a genius. Oh, the *rage* this competitive older sister felt when she got two points less: I wasn't a genius. Ross wasn't up there at all — and felt it all his life, even though he went to university for the first time when he was forty and qualified as a medical doctor.

But I presume those early IQ tests were measuring intelligent intelligence, not emotional intelligence (a phrase that as far as I know wasn't even invented then), and it wasn't easy being the daughter of a judgemental, frustrated genius in the 1950s who — so clever and original and quirky and interesting in some ways — was also extremely conventional and cared so enormously about what 'the neighbours' might say. The battles with my mother which became more and more stark over the next years were in some ways, of course, the usual mother–teenage daughter battles. But I think there was something much more going on in that suburban house where 'feminism' and 'the women's movement' were unknown concepts; where the advertisements we were surrounded by in newspapers or on hoardings featured all those Happy Homemakers with neat, curly hair and lipstick, using Persil and Sunlight Soap and putting dinner on the table for the happy family. All the advertisements for Cashmere Bouquet Soap, Old Dutch Cleanser, AirWick Odour Remover — all for keeping the dirt away — meant that so many of the pictures of women we saw were women in aprons, smiling and smiling at cleanliness. (Men featured often in cigarette advertisements, smoking relaxedly and looking manly.)

I am conscious, always, of the dangers of a story being told only by the one still alive, and that the story told in these particular diaries is also a story about my mother. I am also aware how complicated and convoluted our relationship was. And sometimes now of course I find myself taking Mum's side: she was born into a time when marriage and children were absolutely considered to be a woman's joy and pinnacle — even for a woman who felt cleverer than almost all the men she ever met. Including my father's colleagues who — she screamed at Andrew and Ross and me after our father's funeral — thought of her as 'a silly little typist from Newtown'. Yet although she judged and blamed us for many things, and manipulated us also — the teenage me in particular and ultimately, and dramatically, my father — she must have known, or perhaps she had blanked it out, that her intelligence *had* been recognised: unusually in the 1920s she had been given a chance, sent to university when she was very young, long before she knew any of us. And she had been unable to cope — and maybe that was the most bitter knowledge of all. Yet some fifteen-year-old girls might possibly find it difficult even today to be thrust into a university science class of all boys. In another time she possibly would not have had children. She had a brilliant scientific, logical mind, but by the time I started college the only things she had had to use it on were her three children and a husband who was doing so well in his own work — and all around her advertisements that really did exhort DON'T LET MRS NEXT-DOOR SNIFF TWICE — USE AIRWICK.

And she was *angry*.

So life became more and more difficult in our house, in New Zealand, in the 1950s. Some of the sounds of my childhood echo still: the vacuum cleaner being banged down loudly and resentfully when it was being used, as it was in our very clean house, every day; that loud running cold tap in the bathroom to cover any rude sounds when Mum was going to the lavatory; my father (who avoided rows and confrontations at any cost), in times of tension in the house whistling a kind of innocent, tuneless whistle and going about his business. And the screaming.

My mother was still hitting me — physically and emotionally — when I was seventeen years old and had started studying at the same university she had had to leave (perhaps *because* I had started studying at that same university?): not, anyway, the experience, as far as I know, of my close friends. It is clear that from the time I was a teenager I had to learn to use various strategies to cope — and if I used such strategies I say so in my diary, because I became perfectly well aware of what I was doing: the diaries show how I learnt to a certain extent to manipulate her in my own way. But when she screamed at me the devastating criticisms that became more and more repeated and familiar, when she screamed and wept — all there in the diaries, I would not be able to cohere them otherwise — I was afraid of her. I was afraid of the hysterical, uncontrolled screaming. And when I was afraid of her, the dark shadow of my shouting Uncle Harry loomed and festered, always undiscussed.

We lived near a Presbyterian private boys' boarding school called Scots College, mainly at that time, I think, for the sons of rich farmers or rich businessmen or families with social pretensions that seemed so un-New Zealandish that when as children we first became aware of them we laughed at them, walking every Sunday to church in their grey and red school uniforms, short pants and long socks pulled up neatly. But by the time we got to college they became an important source of 'boys' for the girls who lived nearby. Adolescent entertainment we had to make ourselves, and it often featured the church near the sea, the wooden church hall where Bible Class was held, and the walk home from church through a tram tunnel to our suburb on Sunday mornings — after which the boarders had to be back at school for lunch, and the girls had to go home to help their mothers. Very occasionally, the Bible Class had a 'social', with ballroom dancing (those foxtrots and waltzes we had first practised with chairs), which the boarders were permitted to attend: that was a really exciting evening.

My parents — my mother — kept a very strict eye on any social activities that were arranged. She told me that she had planted a blossom tree by the front gate years ago in the hope that one day it would make a pretty flowering arch over the gate where I could say goodnight to my boyfriend (to whom I would become engaged, and then marry, and then live with happily ever after, with our children), though she did already say, slightly disapprovingly, it was a shame that my nice, first favourite boy from Scots College, who I later wrote to for years, was rather short. In the end of course she must have yearned for shortness rather than other problems, and the blossom never did arch over into a romantic bower.

WEDNESDAY 6 FEBRUARY 1952

College. They're certainly super-duper grounds anyway. I wish I didn't have to take Latin. We've had a few lessons. Guess what came home today – just guess. Yes – we've got a car at last, a beige Austin A40. Of course we went for a ride in it after tea. Our own car. I'm allowed to change my course at the end of the year if I want to.

THURSDAY 7 FEBRUARY 1952

I was having a wash this morning and Mum came in with a funny look on her face. Today is a day that will go down in history for many years. King George VI is dead. He died peacefully in his sleep last night. There was no school. We went to Days Bay in the new car and had a swim. And Viv told me that at Ian McF's party she smoked!!!

FRIDAY 8 FEBRUARY 1952

I like college now. There are some nice girls in our class and there's going to be School Plays and I hope hope I can be in them. I still want to be an actress. Everyone was very amazed at the King's Death. Miss Wilson the headmistress gave a speech about it, and I honestly think she was crying. Wobbles is sick – he wont eat anything.

MONDAY 11 FEBRUARY 1952

Wobbles doesn't seem any better today. On Wednesday the four main colleges are going to the Town Hall for a service for the King. We're having gym inspection tomorrow. Wobbles is just lying in the wash-house.

TUESDAY 12 FEBRUARY 1952

I woke up about 3.30a.m. and I knew Wobbles was dead. Mum went out and had a look at him – and he was. Mum was crying too. At school we're practising songs for the Service. We had Maths today then French. Gosh it was funny, the teacher gabbling away. I only told Pauline and Jennifer about Wobbles, not new people.

WEDNESDAY 13 FEBRUARY 1952

We went with all colleges to the Special Service for the King at the Town Hall. It was awfully hot and silly me – I think I fainted. Went back to school in a teacher's car.

. . . and there we were, on that far side of the Pacific Ocean, summer in February, with a funny look on my mother's face: the news from the BBC on the brown wireless with the yellow dial was that King George VI of England — and of New Zealand — had died. And so had our kitten and I fainted in the Town Hall.

Of course the schools were closed the day he died, *of course* we had a big Town Hall memorial service for all the Wellington colleges. He was absolutely our King too, the man whose face was often in our newspapers and in the newsreels at the pictures with his lovely kind wife and two pretty daughters, and we always stood up at the end of *Annie Get Your Gun* or *Harvey* while they played 'God Save The King', and I knew the words *God save our gracious King* much better than I knew the words *God defend New Zealand*. My only knowledge of God defending New Zealand was when He saved us from the Yellow Peril which (they said) was silently approaching from Japan. My sole memory of the actual war was one night at the very end: a member of the Home Guard coming to our door to tell us there was a chink of light visible through our dining-room curtains. (And one of the men who had tried to defend Our Gracious King and defend New Zealand was my uncle fighting in Egypt who later wielded a knife in that same dining room.)

I had saved their photographs once, but presumably it was not grief for the Royal Family that caused me to faint at the King's funeral service. Seemingly out of the blue, I started having what would now be described as severe panic attacks. And the insomnia that had been nibbling at the edge of my nights turned into a life-long problem. I couldn't sleep at night and in the daytime I couldn't bear to be in any enclosed space that might get hot or crowded, and if I ever had to stand for very long — in a choir, in assembly singing hymns, in church, anywhere where I couldn't get out — I was terrified of fainting: the only way I can describe it is that suddenly every day had become an obstacle course of fear. Over and over again I became dizzy for no reason; perspiration ran down my body and my legs as I tried not to pass out. I, who was so looking forward to appearing on the *real stage* in the school Assembly Hall in the 'school plays' I'd heard so much about, became terrified of even entering that Assembly Hall to sing hymns, which we did every single morning.

So: I lay in my bedroom all night, frightened, panicking and awake, with no idea what was the matter with me.

My poor parents, puzzled, tried to help me, and made an arrangement with me. If I was still awake at 3 a.m. I was allowed to go into their room; my father (who now had to travel a lot round New Zealand with his work for the Education Department) would stagger into my thin bed with the pink bedspread, and my mother would turn away from me on her side, and instruct me to lie still next to her back in the bigger bed with the green bedspread, and breathe in and out in time to her breathing. I suppose I often finally dropped off for an hour or two, and then staggered off in my college uniform when morning came. Also: my mother had just, at last, started a part-time job as a typist in a place she loved called the Applied Maths Laboratory. So she had to stagger off too. My poor parents.

I lost weight, lost courage: the cycle-riding, tennis-playing, Bartholomew-starring, friend-pinching, bell-ringing head prefect had become (we didn't know this word) a wimp; a cowardly girl with a pale face who had, so foolishly and fancifully, wanted to be an actress. How could anyone be an actress if they were scared of standing in public? And some days I couldn't even go to school. There are sad little day-after-day entries . . . what is wrong with me? . . . what is happening to me? . . . couldn't go to school today have to catch up with subjects . . . Mum stayed home with me today . . . don't like being sick, what is wrong with me? . . . How ridiculous and childish all this sounds as I try to describe it, but anyone who has suffered from panic attacks knows they are often totally un-understandable — that is the point — and totally terrifying. And the reasons they were so suddenly happening were never explored or talked about: I was obviously just being a bit silly.

There is so much more emphasis these days on recognising and dealing with anxiety and panic attacks in children and teenagers; many schools — and universities — have student counsellors. In the 1950s it was more of a matter of 'pulling yourself together'.

In my diary I called my fear of fainting aa..xx..hh. I slept very badly night after night after night, and the most common entry in all the diaries is . . . I am so TIRED. I was often ill with flu and sore throats and coughing fits, had teenage spots all over my face, and had interminable dental appointments: sometimes teeth broke or fell out. Presumably, as well as eating bags and bags of 'lollies and chocs', I was madly clenching my teeth a lot of the time.

Finally Mum went to see the headmistress and she allowed me to miss Assembly: I could stay outside the hall with the Jewish girls until the standing up and hymn-singing was finished and just go in with them for the School Notices. I loved singing but left the school choir because you had to stand. I wouldn't go to Bible Class because we had to stand and sing hymns even there, and I gave up church altogether. I'd lose days of school, then I'd go back, try and catch up the lessons I'd missed, sit with the Jewish girls outside the Assembly Hall, and stare at the wind-blown sky while 'Praise My Soul the King of Heaven' echoed out.

And yet, and yet . . .

The diaries show I was deeply disturbed in one way but the permission to miss Assembly immediately gave me some respite. And what I obviously had, deep down somewhere inside me in the middle of all this frightening upheaval, was some kind of mad, determined resilience. There were school sports races that I at least entered . . . I came fourth in the walking race . . . I came 2nd to last in the 75 yards and nearer the end than the beginning in the 100 yards . . . My English teacher liked my essays. My friend Viv of *The Red Shoes* bathing-togged ballet had moved to Days Bay across the water of Wellington Harbour: she came to stay one night and we wore nylons fastened to our suspender belts instead of scratchy school stockings to go to see

An American in Paris, came home and danced like Leslie Caron, and argued about which of us would dance with Gene Kelly before we died. (I never did dance with him, but I auditioned for him once and he was so charming that I couldn't stop smiling, thinking of his photo tacked on to my bedroom wall, even when I suddenly realised he assumed — of course — that I could tap dance and I had to confess I could not. I did not add that my mother had thought tap dancing 'common'.)

And then. In our English class we performed *The Merchant of Venice* and I was cast as Bassanio and the teacher lent me her red evening cape as part of my costume. I was so nervous that I of course couldn't sleep . . . I have to stand for a long time . . . I hope I'll be all right . . . I'm scared . . . I'm so tired . . . But: I so, so wanted to act, and *that* made me fight my panic attacks instead of running away. And, with this performance in our classroom in my teacher's red evening cape taking on in my head the importance of a first night at the Royal Shakespeare Company, I did it. I worked out that *if* I could screw up my courage enough to go on stage (in this case, a partially cleared third form classroom) then — because there, where I wanted to be so much, I knew exactly what was going to happen, where I had to stand, and for how long — I could win . . . I did it! It went all right, I perspired like anything down my clothes but I didn't faint, it went all right, it went all right.

I thought I had found a way to beat that aa..xx..hh.

I wasn't miraculously cured but I had, by myself — and inside my head, inside my *brain*, I suppose I mean, not sharing this particular battle with anybody but my diary — made myself take the first step. But I still didn't go into Assembly while the hymns were ringing out. I longed for the weekends, hated and dreaded Mondays — and then that same odd, determined, mad resilience would break out and I found myself enjoying things after all . . . school's not so bad really . . .

Then to my terrified excitement I was cast, the youngest of only four girls from our school, to be in a play about Alexander the Great, *Adventure Story* by Terence Rattigan, at a boy's college: Rongotai. We four girls went there every Friday after school for many weeks to rehearse with more than a dozen boys, and I was in heaven and I was in hell: acting and boys — and terror . . . what will happen, I am so nervous will I faint? . . . I am much more nervous than all the others . . . will I be all right? And then, knowing exactly what I had to do, pulling it off again . . . I was so nervous, but I think it went ok and I didn't faint . . . Then I was cast in our 'House Play Competition' held actually *in* that dreaded school Assembly Hall, to play Arthur in Thornton Wilder's *The Happy Journey* (where, most fortuitously, the characters are sitting in a car most of the time). And was singled out by the judge, Richard Campion (who was just setting up the New Zealand Players, New Zealand's first professional theatre company, with his wife, the actress Edith Campion), who . . . told me to keep on with it . . .

And so, peculiar as it seems, it was my early desire to be an actress . . . I'd love to be an actress when I grow up and that's what I'm going to be (I hope) . . . that seemed to save me.

But I still waited with the Jewish girls to go into Assembly only for the School Notices, after the hymns, and I still didn't go to church, and as to *why* all this had happened to me there was never any discussion.

WEDNESDAY 4 JUNE 1952

Today we had four subjects. Ruth's lent me a murder book and it's beaut. I got 24 for English test but Ruth got 24 and a half. I must try and come top in English. I've decided I quite like school after all and when I get over this aa..xx..hh I'll love it I should think. We've started Genetive, Dative and Ablative in Latin (worse luck).

WEDNESDAY 25 JUNE 1952

Went to the library. Nearly froze to death. Dad has promised me £1 if I can go to full assembly six times running. Of course they all think I'm just silly. And – Mum is to be a relieving teacher at Scots College starting on Tuesday!!! (hmm). She's getting her driving licence. Got a letter from Bev, wrote back straight away. I never see her now.

I caught up in most of my school work (except Latin). Bible Class slowly begins to feature regularly again. I was still at the library at least twice a week getting armfuls of books; Mum and Dad still went to visit Uncle Harry in the Porirua Mental Hospital on Sundays, never discussing it, and I had to look after my brothers. So we usually made fudge or hokey-pokey.

In October a diary entry says that one morning I went into the Assembly Hall after hymns — and a School Notice read out was about me. I had won the School Prose Competition even though I was only in the first year. I have absolutely no memory of winning that prize; I only remember, so clearly, the rest of that day's entry: on that same day, the headmistress told me, very firmly, that I would no longer be excused from attending Assembly. I had been in school plays — and from now on I was to attend like everybody else. I told myself over and over and over and over, in the middle of the night wide awake and sweating, that I had been in two plays, and won a writing prize and so . . . I HAVE to manage assembly as well . . . How oddly it all reads now. How terrified I was then . . . what will happen? Will everything start all over again, I'm dreading it. I'm dreading it dear diary . . . will it all start again? . . .

TUESDAY 21 OCTOBER 1952

Oh oh CHEERS! I was Okay in Assembly. I just held tight to the seat in front and perspired a lot when we had hymns. Thank goodness. Looks as though I am getting better at last at last. Only got 30 out of 70 for Latin test and 21 out of 30 for Social Studies test. O dear. Mum got me a brassiere. I've got 47 'Picturegoer' magazines now. Oh thank goodness thank goodness thank goodness it was okay.

WEDNESDAY 22 OCTOBER 1952

OK again in Assembly. I hope I'm really all right now. Tonight, for winning the Prose Comp Dad gave me 'The Collected Stories of Katherine Mansfield'. It's super. Win and I are going to try and get a job at Whitcombs and Tombs Books in the school holidays to earn some money. Mum gets a heck of a tired now days. She says the boys at Scots College are totally out of control.

Mention still every now and then of aa..xx..hh and occasionally still I simply couldn't go to school because I hadn't had any sleep at all, but I now gritted my (poor) teeth and went into Assembly most days as if it had all just been a funny little episode of puberty; of course I didn't know that word, or the meaning yet of puberty — we didn't speak of such rude things — even though Mum had just bought me my first brassiere. When I got my first period she spoke of the matter distastefully, and introduced me to a sanitary belt, and to sanitary pads which were fastened to the belt at each end with large safety pins — but we didn't speak about sex. Nor did we at school. (Things changed eventually: recently a younger woman I know told me that in New Zealand in 1992, when she was leaving primary school in an area that had far too many unplanned pregnancies, a teacher demonstrated sex — in separate lessons for boys and girls — by showing the children how to put a condom over a banana. My Norwegian niece advised me that the same kind of thing was going on in Norway round the same time: in her case it was a condom and a latex oblong.)

And I still have the copy of Katherine Mansfield's short stories, indeed inscribed *To Barbara from Dad, 22/10/52.*

Of course very different New Zealand writers now have their own subjects and their own confidence — and I've heard younger Pākehā writers say that Katherine Mansfield was of no importance at all in their development. But, as I've already said, I realise that this confidence we proudly take for granted now was being hard fought for and hard won by an older generation of New Zealand writers, who were writing about New Zealand at the very same time as I was devouring *The Lark on the Wing* and *Carol in Repertory* (set of course in England). The only New Zealand writing I had ever seen was in the *School Journal* that Dad used to edit, in which there were little New Zealand stories and poems. Dad himself wrote a small thin pamphlet-looking book called *Pitama* with a Māori design on its cover because the Education Department thought that Native schools should have a book in which the hero was a Māori warrior, and we were all very proud when he brought this little book home with his name on it. But that was a special case, a school book. Also, at home, as well as *The Laughing Cavalier* and a Vermeer print, we had on our walls several woodcuts by New Zealand artists which had been used in the *School Journals*, I think by E. Mervyn Taylor and Russell Clark. But that was all I knew about New Zealand art. New Zealand art and literature didn't count, not really.

Art — like literature, like cars, like refrigerators, like most things — came from Overseas.

So Dad's gift of Katherine Mansfield's stories in 1952 had a huge, incalculable effect on me. Here was the first of all those devoured books — a big fat book — which had lots of stories set in New Zealand. When I realised that the bay of 'At the Bay' was near where my friend Viv lived, where we went swimming the day King George VI died, I was astounded.

I hadn't understood.

You could write about anywhere . . .

However, those ongoing diaries also narrate that, seemingly 'cured' of my strange little difficulty and even winning a prize, I was becoming what Mum labelled 'rebellious'. She sent me to bed early one night . . . with the light off as if I was a baby . . . for quarrelling with Andrew, so I put the light on again and wrote, enraged, in my diary. No corporal punishment at secondary school, as I've said. But these rules did not apply at home, and — especially — did not apply to me.

My brothers and I still listened to the Lever Hit Parade, and England may have been 'Home', but almost every pop song came from America: 'Wheel of Fortune', Johnnie Rae singing 'The Little White Cloud That Cried', and as usual Andrew and Ross and I knew all the words and sang them loudly while doing the dishes. Little girls began to ask me if that handsome boy Andrew was my brother, and it was already quite clear at school how bright he was. Ross, now aged eight, still spending a lot of time being an aeroplane, already had the same sense of humour as our father: he and Dad used to sit together listening and chuckling to radio programmes like *Much-Binding-in-the-Marsh* and later *Take It From Here* and *The Goon Show* and Ross could do all the voices. Kindergarten teachers had earlier told Dad (visiting them from the Education Department) that when they had asked each child what their father did, Ross had said casually, 'My father is a Burglar.' He perfected a marvellous imitation (just among the three of us, of course) of our parents: he would make a contained high-pitched screeching sound followed by a mumbled male undertone: Mum and Dad having a row. For years we three directed a quiet, short-hand version of this sound at each other if we sensed there was trouble brewing.

I emerged not terribly well from the first year's college exams, but I got a prize: *Flush* by Virginia Woolf. I played, yet again, the Virgin Mary, this time in the Bible Class nativity play — and there is no reason to believe that the real Virgin Mary wasn't hit by her mother also, who may have had some trouble believing her daughter's story.

SUNDAY 14 DECEMBER 1952

There wasn't any bible class. Mum gave me a hiding for

nothing and that's true. And then went mad when I didn't get the lunch. Apparently I'm not good enough for Her Majesty. I was nervous at the beginning of the Nativity play tonight, but ok. We had to rope in those three boys to play shepherds. Even though we were always laughing at rehearsals it went all right tonight except for a snort from one of the angels. We went to a party at Wesneys afterwards. Mum said I was too late back. Wot a pity.

Still over two years before rock and roll really exploded through New Zealand radios and jukeboxes, so we weren't quite yet the phenomenon of 'wild teenagers' (though there were hints: when we went to the pictures we saw newsreels of young people in America and England 'jiving' to — somehow — different music, which seemed exciting). I was growing up like a million young people, just one of them, recalcitrant, finding our way.

But not quite.

Because somewhere at the bottom of my soul a fragment was half-formed that I wasn't able to articulate and certainly didn't yet write about in my diary — writing might make it true. I wondered whether those panic attacks that now read so pathetically but then loomed so large meant — again the shadow hovered — that maybe *I* was somehow mad, like Uncle Harry.

IV

WHEN I WAS FOURTEEN I met a woman who — literally — changed my life. Right then in 1953: seeing me, my enthusiasm and perhaps talent, encouraging me, stretching me, making my dreams. But the diaries have told me something else (plot and threads do all keep appearing after all . . .). Very importantly — and I had not completely understood this until now — she influenced me in another chapter of my young life: when things had changed.

Madame Maria Dronke, a successful German-Jewish actress, had had to flee Germany as Nazism grew and, with her family, been given sanctuary in New Zealand in 1939. Were they called, sometimes pejoratively, immigrants? Statistics and newspaper accounts anyway show that New Zealand with its population of something over one and a half million took in 1100 Jewish refugees, and there was some dissension in the country about this number: *after all they are Germans* echoing the words today about Syrian refugees: *they might be terrorists.* Maria's beloved (non-Jewish) husband, John Dronke, had been a German magistrate: in New Zealand during the war

I believe he was given a job making artificial limbs for injured soldiers; he never worked in New Zealand law courts. Later he played the cello in New Zealand's first National Orchestra and finally worked in a government department involved in patents and copyright where he could use at least some of his legal knowledge. They had two now college-age children, Peter and Marei. I can remember being scared almost of Marei, who was sometimes there in Maria's studio in her college uniform; older, she seemed so beautiful and so composed — all the things I wasn't. Presumably Maria needed to add to the family income but of course that fact never crossed my mind; she was a famous actress, she was giving real 'drama classes' and I begged to be allowed to go.

A number of young people in Wellington enthusiastically enrolled for these classes. Maria was a terrific teacher, with a big theatrical personality of a kind we certainly hadn't experienced before. At first we called her Madame Dronke and were overawed by her. She had a beautiful voice, and a fantastic knowledge of rhyme and rhythm in words, as well as of the craft of acting, and she wore flowing scarves and long, dangly earrings. (Of course some people in Wellington laughed at her behind her back, imitated her.) We read plays from all over the world, from *Antigone* to *The Madwoman of Chaillot* to the new *Waiting for Godot*. We worked in detail on *The Importance of Being Earnest* and *Saint Joan*. We worked on how to use our voices and how to move on stage. She also knew so well how to read poetry and was particularly interested in New Zealand poetry: one of the poems she, unforgettably, read to us one day was 'Wild Iron' by Allen Curnow.

Sea go dark, dark with wind,
Feet go heavy, heavy with sand,
Thoughts go wild, wild with the sound
Of iron on the old shed, swinging, clanging:
Go dark, go heavy, go wild, go round,
Dark with the wind,
Heavy with the sand,
Wild with the iron that tears at the nail
And the foundering shriek of the gale.

When she read that poem to us — a 'foreigner' whose first language wasn't even English — I could hear it, the wind and the echoing iron; felt that heaviness of dark sand as you trudge through it. New Zealand.

From this time with Maria I learnt what I never forgot: a way of using the words, the rhythm of a good poem so that, no matter how difficult it is, it makes sense. Sometimes now, locked into a recording studio with the Professor of Egyptology at Oxford University, I record rhythmic, beautiful translations of words written aeons ago in old Egyptian hieroglyphs found on old, lost papyri. I read them the way Maria Dronke taught me.

Maria also made me more aware of my body as something to be used properly. I think I've always walked slightly oddly — thin legs and tension in funny places. (Oddly enough anyway to have been imitated years ago, I've been told, in a comedy programme on New Zealand television.) 'Walk from the hips, Barbie darling,' she said. 'Walk from the *hips*!' This was an interesting contrast with Madame Fedro's later comment on my inappropriate stage movement in English Restoration plays at the Royal Academy of Dramatic Art (RADA) in London: 'Open zee groin, Barbara! Open zee groin!' I tried to combine the two at one point: walking from the hips and opening the groin: this was such a disaster that I was given several private classes with Madame Fedro to try to perhaps remove a little of my 'colonial' gracelessness (just as the RADA teachers worked, with special classes, to remove the colonial sounds from my voice and I complained that they were taking away my *heart*).

Maria Dronke enlarged the world for me, while never ever saying New Zealand didn't count. She had become, though outside the classroom, one of our teachers.

In 1953 the Stratford-upon-Avon Shakespeare Company, precursor of the Royal Shakespeare Company, came to Wellington from England (after touring Australia) with, among others, Anthony Quayle, Barbara Jefford and Leo McKern in the cast. A group of us from my class, influenced by Maria's enthusiasm, queued to get tickets in the Gods to see them in *Othello* and *Henry IV Part I* and *As You Like It*, and hung round the stage door for autographs. A critical review in the *New Zealand Listener* said Anthony Quayle played Falstaff like Father Christmas — I was outraged and wrote my first public letter to the editor in protest, which was published. Somebody heard Anthony Quayle saying that he thought New Zealand must be a very religious country because there were so many religious chants on the radio: it was explained to him these were horse-racing commentaries. On their last night we were given streamers at the Opera House to throw down from the Gods on to the stage, and next day we waved them all goodbye in our school uniforms and took photos of them as they departed back to Australia on a flying boat. Some years later Barbara Jefford presented me with the Bancroft Gold Medal at the prize-giving at RADA. Later, making a film with her on the Scilly island of Bryher, I presented her with the black-and-white photograph of herself that I had taken with my new camera across the world all those years before, her hair flying wild in the Wellington wind.

Also in 1953 many of Maria's students were present at the very first performance of New Zealand's first professional theatre company, the New Zealand Players: *The Young Elizabeth* starring Edith Campion who had trained at the Old Vic School in London, directed by her husband Richard Campion (who, judging those school plays, had told me to 'keep on with it.') . . . Oh they were super! Wish I was one of them. Hope they're successful . . .

Edmund Hillary was successful.

TUESDAY 2 JUNE 1953. CORONATION DAY

EVEREST WAS CONQUERED BY A NEW ZEALANDER – AND ON CORONATION DAY TOO. Super isn't it. I'm glad it was today. Holiday. Didn't go to the Coronation Day Parade with the family as was asleep. Went into town and saw the lights after tea. Listened to a little bit of the Coronation on the radio. Only allowed to go to one dancing lesson with Wellington Boys' College this week. Huh.

THURSDAY 23 JULY 1953

Well I'll be . . . I'm in The Quiz Kids!! I've got to do two programmes on trial – and then I'll be kicked out I expect for being dumb. Still I'm in for twice. I had an audition with another little boy. We had to answer lots of questions that Selwyn Toogood gave us.

It was from Maria Dronke that I had my introduction to audition for *Quiz Kids*, a weekly radio programme in which a regular team, made up of Wellington college students, had to answer — sometimes quite difficult — questions from the quizmaster Selwyn Toogood, and so many diary entries show I spent the whole time I was a Quiz Kid in terror that I wasn't brainy enough . . . gosh it's super super fun being on the radio, being a Quiz Kid. I do hope I don't get kicked out . . . I answered a couple of questions correctly tonight . . . they're all awfully nice – but I might get kicked out because really I'm not clever enough . . . I'm not as clever as the others, I was awfully nervous tonight, and dumb . . . I remember one question: 'Who lives at number 11 Downing Street?' and from some recess in my brain I answered 'The Chancellor of the Exchequer'. But I twice, in our relatively class-less society, muddled the meaning of 'hoi polloi'(!).

And we got paid. I record sums like £1/11/0 and £1/14/0 and a copy of the *Oxford Companion to English Literature*, and once, for three broadcasts, we all got £5/2/0. I saved and saved and finally put all the money towards the greatest possession I record us obtaining in all my young years, even greater than a car: a gramophone. We could buy our favourite songs from the Hit Parade on records and play them over and over again in our house. My diary notes I bought 'Terry's Theme' from *Limelight* — a film made by an older Charlie Chaplin. And Orson Welles stared malignly down over Vienna as Harry Lime in *The Third Man*, and I bought the theme tune, played on a zither.

But a gramophone didn't turn me into a 'nice' and 'grateful' and 'supportive' fourteen-year-old daughter. Poor Mum. Horrible, horrible me. This is the year she went back to university, sat

Zoology I, and won the Kirk Prize awarded to the top student, of which we were very proud. This is when she cut up dogfish wearing violets. And I was expected to do much more as a 'Homemaker', more housework, more polishing, and I had to make quite a lot more of the meals . . . why me all the time, why not the boys? . . . and my diaries make it quite clear I was resentful . . . she went to Varsity this morning, said I had to do all the housework. Then when she came home she went mad at everything I'd done because it wasn't good enough and I had tried hard . . . I was unlike — as Mum told me so very often — all my friends 'who are not lazy like you and always help their mothers'.

At school I also became more badly behaved than giggling in a Nativity play. Underneath everything that was happening, including the good things, there was still the frightening fear of falling, nervousness about Assembly, and the unceasing insomnia — so tired sometimes that my legs would hardly work. The words I hate school appear in the diaries more and more, and I 'hated' the form mistress, who was also our Latin teacher and who told me I was a disgrace and unsuitable to be the class captain (I have absolutely no memory of being class captain). Also I now began blushing for no reason. Mum had somehow started making me feel guilty of something even if I was guilty of nothing at all, so now I began to blush on a daily basis: it was horrible and deeply, heart-beatingly embarrassing — one of the worst things about adolescence that I remember. I started refusing to do homework, had already managed to get zero in a Latin paper, didn't want to get out of bed, began to fight regularly with my mother — over and over again never doing the housework to the satisfaction of her very high standards.

Refusing one night to do any homework at all, I was finally locked in the kitchen to do it, *and* to eat gratefully the semolina Mum had made that night for pudding. I snuck out the back door and buried the semolina under the hydrangeas.

My belief in life's narrative requires a move here from semolina under hydrangeas in Wellington to the conservative *Daily Telegraph* newspaper in Britain, because the person who most affected my early diary-writing now appears. By now, like many of my friends, I had my first 'sort of' boyfriends (including the 'short' one from that nearby Scots College) who came in suits to the front door and rang the bell and escorted you to Bible Class or school dances and escorted you home again. But I had an English friend at college called Sally Garland; her father was a doctor and her mother made several trips to China, which she told us all about, though that troubling word *communist* floated again in the air. There were six children and I observed that Mrs Garland treated them like adults, not like children . . . they seem so free . . . Sally had four brothers and one of them, Nick, older than me but still at school, also kept a diary, but his was a large, lined notebook which he carried with him everywhere and in which he wrote in public places, making clever pencilled drawings down the side and saying 'Hell' quite often. I thought him so sophisticated. He sometimes arranged to meet me in milk bars with jukeboxes, and assured me that little Collins diaries weren't nearly big enough to contain all the interesting things one thought about life, and persuaded me of the absolute importance of my acquiring a big notebook also. Then his real, older girlfriends who would have been instructed to meet him at the milk bar appeared, frowned at me, and off they would go together. And then off he went to London, to Art School, and finally became Nicholas Garland, the *Daily Telegraph*'s long-term political cartoonist. We met at a funeral in London many, many years later; we both remembered the milk bars and I thanked him for the notion of big diaries: by then I had had eight novels published. Well: I suppose I am grateful to him. I have filled very, very many large lined notebooks and I must have honed some of my ways of writing therein — but I have also had to trawl through thousands of boring entries of adolescent detailed angst about very, very many matters including burying semolina under hydrangeas.

But Garland boys were just as unacceptable to my mother as short boys, and more rows ensued . . . I've had rather a shock. I – well I didn't know Mum was like that. She warned me that the Garlands were Communists (which they're not) that's all. Hell – I was angry. If they were it wouldn't make an ounce of difference anyway . . . The most ludicrous thing about this entry is that I still didn't know what communists were.

THURSDAY 20 AUGUST 1953

Sally had a letter for me from Nick this morning, with drawings down the side. A super drawing of Orson Welles as Harry Lime. I read it instead of doing Science! At sewing my pattern blew out of the window and Miss Herrick wouldn't let me go and get it so I sat in a corner and wouldn't do any work and when, at the end, she told me to get it, I stalked out and slammed the door!!! Dramatic exit. At the Majestic Theatre Sir Edmund Hillary and George Lowe told us about the journey to and from the 'Ascent of Everest' and showed us slides as they unfolded the story of their huge adventure. Everyone's knucklebone crazy.

MONDAY 16 NOVEMBER 1953

Today in the Lab Joyce accidentally made some stuff go all over me. Miss Yates rushed over and absolutely poured ammonia all over me to neutralize the acid. The fumes are still in my throat and everywhere and burnt my school jersey. Ugh.

My father was awarded a grant to go to America for six months at the end of this year to study education methods, but Mum didn't want him to go: '. . . why should he have gone without me when I helped him so much?' my diary records her telling me later. He compromised by arranging to go for four months. My parents roped in some of their friends to speak to me about my friendship with 'communists', but Nick had stopped sending me letters to school anyway. I got hot in crowded rooms, had to get out, still felt 'funny' sometimes, blushed all the time, couldn't sleep, wouldn't work, teachers complained, and I was now taking Aspros regularly at night, exams looming.

FRIDAY 11 DECEMBER 1953

My report came and it was terrible. Miss Gordon wrote everything awful she could. As bad as possible. So Mum says I cant go to Maria's next year. If I don't it's just because Miss Gordon hates me (and me her!) She's going to be bashed!

Almost fifteen, along with all this rage, blushing and drama, and the reiteration of 'definitely no more Maria', I also got my first 'proper' boyfriend, Don Neely: not at all communistic or short. He was deputy head prefect at Rongotai College and he was a rising cricket star, and he came in and met Mum and Dad the way boyfriends were supposed to and they liked him and he began quite relaxedly to make our house his second home and would just appear, often. He was very kind and reliable and respectable and said he didn't mind me being so skinny, and my diary records that if I talked too much, which I did often, he teased me by saying, 'Give the gums a rest.' My college friend Win and I got holiday jobs in shops, Dad got ready to go to away to America, Mum cried a lot, I went to watch Don playing cricket at the Basin Reserve and liked, ever after, that 'pock' sound of the bat hitting the ball.

And the new young Queen Elizabeth and her consort Prince Philip came to New Zealand.

FRIDAY 25 DECEMBER 1953

Christmas Day. But something awful has happened. Last night between 10–11pm the 3.0 Express from Wellington to Auckland fell into a flooded river, Tangiwai, because of a weakened railway bridge and there's still 100 people not accounted for. There's 26 dead for sure and farmers and police and army have been searching for survivors but they think many of the bodies may have been swept out to sea. It's horrible – the worst disaster ever in NZ and the Queen here too. In her Commonwealth Message she expressed her sympathy to relatives and friends. I hope they find more survivors – what a horrible Christmas some people must be having.

That New Year's Eve I had a 'date' with Don where (my diary advises) other young people were drinking alcohol and I was shocked, and we came home and had midnight with Mum and Dad, and they all had a sherry but I wouldn't.

And Dad went to America the next day, and now it was 1954.

New Zealand still didn't have television.

We had followed the funeral of King George VI — and later the coronation of Queen Elizabeth II — on the wireless. Later we saw newsreels of these events when we went to the pictures, and so it was now with the Royal Tour: wherever the Queen and Prince Philip went they were followed by the National Film Unit and so we went to the pictures and saw the newsreels of the Royal couple touring our own country.

But other countries did have TV, so New Zealand trials were now being done, and a few radio programmes were being filmed and simultaneously shown on screens at big places like the Winter Show Buildings in Wellington. So by a fluke I was in some of these early live TV broadcasts in January 1954 because they had decided to televise the Quiz Kids during the summer holidays; as usual I report that I was dumb — *and* absolutely terrified. Strange big cameras poking at you and stopping your concentration, and wires and lights everywhere . . . I only answered one whole question by myself – the rest I put in a silly word here and there and generally made a fool of myself. Gosh I was soppy. Never mind, I had two hot dogs . . . I also report seeing the Queen 'in person' several times when she was in Wellington and how odd it was to see someone you'd always read about and saved the pictures of, and that she was very beautiful and the Duke of Edinburgh was 'super', although I also wrote . . . she always looks – I don't know – sort of fed up and everything – I cant explain it but she does . . . When I later met her, following the Royal Academy of Dramatic Art Jubilee Performance, she looked rather fed up also after the long evening; we understood by then that theatre was not her greatest interest. (I seem to remember that our RADA Vanburgh Theatre was set up for the occasion with a Special Royal Toilet.)

The diary records that kind Don came nearly every day of that 1954 summer while Dad was in America, and he and Mum did a lot of smashing of concrete to make another crazy-paving path and I sunbathed . . . in my new bikini . . . and he and Mum and I turned my bedroom into a room with a desk and a reading lamp as well as a radio, and then I got into trouble for liking it so much and wanting to stay in there and write letters to Dad and to friends instead of coming out and being sociable. Mum liked Don and relied on him quite a lot while Dad was away.

But, as summer was ending and the March winds blew, my diary also records that I wished Don was my brother instead of my boyfriend, a pattern that was to repeat itself over and over again; I told him I wanted to 'just be friends' and go out with other boys. The rows between Mum and me — with Dad not there, nor Don either — became screaming, weeping matches . . . Mum wants to ask Don to come camping with us. I don't WANT him to come camping with us. What she wants to do is miles worse than what I want to do. 'No-one can come on holiday with us who isn't going to work.' 'You cant be rushing around all the time.' 'You never do any housework.' 'You never do any sewing.' 'Isabel and Win are always working and helping their mothers.' Etc etc. Mum just picks on me all the time – on and on and on. Oh – now I'm feeling sorry for myself. Shut up.

And although I had made written resolutions on New Year's Eve to be a better person and a better school pupil and try and pass the big external School Certificate exam that everybody in the fifth form had to sit, the diary shows that as soon as I got back to school I hated it all over again. Free of Don, I had as many boyfriends as one teenager could possibly manage, extricating myself over and over again and looking for the next one.

And perhaps there was a reason for this.

I was criticised by my mother so much and so often at home that presumably, more and more, I was looking for affirmation everywhere, anywhere, else. For lots of boys, hormones raging, wandering about after Bible Class dances with girls, riding in cars with girls, was probably about early sexual experiences; in my case, I may have had hormones raging that made me so unbearable, but it was some time before I fully realised the power of sex (and when I did I got pneumonia). I kept writing that I wanted to be friends with everybody, I wanted everybody to like me . . . *I like being liked. It's so nice when people like me . . .* says my diary. (It is expounded that all actors want to be liked: that's why they turn to performing.) But if I'd been wiser about myself — only I was fifteen and it was 1954 and a lot of us didn't really know how to be wise about ourselves — I might have been able to articulate better what I also wrote but came to understand only later . . . *it's nice when people hold me . . .*

I longed to be held, and nobody, including — perhaps especially — Mum, had ever really held me in their arms until I started going out with boys. Perhaps some other young people's experiences were similar then, for apart from Mum not being a very maternal person, it was also of course such a different, restrained era when I was growing up — for instance Andrew and Ross and Dad all their lives shook hands when they met; I never saw them meet in any other way.

So when, years later, Dad actually put his arm round me in London and said that he loved me it was such an extraordinary thing that I wrote of it in my journal. My un-holding mother on the other hand said, very often, as she was angrily criticising me for something, 'It's only because we love you.' But that almost certainly meant 'What will the neighbours say?'

My father was in London, staying with me, because Mum had left him.

In the late 1970s when she was nearly seventy and he was four years older.

Or, rather, she had moved him out. At first she kept their new Wellington house with its large windows overlooking the city and moved him and his belongings to a flat she knew of: I had rented it while I was making the NZTV series *Rachel*. Mum felt, she said to us children (as she had often said to me previously), that she had always been unappreciated, unacknowledged. And that Dad, a much-liked and respected figure in the Education Department, who had had a very successful career, had never publicly thanked her in the education books he could *not* have written, she said, without her assistance. He wrote several books about education in the years after I left home; what my mother's input was I don't really know. I guess that, in New Zealand government departments in the 1950s and 1960s, senior public servants (men) didn't, on the whole, publicly thank their wives. Dad agreed to us morosely that he should have shown more gratitude. Being so much more aware of so many things by the time this happened, I simply wished that, feeling so strongly, Mum had taken that decision earlier so that they might both have had a chance of a new life — but that's not what people of their generation did in those days. But: Mum did do it. It was a terrible, terrible shock to someone of Dad's generation and age. Whose father had left him also, when he was fifteen.

Ross, the only one of us still living in New Zealand then, described to Andrew and me the experience of coming to Wellington and finding Dad sitting alone in the flat, not watching television or listening to the radio, not reading, and cod-in-a-bag boiling and boiling in a small pot on the small stove.

We three suggested Dad should travel; first he'd been staying with Andrew — now working at the World Bank in Washington DC. Then he came to stay with me in London for six weeks. I lived in a small old Victorian flat with a bath in the kitchen. The wooden top over the bath was the kitchen working space for chopping onions, peeling potatoes, preparing meals. Then I could clip the wooden top up — and have a bath; I could also make toast under the grill while *in* the bath. None of this fazed Dad in the least; we had a good time, those six weeks, and talked, a little, of personal things. I had work sometimes with the Central Office of Information, making short films to be shown round the Commonwealth: *This Week in Britain.* I could find myself trout fishing or down a coal mine; I also interviewed all sorts of well-known people. I quickly learned not to leave Dad home on his own, for he would just sit, bereft, so the whole time he was in London I simply took him with me at all times: to work, or to share my social activities.

I took Dad with me to Ronnie Scott's Jazz Club in Soho one morning, telling him excitedly that in this very club I had once ('touching history' again) actually shaken hands with Ben Webster, the tenor-saxophonist who used to play for Billie Holiday. I had also heard Ella Fitzgerald sing there. And now I was to interview Ronnie

Scott himself. Black-and-white photos of famous jazz musicians on all the walls, and there was my dad, looking interestedly about him, sitting with a cup of coffee at one of the little club tables as sunshine drifted in through the daytime windows of that usually dark and smoky place while the interview was filmed; music played somewhere, great jazz stories were recounted; I saw Dad smiling with enjoyment. Later that day he and I sat on a sofa in the foyer of a London cinema, waiting to go in to see Woody Allen's *Manhattan*. A man who joined us said, 'The thing is, John, I love your daughter.' And Dad put his arm round me on the sofa under the Woody Allen poster and said, 'I love her too,' and although I knew perfectly well that he loved me, this was the only time he ever said the actual words to me, and I had never, ever before sat with my father's arm around me.

I waved goodbye to Dad as he disappeared through the departure gates at the airport at the end of January 1980. 'See you soon!' I called.

A few months after he got home he died suddenly.

I got the news the same day Donald Sutherland broke one of my ribs while rehearsing, with his fist, instead of a knife, for a scene in a film where he was to rather violently stab me. The film director very kindly scheduled the take of that scene first thing next day so that I could fly home at once (luckily it was a very small part; I was stabbed before the titles came up). Donald gave me a magnum of champagne in apology and then stabbed me violently again, this time with a blade-withdrawing knife on my broken rib, and I screamed extremely loudly as I was murdered. Home from the film set for a bath in the kitchen; out to the airport on a bus; economy class, broken rib, twenty-eight hours; on your way to your loved father's funeral. The glamorous life. The leaving-home life.

To me my father left the absolute belief that he and his colleagues had held always: that good education provided and paid for by the state was a right for all New Zealanders.

MONDAY 10 MAY 1954

Daddy's home from America!!!!!!! Guess what I'm writing with – oh just A Parker Fountain Pen – MY PARKER PEN – a Parker 21 straight from the US. My BIG present from Dad from America, along with lots of other interesting things. Gosh! Am I lucky! We arrived at Paraparaumu Airport at 4.40 and Dad's plane from Auckland arrived exactly on time at 4.50. We were so glad to see him. Now that he's home it seems he's hardly gone – except that Santa Claus must have just come down the chimney now, by mistake. Mummy has got a Swiss gold watch, Andrew got a flash-light camera, Ross a model aeroplane, with a proper engine. Well! Also we've miles of bubble gum – different sweets, a secret box from Chinatown, jewellery, Ross an engine-driver's cap, and other things. We're awfully, awfully lucky. Oh – and I've got a little purse that plays a tune when you open it. And we've got an LP Cowboy record. Good old Pop! Lucky us! Gosh – this pen is super. Lucky, lucky, lucky me. I smoked an American cigarette tonight! I'm so glad Daddy is home.

TUESDAY 1 JUNE 1954

Tonight was Maria's Poetry Reading, at which I was an usher which was fun though I showed miles of people to the wrong seats. The reading was absolutely super super super – I'm so proud to learn from Maria – I've learnt so much from her. I enjoyed TS Eliot's and NZ Poets' poems the best. But I've also done an hour's homework – exams so soon – me so dumb. Everyone nice was at the theatre, near us were the Campions, downstairs the poets Anton Vogt, Louis Johnson – all those interesting people. O listening to Maria I wished it would go on forever – her lovely voice.

When Dad was home things were easier between Mum and me for a while but not for long. Instead of the promised studying for this dreaded SCHOOL CERTIFICATE I met boys at tram stops; I lingered after Bible Class; I wouldn't do homework. Almost every single night I lay awake unable to sleep. By now I was a horrible, fully fledged adolescent. The height of my unbearableness was when I got into trouble with Dad as well.

SUNDAY 20 JUNE 1954

At the moment I am 'in disgrace'. Dad was hearing me my Science for which I've been half-heartedly swotting all day for an exam tomorrow and Ross wouldn't turn the radio off and I hit him – so Dad hit me and comforted darling wee cry-baby who I hardly touched, chucked my science book down and refused to hear any more. (Excuse me while I put my hotty on my feet. Thank you.) But I'm in a spot – I don't know my Science hardly at all. Mum of course went mad – I'm sick of my family at the moment except perhaps Andrew who is at least decent to me and never tells on me. Anyway I've paid Dad back by running off all the hot water. Hope I've run off enough! Oh dear, this exam. I hate everything.

'Est-ce que une coquette dans cette classe?' asked the French teacher to that class of fifth formers with seeming innocence one day. My behaviour had deteriorated even further; the diary records the question and adds that I blushed red and the other girls nudged each other; she knew perfectly well what she was doing. (I had already been given a kind but firm lecture by the headmistress about study being more important than boys.) For by then I was indeed a *coquette* or a 'flirt', as the fifties named it — and there could possibly be a number of older gentlemen who once knew me nodding sagely at this point.

The black dial-up (now 'retro') telephone lived very publicly on a tidy, polished table in the hall under the print of *The Laughing Cavalier* and started ringing for me very often. Mum listened quite openly to every phone call and wanted to know about everybody I talked to. The diaries record, over and over, that she also used to suddenly just walk into my bedroom, with its lamp and its desk, at all sorts of odd times and stand there and watch me and ask me what I was writing, who I was writing to, what I was saying — and by now I would always blush whether I was 'guilty' or not. I had lots of boyfriends, but didn't want to 'go steady' with any of them (which seemed to be the expected progression). I had got back into Maria's classes, probably to keep me out of further trouble. I hardly ever slept properly and I was tired all the time but always told the teachers I wasn't. In class we were weighed: I record I was 6 stone 9 lb aged fifteen. I flirted with all the boys including, my diaries inform me, other girls' boyfriends; I fought with teachers; I hated everything: an unbearable adolescent, the star of my own life. The fact that I still have several close friends from that time shows the forgiveness and tolerance of teenagers.

Now in the diaries I also begin to write more and more about being no good at things — even the things I was supposed to be good at. One was being no good at writing — Miss Gambrill gave me 3/20 in a rage for an essay I'd written without proper thought. Another was being no good at acting: about forgetting my lines, doing badly now in Maria's classes and she didn't like me anymore and other girls in her classes were so much better than me. Yet another was doing badly in tests at school — I would never pass School Certificate. At home Mum went on and on being critical and I went on and on being unbearable. And the diaries go on and on describing boys and spots and sore throats and blushing and failures and rows with Mum and tiredness.

TUESDAY 10 AUGUST 1954

Well – it's happened. It had to eventually I suppose – I went too far – was too rude – and Mum first went mad, screaming and screaming at me – then broke up and was crying like anything. I was a bit scared – but apparently I've been awful lately – I suppose I have, I don't know. So I was repentant and – well now I don't know if things are better or – what. I'm all feeling queer, I've been howling like anything – and Mum – I was scared when I saw her. Her face goes all funny.

Yet the following week, as an important mid-term maths exam approached, my diary records Mum giving me and a boy down the road some maths lessons, explaining things to us carefully and absolutely clearly: neither of us would have passed without her.

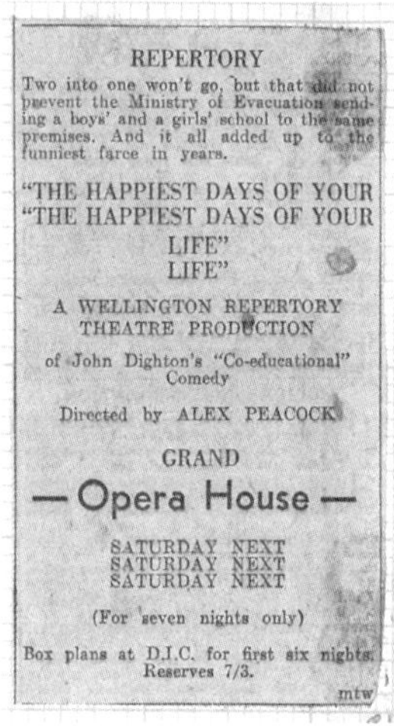

REPERTORY

Two into one won't go, but that did not prevent the Ministry of Evacuation sending a boys' and a girls' school to the same premises. And it all added up to the funniest farce in years.

"THE HAPPIEST DAYS OF YOUR
"THE HAPPIEST DAYS OF YOUR
LIFE"
LIFE"

A WELLINGTON REPERTORY THEATRE PRODUCTION

of John Dighton's "Co-educational" Comedy

Directed by ALEX PEACOCK

GRAND
— Opera House —

SATURDAY NEXT
SATURDAY NEXT
SATURDAY NEXT

(For seven nights only)

Box plans at D.I.C. for first six nights. Reserves 7/3.

mtw

Despite all my sins, I somehow (and with Mum's help in maths) did all right in mid-term exams, so, after much begging, and promising to study hard for School Cert and not go out anywhere else I persuaded my parents to let me play the small part of a schoolgirl in a Wellington Repertory production performed in the Wellington Opera House: *The Happiest Days of Your Life* (ha). I loved, absolutely loved being part of a 'proper' theatre production (and in no part of the play did I have to stand unsupported for a long time, but that fear I always kept entirely and utterly to myself). I took homework to the theatre. And in my small part on a big stage in a 'real' theatre I record being involved in one of the kinds of dramas that sometimes can happen unexpectedly during a performance.

WEDNESDAY 8 SEPTEMBER 1954

Whew! 'What a performance'. My hands are still shaking a bit – well no, not now really I suppose – but they were and my heart was going very fast! 'The Happiest Days of Your Life'

was going happily – the audience were laughing – and then – I went on stage with my flowers, talked to Kevin Woodill just as in the script. And then – Pauline Barnao didn't come on. For about a sec we just stood there – then Kevin just walked off, LEAVING ME ON STAGE BY MYSELF. Oh gosh – I suppose it was an 'experience' but – !!! I just mucked around, smelling the flowers, putting them in the vase – I didn't know what to do, I could hardly walk off too – then on came – Davina Whitehouse who plays the Headmistress! She made up a glorious conversation – told me off for going gardening or something – there were footsteps running all round backstage – then on came Pauline – she'd been in her dressing-room and hadn't been called, and Davina somehow got everything going again, and the play went on. When I got off stage I felt a bit like crying and I was shaking like a leaf, Davina though was wonderful, fixing everything like that – she said I had been good – being sensible – but she though – well there's the professional actress coming out, no one could've gone on like that for 3-4 minutes but her. She was super!!! The Stage Manager was crying and poor old Pauline on stage was trying not to cry too. Gosh I admire Davina for that. Then if that wasn't bad enough the phone didn't ring when it was supposed to and afterwards Davina had me collapsing with laughing when she told me that at that point she looked down on the stage floor and saw a puddle – hers! Such is life on stage I suppose!
Nick Garland went to England last Saturday, I believe to go to Art School.

THURSDAY 23 SEPTEMBER 1954

I've finished my things for the school mag. Miss Gambrill said I was inclined to be drawn to the 'pathetic' after she read that short story I wrote – so, right! As well as giving her one I've written about Maungatapu, I've given her something to chew on – 'The Women's Angle of Football' – that may be pathetic – but not in the same way!!!
We're going to Maungatapu after Christmas!!!! Sally is coming hurrah! But fancy going on holiday when we wont know if we've passed School Cert. I was meant to learn a theorem tonight but I left it at school – wonder if I can get it to sit in my head in the morning and keep it there till the test in the afternoon.

MONDAY 11 OCTOBER 1954

Last night when I had my light off Mum was yelling and screaming at Dad – I was quite scared. Today I was awfully tired and felt awful. Summer uniform was good. School was awful. I know I'll fail School Cert. I'm dumb. At Maria's we did the Epilogue – it is awfully tiring – I just have to stand and stand and I've had it by the end. I got home fagged out and disgraced myself by howling. I'm in bed now – I just feel too tired to work. I have to take a tonic. The chemist said to Mum no homework before bed.

And one Sunday, out of the blue (maybe to pray for help in these so important exams!), I went back to church for the first time since I'd first had the panic attacks over two years earlier . . . I went to Church tonight. Just like that. And I was ok. Funny isn't it . . .

MONDAY 29 NOVEMBER 1954

WHACKO! SCHOOL CERTIFICATE EXAMS ARE OVER.

Tonight Ross and I were 'jiving' in the lounge, we've been seeing this dancing on the newsreels a lot, we love LOVE it, we just love it. Mum and Dad do not.

MONDAY 6 DECEMBER 1954

At Maria's tonight I was good as Saint Joan. Something happened to me. Maria said it was the first time I had moved her while playing this part. 'It's come back Barbie' she said. Something happened – I felt it – but I don't know what it was. Is it – God?

THURSDAY 9 DECEMBER 1954

I found a Christmas job today – yes, starting on Monday at Farmers Department Store. Good show (but only £2/2/- per week, what a beastly swiz.) (Every now and then the Mater is going off at the deep end about Dad and I getting wet when we walked home in the rain because the car broke down while I was having a driving lesson!) I've already got 7 Xmas cards – and I've decorated my room with pine cones.

MONDAY 13 DECEMBER 1954

Well! Adventures befall even a poor working girl. Today has been very enlightening but – as long as I have my sense of humour – I think I'll survive. I arrived at my new job at Farmers Department Store but – when I was introduced to the woman in charge of the china department she started putting her coat and hat on. 'All right,' she said – 'I'm going.' I stood there flabbergasted! She apparently didn't want a girl!

I felt a bit of a fool – but in the end she calmed down a bit – and I just did what I was told and by the afternoon she was a bit friendly anyway. There was also another woman, who was particularly nice, trying to make up for 'the gorgon'! I have written out all my Xmas cards – a job I love doing. I guess I'll make out – as long as I can laugh!

On Christmas Day I compared, in my diary, Dad's face coming back from 'Morning Xmas Drinks' with the neighbours (red cheeks and shining eyes), with my own face that had smiled back at me from the mirror the night before, when I'd joined in Christmas Eve drinks with the boys in the Farmers stockroom, got kissed by one of them, and had my first taste of whisky.

A couple of days after Christmas, off we went in our mustard-coloured Austin A40 full of Mum and Dad and Andrew and Ross and me and my friend Sally Garland (apparently girl communists were not dangerous), with a packed trailer attached carrying a big 'three-roomed' tent and all our luggage, on our way back to magic Maungatapu. The trailer sparked, and then we had to stop along a faraway road where people were kind and a shut café opened and gave us free food, and a mechanic fixed the trailer, told us to drive slowly, wouldn't take any payment. We put up the tent nearby and all fell asleep. On New Year's Eve, lying awake writing by torchlight in our shared canvas accommodation while everyone else was asleep, telling myself it was time to use better adjectives than 'super', I heard Mum crying about something Dad had done, and wrote that down too. And lay awake much longer.

Maungatapu, my descriptions of which had now won a prize in the *Wellington Schools' Magazine*, was its beautiful self: the sun shone, the sea was just below, the cicadas sang along the dusty road, and I waved to my old Māori school friends. Auntie Ellie was as beautiful as ever as she and Uncle Erling and the twin boys waited at the gate; the sisters were so obviously happy to see one another again and we loved the modern house my Norwegian uncle had now built. We swam and sang and sunbathed and laughed. Sally and I had a wonderful social life with the neighbours' sons, all of whom were home from boarding school (we called them the 'sons and heirs'), one of whom, Anthony, had been at the Native School with me before he was sent away to a private school — and it was his father who had the vineyard. We played tennis, played cards, went swimming, sunbathed more, listened to classical music records in one of the houses, and even took turns at cooking. A cousin in one of these families arrived from Eton — '*Eton*!' we said — and my diary says that he and Sally did maths together and later, during a sophisticated evening listening to Beethoven at the vineyard, he began a discussion (as we were given a thrilling, first taste of Maungatapu wine) about the meaning of 'A

Great Lover' to which we all added our vast store of knowledge.

And sometimes I went off by myself, walking down the unpaved road.

SUNDAY 9 JANUARY 1955

There it flies, time. Early this morning I walked by myself down the dusty road, saw some of the Maori kids again. We all remember each other and talk about those days and laugh and sometimes we sing. Later I walked along the 'dry dusty clay track that led to the school' and went in and peered in all the windows – and I saw the very desk that Anthony and I used to sit in. O Maungatapu is so wonderful and time is going so fast.

And then something happened that allows 'plot' — the threads — to saunter by again, as yet unrecognised. Wanting Auntie Ellie and Uncle Erling and the twins to have a holiday too, we left Tauranga and magic Maungatapu and went camping together further along the east coast. There were a number of tribal Māori settlements, just like the one at Maungatapu, along the coast road. Over the hills way past Ōpotiki we set up at a 'camping site' near one of them.

TUESDAY 11 JANUARY 1955

Well! This place – a few miles from Te Kaha – where we are going to be staying for three nights is about as near to the end of the world as one could get. Friends recommended it to Auntie Ellie – for some unknown reason – and it's a 'hole' if ever there was one. We didn't get here till after dark – it may possibly improve by daylight – though frankly I doubt it. The place smells strongly of bad fish – is miles from nowhere – and of course Sally and I who did not want to leave Maungatapu view it with mournful eyes. We are by the sea – but it is rocky and dangerous. (Cheerful me!)

THURSDAY 13 JANUARY 1955

Every now and then it rains and everything that was hung out to dry gets sopping wet again. And the last blow has fallen. My back – the brownest and nicest of everybody's – has started peeling in a big way! Blast. I am sitting in the car as I write this. If I look out the door I can hear the roar of a very unfriendly sea – I can still smell dead fish – I can see the campfire smoking and I can see Auntie Ellie and Mum getting the lunch. Sally is asleep somewhere, dreaming of being a ballerina which she has decided she is going to do, she is a really good ballet dancer now. The men are trying to fish and the boys have gone off to get water. I must say this is a marvellous place, and a marvellous frame of mind, to wake up on my sixteenth birthday tomorrow!

Later: Dad and Uncle Erling tried more fishing off the rocks this afternoon – but only managed to catch two old catfish. But tonight Uncle Erling, Dad, Sally and I cooked 'barbeque style' steak for tea, then we had a big campfire after tea which we all sat round for a while and tried to have a sing-song but it fell a bit flat. This afternoon we walked to the Te Kaha store which hasn't got much in it and to pass the time away – for want of something better to do – we sat up on a railing and spat chewing gum on to the road (?) below. We're leaving tomorrow!!!!!!!!!!!!!!!!!

But.

I'd be back there, years later — very, very often. Right there along the very same part of that eastern coast.

If I had known.

If I had known that one day far, far into the future I would look out at glittering blue and gold sea, crayfish boats coming in to shore with the wedding breakfast for about four hundred people where I was The Bride; if I had known that my husband and his family would sing old 'Blue Hawaii' to me, but written in romantic Māori . . . *mokemoke, te po nei e te tau* . . . written by my late father-in-law who I never met, but who thought fine Māori oratory and Shakespearean language had much in common, and quoted Shakespeare often: his family always remembered Shakespeare echoing out from the milking shed while he was milking the cows — if I had known these things as I spat chewing gum outside the Te Kaha store, I would simply have expired in disbelief.

We ended this camping holiday on my sixteenth birthday, said goodbye to our loved relations along a lone road in a lone place called Te Teko (it's still there, lone Te Teko, the locals call it Texas), and drove through the night all the way to Wellington, arriving before dawn and running out of petrol about two miles from home so that we had to walk home as the sun rose and then found out that . . . Sally and I have PASSED SCHOOL CERTIFICATE!!!

V

LONG, HOT, DROWSY FEBRUARY DAYS in 1955 as my last year at school began. I tried valiantly to get more sunburnt over my peeling sunburn whenever I got the chance: we don't seem to have used much sun cream, and we had heard of neither melanoma nor the ozone layer. When we wore sunhats we were told it was to protect us from getting 'sunstroke'.

The MCC cricket team toured and sometimes Dad and I listened amicably to the cricket tests on the radio together, that familiar, hollow 'pock' as the ball hit the bat and, from the Basin Reserve, respectable applause. Andrew too became a teenager and girls all over Wellington smiled adoringly at him, and he and I became conspiratorial. Ross set up some sort of walkie-talkie in the house so that we could all talk to one another. Somehow local truck and taxi drivers occasionally picked up the wavelength and, alone in the house one day, I was startled out of my skin to hear two men laughing loudly in our dining room, then one giving the other a pick-up address in Cavendish Square.

In the sixth form year the school itself made the decision, through tests throughout the year, about whether you would be accredited with University Entrance or whether you had to sit the actual exam. I had discarded dreaded Latin the moment I was able; I'd given up Science; but in History I suddenly became fascinated by Napoleon and quoted H.G. Wells on him, at length, in my diary (and years and years later made him a character in one of my novels). Encouraged by Miss Gambrill, I also wrote a 'thesis' on 'The Effect of Landscape and Life on New Zealand Poetry'. Also we were now having to consider seriously what we might do when we left school — being an actress was only a dream after all. My diary records that the Plymouth Brethren teacher who was our career guidance person suggested careers to me: teaching, library work, clerical work or nursing, and I said 'thank you', and on the same day Mum slapped my face for saying Ross was mad.

And: the music changed.

I can't find the right words to describe the effects of that change on many teenagers: how different, how wild, how loud, how *ours* and exciting the music became. The Lever Hit Parade, almost always American music, still gave us, at the very beginning of that year, songs like 'Love Is a Many-Splendored Thing' and 'A Blossom Fell' (and very *soon*, his girlfriend would be kissing someone else in the *moon*-light) — same old stuff — *but* 'Sh-Boom' echoed out as well: American doo-wop was already permeating. We heard The Platters: that insistent slow piano beat and voices singing, hips swaying *doop-do-wah, doop-do-wop.* The beat got faster; gone was any interest I might have had in waltzes or foxtrots: that year Ross and I were jiving more often in the lounge when Mum was out; he, aged eleven, was already larger than me and could twirl me about, loud gramophone playing 'Shake, Rattle and Roll', annoying everybody but madly enjoying ourselves, and by the end of that year we were wildly and joyously rocking and rolling to 'Rock Around the Clock' and we broke Mum's china tulips in our enthusiasm.

Teenage pop music and Rock and Roll had truly arrived.

Andrew and Ross and I now became so besotted with pop music that it went on resonating through the rest of our very different lives. Well, of course it did: it was in the mid-1950s that the word 'teenager' really emerges: we heard Bill Haley, Buddy Holly, Fats Domino, and in particular Elvis Presley — *sex*, it apparently seemed to our parents — blaring out of the wireless. Later we three children might have been scattered to the New Zealand Air Force, the World Bank in Washington, the Hammer Horror film studios outside London or Granada's television studios in Manchester, but we only had to be in the same room again, *anywhere*, and we were singing the old songs: 'Rock Around the Clock', 'Peggy Sue', 'Blue Suede Shoes', 'Heartbreak Hotel', 'Blueberry Hill'. Later we found our absolute favourite song: 'Sad Movies (Make Me Cry)', complete with every *do-wop*, which we always included in our own rendition. This was usually the first song — after not many drinks — the three of us would be singing together, no matter where we met up again, all our lives. I have learnt, to my financial cost, not to quote pop songs in books, it is a very expensive business, and the last time I wanted to quote a number of them (and was mostly refused unless I paid thousands of pounds) I was outraged to then hear one of 'my' songs, 'Crazy', being used on television to advertise hamburgers. (I have gleefully been aware that fifties–early sixties music has been having a bit of a renaissance as I've been writing this.) Anyway, in our favourite 'Sad Movies' song our heroine went to the movies by herself because her boyfriend said he was working, and just as the lights went down in the cinema she saw her boyfriend come in with her best friend who he kissed, so she went home crying and didn't want to lie to her mother so she just said that sad movies always made her cry *doop-do-wah, doop-do-wah.*

Now all the next generation of our family, by osmosis, know all the words of that song and every *do-wop* also. (I sang it not so long ago with one of my nieces as we staggered jollily out into the New Zealand night from a bar where — by wearing what I was wearing anyway — I was presented with the first prize in a fancy-dress competition for the best hippie.)

Occasionally now I also became aware of the blues that I heard on the radio or on other people's gramophones. Some of them seemed to have some relationship with the doo-wop songs, that slow, insistent beat, and very occasionally I was stopped in my tracks by the strange, unforgettable, broken sound of Billie Holiday's voice. There was still no television but if there wasn't a Bible Class or school dance somewhere, then going to friends' houses and, if not permitted to wildly dance, at least listening to gramophone records of the latest pop music, was now the heart of our sophisticated Saturday nights; supervising mothers made pikelets.

My diary also records that I gave a talk on 'Mohammedanism' at Bible Class and played Lady Precious Stream in a school play.

My sixth form education was greatly enhanced by Maria Dronke's ongoing drama classes: the diaries advise we worked that year on *Lycidas, The Confidential Clerk, Medea, The Playboy of the*

Western World — and she also gave us *real coffee*. Dark, smoky, exciting Coffee Bars had just begun to take off in Wellington: there was already one by the cable car called The Buttery where we knew Arty Persons went, and other places were opening. But Maria in her new studio up some stairs along Lambton Quay also had 'real' coffee which she shared with her students — this rates several mentions in my diary, because we only knew coffee powder. We, who had probably eaten fish and chips out of newspaper in our school uniforms (forbidden) as we walked to the studio after school, drank real coffee and talked of literature and life with Maria, and felt so very sophisticated.

WEDNESDAY 20 APRIL 1955

I can never say that I didn't know what happiness feels like. It feels like Maria's classes. I know that sounds a bit soppy but it's what I feel. Trouble is time wont stand still, even for a moment, for me to – sort of taste the happiness. Win and I went to class – as usual I left there as up-in-the-air as possible. I live for those classes.

Tonight we read 'Playboy of the Western World' by John Synge. An Irish play – my accent is frightful but it was fun. And fun too trying to learn to laugh at will: we did a mime of some people in church seeing a fly on a bald man's head, laughing so much that they had to go out of the church and Win and I still giggling like a couple of schoolgirls on the tram home.

And at Bible Class I went to lessons in preparation for being 'confirmed' into the Church, and Mum was scathing, calling it all a lot of nonsense.

The emotional relationship between my mother and me had grown more and more byzantinely complicated. I was so clearly sometimes scared of her, this unpredictable, domineering personality in our house. And it is obvious from the diaries that I got fond of several other people's mothers who were so much more 'motherly': that many other friends' mothers were not like mine. Over and over again I write about how she stood in the hall and listened openly to all my (many) phone calls, sometimes actually hovering in my eye-line with an oven cloth or a tea towel. Up until I left home she always made me 'report' to her, in their bedroom if necessary, when I got home late at night, and often — I don't know how else to put this — 'carefully looked me over' when I did so, so that I blushed guiltily even if I had only been eating pikelets.

To try and conquer the agony of blushing all the time, and because it was so hard to know how Mum would be from one day to another, it is clear from the diaries that this is when I first began to instinctively learn to somehow, sometimes, 'feel' what another person was feeling. I don't in any way at all mean to imply I became 'psychic' — simply that I learnt to come into a room and sort of feel the air, the atmosphere, what to expect: somehow picking up on other people's 'moods' (usually Mum's). I, of course, didn't know that that was what I was learning. When I wrote my novel *The Mesmerist*, I thought mesmerism was just a trick, a scam — but as I researched it I realised it was the forerunner of hypnotism, and at last understood that all these things were about energy, and feeling the transference of energy. Over years I learnt that this energy connection can also happen in the theatre occasionally and it is tremendously exciting for both actor and audience when it occurs. Something, some version of picking up that energy in the air, developed in me in these teenage years as a kind of protection, a sixth sense.

Presumably Mum was trying to bring up a 'nice', respectable, conventional daughter: she was instead nurturing someone who would never do the things she had ordained. But, so influentially, she also talked enough about 'nervous breakdowns' for me to be frightened I had inherited some of that fragility from her — or from her brother, my Uncle Harry. So over and over when I couldn't cope — and knew something was wrong inside my head, especially when I simply couldn't sleep at all — I still ran to her, and depended on her absolutely.

I often write almost as if Dad wasn't there. He was away with work sometimes, but he was there too, always very busy at the Education Department. But as is clear — and becomes clearer — he hated and avoided conflict of any kind: it was always my mother who made the decisions in our lives at home, so what he thought about things, what he thought about what happened later in that house, I have never been sure, except that he never — in front of any of us — disagreed with our mother. Sometimes, my diary records him, inarticulate but kind, quietly bringing me a cup of cocoa, or a hot-water bottle, when home was turbulent. As it often was. When my insomnia was particularly bad he would sometimes try to read me to sleep. Once he came in with a heavy tome, *The History of the Decline and Fall of the Roman Empire*, which he assured me would make me sleep, but he was so tired that he fell asleep while reading it aloud and I had to get up and wake him and we laughed and he went to bed.

All that last year at school I wrote, as usual, pages and pages and pages in my diary of frenetically flirty and flighty relationships with boys, 99 per cent of which I have spared us. Sometimes the entries are so wild — though still so very innocent as to be almost laughable — that re-reading them I seem actually drunk on something — yet we so seldom drank anything stronger than Coca-Cola and knew nothing of drugs at all (though there is very much mention of Valderma Ointment for spots). I had a few spurts of doing a lot of school work, and simply learnt to survive on much less sleep than most people and just stayed awake, in my own bed, waiting for morning to come. Andrew also had trouble sleeping: maybe our same whirring minds unable to slow down. A diary late at night didn't help: just as these days people are advised to keep their electronic devices away from their sleeping places, so my sleep-disturbing machines were a pen and a notebook. Years and years later a doctor asked me to write a paper on our experiences — he was investigating, I think, whether insomnia might have any genetic, as well as environmental, connection. Whatever insomnia is, and neither my father nor my mother had trouble sleeping, it affected Andrew and me all our lives. I have survived with the help of sleeping pills; Andrew, chemical engineer and personal assistant to the head of the World Bank, kept a bottle of whisky under his bed.

And very occasionally now, although we children still never saw him, I actually wrote a few words about Uncle Harry.

FRIDAY 22 APRIL 1955

The school Anzac Service came and went . . . I was dizzy but didn't faint. It's a long weekend thank goodness. But I will try to remember why. Poor Uncle Harry. That's what War did to him . . . I hope there is NEVER NEVER another war. Surely there wont be. But that's what they said after World War I. I can suddenly exactly understand Katherine Mansfield's feeling towards the wind – the wind in Wellington that blows and blows and blows. Today has been just like the day of her story, and I cried because I couldn't make my hair go right . . . Last night I had 3 nightmares: all different, and all about war. I kept waking up, terrified . . . there mustn't be another war.

THURSDAY 5 MAY 1955

So I am in disgrace again. In fact Mum is – what was it – 'absolutely nauseated' by me. The phone kept going for me; Don to have a friendly talk, and I so like that we are still friends, Warwick to ask me to the pictures, James to ask me to the school dance – I said I'd arranged to go with someone else though actually I haven't. Then while I'm still talking Mum who has been all ears yells out something or other, and when I hung up she went absolutely mad about being silly, talking rubbish to a whole lot of boys over the phone. And just now, as I was writing this she comes in to my bedroom and I get another pep talk – yap yap yap – going along the wrong track – silly, giggling girl, lot of nonsense with boys. When Mum went out just now she left me 'heaving with wracking sobs' – I've stopped now. Huh. Oh HELP! I can see that my flirtatious nature is going to be troublesome . . . but I cant help being friendly – why cant I be friends with boys like I am friends with girls.

The very next day it was finalised (no wonder she was so angry and nauseated and ashamed about the 'wrong track' I was taking): my mother, after two weeks 'studying teaching methods' at another girls' college, would suddenly be on the permanent staff as the Science and Biology teacher — at *my* school, Wellington East Girls' College. It wasn't long before she was straightening my tie — me, a *prefect* — in the school corridor, as recorded furiously in my diary.

But the girls in the Science class liked Mum teaching them; they respected her, felt they were learning properly. (Although Biology classes with Mum, I assume, meant cutting up rabbits, not discussing any intimate human anatomy.)

THURSDAY 14 JULY 1955

Today it was absolutely freezing cold – and I had to wear my skirt and jersey to school because I'd had to leave my school uniform there overnight. I was so cold I wore my red jersey and a pair of Dad's grey socks over my stockings to get warm. And when we got home Mum said I was disgracing her in public again – she called me a 'dirty little girl trying to make yourself conspicuous'. Mum is tired – I should make allowances. If I was all the things she calls me, 'selfish little egotist' was the final one – I'd be quite a character. I'm trying to take a blasé attitude but I must be sorry for myself because Dad just came in and he smiled so kindly and brought me a cup of cocoa, and now that he's gone, he was so kind that I cried, I'm a drip. Mr Wiseley told me that it is always Dad who settles arguments in the Department and I can quite imagine it. I'm almost tempted to be a school teacher, Dad would be thrilled.

SUNDAY 24 JULY 1955

Dad has gone to Auckland until the end of term and Mum

is awfully tired – she had another crying fit. I didn't go to Bible Class this morning in fact I didn't get up till 12.30. Mum stayed in bed all day – she says she is so tired she doesn't know what to do with herself. I cooked lunch and tea. Went to Confirmation class. We all look at each other when Mr Robson talks about Love (whatever it really is).

By now I had occasionally written in my diaries about 'remembering things' — this idea of the significance of memory — and I found an entry from this year about an evening when Maria also talked to us about memory, which I think must have influenced me more than I realised: all my life I have remembered the poem, and the rose. Maria and John Dronke, feeling so unsafe at 'Home'; escaping from their country with two little children: what memories did they have? We sometimes heard her speak German, because they had also brought with them Maria's old Nanny who could not speak much English, but Maria hardly spoke of Germany to us, and she loved New Zealand, I always felt. But this conversation must have seemed so relevant to her.

THURSDAY 6 OCTOBER 1955

We went to Maria's at 6pm and discussed 'Look Stranger' – W.H. Auden. She said that although some scenery, a view, may be very beautiful – to remember it always, there must be a feeling, an emotion involved with it at the same time. She said, after she had read us the poem in that beautiful voice of hers, that the poem was reminding us – and I had picked for her a perfect dark red rose from the garden – 'that for instance this rose: it will be gone tomorrow but you and I will always remember, because what we are talking about is important, that it was here'. And she was dressed in black with a white blouse and as she spoke this dark red rose lay on her dark skirt, a spot of colour. And she was – looking away from us. She said some things that made me think like 'things are wonderful to still have in memory when they are the past' – at least she put it much better than that, not soppy or sentimental but – I understood.

TUESDAY 11 OCTOBER 1955

I had my Teachers' Training College interview today; Miss Campion lectured us loud and long on arriving in plenty of time, composing ourselves etc etc. Well – I got lost and was late and arrived puffing and blowing and had to go straight in all uncomposed – not having in the least time to be nervous at all, so felt quite at ease!!! It was fine today mostly, I love summer when it starts to come. Today Miss Powell called me, what was it – skittish! Some of the Science class girls were here at home today, cutting up a rabbit with Mum for school. I'm worrying about next year.

In my heart, even to please Dad, I didn't really want to be a teacher. I also applied at Broadcasting to be a cadet, which would earn me £6 per week — would that help me to become an actress? Maria Dronke, trying to help, said it would be better to train as a teacher . . . which she says will stand me in good stead both in New Zealand and Overseas . . .

But 'Overseas' somehow didn't really exist for me: it was Maria's idea for me, not mine.

I note in November that Princess Margaret announced she

would not marry Group-Captain Peter Townsend. I imagined her being an old unmarried Princess . . . poor thing . . .

Someone from our class had a baby. Mum kept telling me it was 'awful' and 'terrible'. How little I needed the warning. How naïve and innocent I still was.

SATURDAY 5 NOVEMBER 1955

Ewen and some of the boys took Ngaire and me out sailing, to Ward Island and when we got becalmed Ngaire and I rowed! We enjoyed it! We found a penguin sitting on eggs in a little cave. Then we found ghekos (?) from under stones! I like to think of the warm warm place where we had lunch with beginning-summer sun. I think I am a sun-worshipper – I love to feel the sun sort of seep through to my bones. I lay in the sun, in the crook of Ewen's arm – gosh it was comfortable and lovely. Does it sound very bad?

SUNDAY 6 NOVEMBER 1955

Punished. As if I was five – 'forbidden' to go to the boatshed with Ewen. Yet this five-year-old has been accepted for Teachers' Training College. With all the lists of costumes for Physical Education and Compulsory Games – oh hell. There is nothing I hate more than Compulsory Games.

Then Ewen came round this afternoon. We were talking on the back verandah and Mum came out to see what was going on – tells Ewen I cant go out with him again if I don't get home early. She doesn't mind at all humiliating and embarrassing me in front of him. My habit of 'blushing' is worrying me; it seems to be getting worse (if that's possible) – I blush at simply anything at all it seems. But what can I do? How does it stop? If I think of blushing I blush – almost blushing now because I'm thinking of it. It's horrible. O god I just cant stop crying about everything, about life. If only I had an elder sister or someone. Someone I could confide in completely, and ask advice from. But I suppose part of growing up is learning there is no-one but oneself to depend on. I don't quite know what I would do without this diary. G'night.

FRIDAY 11 NOVEMBER 1955

8.15am Gulp! Just about to depart for school: Accrediting Lists for University Entrance to be announced. I'm hoping for the best. Good luck Honey!

10.45pm. I have been accredited University Entrance. Thank heaven I did though. It was horrible – I'll never forget the deathly silence when Miss Wilson walked into the Geography Room to face the assembled VI form. Seven girls in our class didn't get it. But whacko – good for him, 17 were accredited at Scots College, Ewen was 17th!

After school I went to get some money from Dad and bought at long last my own LP of 'Homage to Dylan Thomas'. Then a crowd of us went to 'Blackboard Jungle' – a film about teaching that I have heard criticised, but I think it is one of the best films I've ever seen. Really well-acted – about juvenile delinquents in a school in US – and it's a film that's making me think again too, about teaching. (And it's got 'Rock Around the Clock' in it!!!) Oh dear – I should feel elated now shouldn't I? but I don't really feel anything at all. Miss Mulvihill told Mum I'd never get French in the first year if I went to University, so then Mum told me. But you have to have a language.

WEDNESDAY 16 NOVEMBER 1955

This morning we went up to the University. I was terribly, terribly, impressed and – I dunno – influenced: I'm dying to go. That wonderful library. Books and books and books and books. That wonderful tall window. O gosh it's awfully difficult and worrying trying to plan the future.

Ewen took me to 'The Sleeping Prince'. Sir Ralph Richardson, Dame Sybil Thorndike, and it was a really good experience – real theatre – of course I'll never be an actress really, I know that, when I look at them. Ewen also wants to take me to a Jazz concert and says he wont go with a whole party of boys – just me – oh gosh I wish he didn't have it so bad. I'm afraid I want to go out with other boys . . . but how can I without hurting Ewen. And – he knows.

Mum and Dad were at 'Blackboard Jungle' but they didn't like it much.

SUNDAY 20 NOVEMBER 1955

This afternoon Ewen came over, terribly depressed – his parents don't want him to be a chemist – gosh they are being awful to him.

And so am I. I tried to explain that I didn't believe 'steady' was right. What I really mean deep down I suppose is that I don't want to 'go steady' with anyone. After all, as Ewen himself says 'we're only a couple of blasted kids.' But I'm ashamed of myself. Ewen is the nicest, kind, person and I have to go and treat him like that. Why am I like this? I don't understand anything. He gave me a little photo of the yacht.

SATURDAY 26 NOVEMBER 1955

I have been inspired to great heights: tonight Pauline and I went to see 'Camille'. I am just as convinced as I was after 'Ninotchka' that Greta Garbo is the most wonderful actress and the most beautiful woman I have ever seen. If only I could be such a wonderful actress – well what rot. How could I? Then we got off the tram and went in to the St James Theatre just in time to hear the final speeches of Sir Ralph Richardson and Dame Sybil Thorndike at their last performance. But . . . Sir Ralph Richardson seemed – I don't know. Maybe it was after Greta Garbo. His farewell speech seemed a bit – hoity and false. My career problems unsolved. But oh – I wish I could act. Like Greta Garbo.

Alas, I never could act like Greta Garbo. But I instinctively picked up something that evening.

I was lucky when I went to London: a new style of less technical, more open acting, promoted so strongly in Lee Strasberg's Studio and other places in America — obvious in the performances of someone like Marlon Brando — was just beginning to influence acting styles in England, which were still very much immersed in technical abilities and beautiful enunciation, especially in such an honoured and established institution as the Royal Academy of Dramatic Art. This was something I perhaps intuited myself that evening in Wellington, listening to Sir Ralph Richardson, long before I had even heard of the Royal Academy, and I was perhaps more instinctive, 'natural', than some of the other students there just when that quality was being recognised and given value. This is not to denigrate the kind of things I did learn (including — perhaps — to recognise concrete splinters in the heart). To this day if I am acting, or speaking in public, or if I am recording anything, I prepare by using the same voice exercises that I learnt at RADA. When I left there I could fill, with my voice, the biggest theatres in Britain. And I still, physically, try to use what one of my teachers, critiquing one of my performances, said to me so simply: 'Diamonds, darling.' Reminding me again that to stand tall it is not a case of thrusting the shoulders back, but, rather, to imagine I wear beautiful, beautiful diamonds at my breastbone, diamonds that I want everybody to see.

And then: towards the end of my course at the Royal Academy I saw the actor Paul Scofield playing King Lear in London for the Royal Shakespeare Company. It was only after seeing this performance that — like a light inside me — I at last understood what could happen on stage, that energy I have described earlier, mesmerising an audience. I was stunned. I had never seen a performance like that. I had at last seen properly what I had half-grasped: what acting could mean. You had to be true. Our job was to understand, to illuminate and to share anything: comedy, tragedy, everything in between — *but always with heart truth.* Not just with technical skills.

Later I was lucky enough to be in a film with Paul Scofield: I walked with him along the sand of that island of Bryher in the Scilly Isles and was so glad of the chance to tell him: *You taught me.*

However, in defence of Ralph Richardson: years later, in London, he too had embraced new ways. I saw him and John Gielgud both being terrific — in a new acting style — in a new play by Harold Pinter: *No Man's Land.*

A long, long way from *The Sleeping Prince* by Terence Rattigan in the St James Theatre, Wellington, in 1955.

❀

FRIDAY 9 DECEMBER 1955

I've left school. I'm not a schoolgirl any more.

MONDAY 12 DECEMBER 1955

'Good Morning, Taylors' Dry Cleaning.'

I am now fully installed as a Telephone Operator till Christmas. I managed everything fairly well, except for cutting off the 2 bosses who were talking to each other. (And walking into the men's lavatory.) It is quite a highly involved modern system actually – with radios to the delivery vans and 3 lines of the telephone. Nice women there.

I am, finally (after much argument), allowed to go back to Maungatapu after Xmas before I start work again. I often think about it and feel peaceful.

MONDAY 19 DECEMBER 1955

I like this job AND I worked 3 hours overtime tonight in Pressing until 8pm. Pressing! (Big ironing!) And I'll work in Pressing tomorrow and Wednesday nights too to earn more for Christmas shopping. Mum and Dad were on at me tonight – they want me to go to Teachers' Training College not full-time University, so that I'll earn some money. Oh heck it's difficult.

SATURDAY 24 DECEMBER 1955

I bought all my Xmas presents, and myself some shimmering

> nail polish this morning Mum says I look as if I've got poisoned fingers. And tonight Andrew and I went to a barbeque. They send Andrew to keep an eye on me, not realising that now I have to keep an eye on him! And ha ha Peter C. – who was the first boy to kiss me, about two years ago, tried to kiss me again, huh. Christmas Eve was the excuse I suppose. I laughed (and kissed him back cheerily), then Andrew and I sang all the way home.

Andrew and I sang all the way home together for many years. We both travelled a lot, especially Andrew for the World Bank — I'd get a brief phone call: 'Scrabble, cheese, grapes, wine, 4.p.m.?' and he'd fly in to London from one country or another. Once he turned up in Scotland unexpectedly when I was in a play at the Edinburgh Festival. After staying up all night at a theatre party and singing our old songs, we went for a walk along the Firth of Forth, I remember chill early-morning sunshine. Suddenly he rolled up his trousers and walked into the water (I assumed he was still inebriated). But there was a plastic bottle in the water, and he walked right out to get it. And gave me my first lesson in one of the new concepts in the air about which I knew nothing: 'environmental degradation'. He explained the word 'biodegradable', and told me how plastic was *un*-biodegradable and would eventually choke the world if we didn't stop using it — this conversation was in the 1970s; today we swallow our own plastic, we are told, inside the fish we eat.

Andrew and I often set up fiercely fought Scrabble championships and we played fiendishly in whatever part of the world we met. In 2002 we had one of those Scrabble meetings in London in December. When he had to catch his plane back to Canada where he and his family now lived, the score was two games all. We agreed to finish this particular tournament when we all met as we had arranged to do, in New Zealand in January; we were going around the Bay of Islands in his new boat. In January, as soon as my plane landed in Auckland there was one of those ominous messages: **Will Barbara Ewing please make her way to the exit at the front of the plane where one of our staff is waiting for her**. About thirty-six hours earlier Andrew had phoned me in London from Christchurch; they were in the middle of a family party and wanted to be reminded of all the words of 'A, You're Adorable', so we sang all the words together over the miles, and said 'See you soon!' Now I was escorted to a small airport room with a telephone where Ross, in Christchurch, told me that while I was in the air Andrew had died suddenly, aged sixty; Ross and his family and Andrew's wife Gill were with him in Christchurch, waiting for me to join them.

I finally emerged — somehow — into the Arrivals Hall; there some of my Māori family, knowing, waited to enfold me.

Andrew had lived an extremely successful — and somewhat wild — life.

At his memorial service at the World Bank a colleague read:

My candle burns at both ends;
It will not last the night;
But ah, my foes, and oh, my friends
It gives a lovely light.

He did give a lovely light, my brother Andrew. The Scrabble score between us remains two–all forever.

SUNDAY 25 DECEMBER 1955

So many presents, 2 guineas from Mum and Dad and a little writing case and some powder and some pants. I gave Andrew a record of 'It's a Sin to Tell a Lie' and he gave me 'Ain't That a Shame' (ha ha!) So much food! Part of the Xmas Pud fell off the table, but Mum couldn't tell anyone off because it was her cousin that did it not her children. Andrew picked it all up carefully, and I saw him casually put a bit with a wrapped-up half-a-crown showing, on to HIS plate! I laughed at him, but didn't tell.

After Christmas Day off I went to Tauranga on my own, finally turning into the dusty unpaved road of my beloved Maungatapu where the air smelled so different and the hypnotic sound of the sea shushed us — even me — to sleep. My favourite place.

The sons and heirs back from their private schools were there at Maungatapu, and the Māori boys on their horses down at the end of the dusty road offering to give me a ride across the hard wet sand were there, and the Māori girls, to teach me more party songs and Māori words beside the macrocarpa trees. There was a rumour (but I closed my ears to it) that a motorway was to be built right through Maungatapu. It sounded ridiculous. And I observed, by watching my ten-year-old twin cousins, the difficulties that could arise from being twins . . . and today we walked down to the Hairini store and Ian bought some peppermints. Paul, after some pondering, suddenly said to Ian: 'Hey, those peppermints are mine. You put on the pants with the money in – but I was wearing them yesterday, so the peppermints are mine.'

SATURDAY 31 DECEMBER 1955

Maungatapu. Listening to the sea. Goodbye 1955. It's finally been decided that, yes, if I work very hard, and take a job again as soon as I get back from here, I can go to Varsity full-time. I am very lucky, they've said I must learn to be appreciative. I am. I do know I'm lucky and I don't say it properly.

Lots of boys this year, as usual. But I still feel bad about Ewen. I liked him so much, yet I hurt him so much. I don't understand myself. I would like to be nicer. In 1956 I want to really try not to argue against life too much, to try – as Miss Gambrill said to me so very kindly when we were saying goodbye – not to kick against the pricks.

It is indeed a good thing that we cannot see into the future.

VI

VICTORIA (OF COURSE) UNIVERSITY OF WELLINGTON, built on one of those many hills overlooking the city below.

Today the beautiful, old ivy-covered brick establishment that the university consisted of then is completely dwarfed by huge, high Science and Technology and Biology blocks: rooms and rooms full of computers, wide light corridors and open-plan stairs, bookshops, student cafés; many floors of car parks. And Dad's education office, 'The Oldest Wooden Building in the Southern Hemisphere', is now the university's Faculty of Law: Te Kauhanganui Tātai Ture. And now Victoria University has a Māori name also, Te Whare Wānanga o te Ūpoko o te Ika a Māui. And a marae on campus: Te Herenga Waka.

So. Many things have — indeed — changed. But . . . an odd shiver, there, late afternoon last summer. I was brought up, of course, not to believe in ghosts. But I am not . . . absolutely . . . sure now. There is after all, I am certain . . . unseen energy . . . Or perhaps it was just a dark, pale shadow probably, or just smoke, there by the main door.

Still students take the cable car up to the Kelburn sports ground that looks out over that beautiful city, or walk up steep steps and steep alleys from the busy main streets below. Still the opening of minds to good and bad professors and tutors? Still the long, winding conversations and arguments that could last all afternoon in a university cafeteria? Still, I am sure, the flirtations and the romances and the broken hearts. And still perhaps, in some departments, the academic language that seemed to me a particular convolution of words that placed us above 'ordinary' persons. The grass lawn is still there, leading up to the steps at the entrance of the old building. A group of us were lolling about in the sun on that grass when the *Evening Post* appeared one sunny day in 1956: they wanted a photo of students preparing for end-of-year exams, and we had not one book there with us. We hastily assembled a pile and were then photographed, lying on the lawn, immersed in learning. After the photo was taken we went off to rock around the clock.

In New Zealand in the 1950s my father and his colleagues in the Education Department believed utterly, and were supported by the government, in the opportunity of free learning for all, boys and girls, from kindergarten until the end of tertiary education. And if your parents couldn't afford to support you when you left school, but you had University Entrance, there were plenty of jobs in government departments that gave young people permission for time off for university lectures at either end of the working day. Teaching students could be trained, paid and take university classes part-time. And, for hopeful lawyers and accountants, many of the legal and commerce classes didn't begin till 5 p.m. Up and down the steep Wellington hills we all buzzed: some young people in suits or neat ladies' attire, hurrying in the early morning or the early evening; some full-time students like me and my friends, not quite so neat, not quite so hurried, lingering long in cafeterias and common-rooms.

How lucky we all were.

The government also sent young people who showed talent to study, in various fields, 'overseas' on scholarships or bursaries — without any bond or written promise to come back (or indeed a return ticket). I always felt so grateful to the New Zealand government of the early 1960s which awarded me a bursary that allowed me to become a professional actress. However, when a later government was uttering the phrase 'user pays' even in the context of education, and at that time I was offered an OBE, I felt I couldn't accept it: I imagined my father who lived and breathed free education sitting up in his grave in horror.

To contribute money towards our parents' support of us as full-time university students, school friends Win and Vanessa and I, before lectures started, took the inter-island ferry to Picton, the small rackety port town full of seamen, near the top of the South Island. From there we jumped on a small launch that took us down the Marlborough Sounds to the landing-wharf of a popular but remote wooden-verandahed hotel where we lived in old army huts at the back and began work as kitchen-hands and waitresses to earn money to buy textbooks and shoes and lipstick.

At first I liked working in the kitchen best — it was a happy place often, because Tia, the big Māori woman who was the head cook, sang as she worked, including the same old party songs that the Maungatapu girls had taught me (though Tia also, waiting till she knew she had our attention, ate fish eyes with great relish and laughed at our faces). Scrubbing great piles of huge pots and peeling potatoes was nothing if you were singing. I learnt on the job and certainly never scrubbed so many pots before or since. I did get a faint exclamation of surprise from the owner's wife who came upon me straining milk through a colander because it had skin on it. And Tia put awful chicory in the coffee, and I made a note in my diary about how my Norwegian Uncle Erling would hate it, being foreign and knowing about coffee. Waitressing made me nervous but Vanessa liked it; however, one day she got so angry with a very rude guest that she spilt soup over him and pretended it was an accident. In the evenings after dinner we were encouraged to sit in the bar with guests and — this is where I first started drinking alcohol properly — we had Pimms and sherry and I write that one man bought us all some 'Quianti'. And I flirted with all the male guests and the male staff.

It was very hard for someone who was growing up in 1950s New Zealand to write anything about sex at all — I didn't even know what words to use — but I did try to write in my diaries about things that happened as honestly as I could. Of course sexual feelings developed in young people, but we didn't understand them properly: all that girls like me did absolutely understand was that you could have a baby if you weren't 'well behaved'. And girls who did anything 'bad' either got married very quickly, like the girl in our sixth form class, or were, as I have said, 'sent away to the South Island' (though who knows what they said in the South Island — 'sent away to the North Island' perhaps). In 1956 the concept of an unmarried woman with a baby being Prime Minister of our country — even maybe in a dream sequence of a Walt Disney film with animated figures — would have been so shocking that the film would have been censored. In 1966 when I returned to New Zealand with the Royal Shakespeare Company in *The Comedy of Errors* I stayed on to be in a Downstage production in its early small space off Courtenay Place: a production of *The Knack*, directed by Dickie Johnston. Clever old Dickie: the film of *The Knack*, released the previous year, had been banned in New Zealand, and although the ban was lifted before our production opened, each night before a performance we looked out of the window and saw crowds queuing right along the street and round corners to see the play live. The following year the film of James Joyce's *Ulysses* was shown in New Zealand only to over-twenty-one-year-olds; the New Zealand Censor also decreed that these showings be gender-segregated, with a rope down the middle aisle of the cinema to keep males and females apart.

Because both these films were 'about sex'.

At first I thought to censor in this account all mention of the fumbling ignorance and confusion about sex, and the continual anxiety for girls about pregnancy, and about what was 'right', as too personal, too embarrassing — even though I'm writing over sixty years later, when information about sex is available to younger and younger people, illustrated with moving pictures and sounds at the touch of a computer key. But finally I have concluded that perhaps, in different ways, mystery and confusion about sex and relationships is part of our lives always, whatever knowledge is available, whatever century we live in. At least by 1956, just turned seventeen, I had begun to sense that many boys — men — wanted things that alarmed me and that I 'knew were wrong', though I didn't really 'know' anything at all, and that ignorance is part of this 1950s story. Except for forcefully repeating how terrible it was when girls we knew 'had' to get married, my mother had explained so little: once, years later, I heard her call sex, distastefully, 'that silly business'. We certainly weren't shown condoms on bananas — I didn't even know the word 'condom'.

One guest at the hotel where we were working — an old man in his thirties — knew I had just left school and talked to me seriously in the Guests' Bar one night about how I mustn't flirt all the time and how I must consider what kind of person I wanted to be, and about platonic friendships: he seemed very wise, and an expert on the word 'platonic'.

TUESDAY 14 FEBRUARY 1956

Ron told us about Plato's idea of each spirit going for a moment to heaven, some seeing little, some seeing God – and by that vision, so there is nobility of character and spirituality in life. And then we talked about re-incarnation. And we talked about what animal or bird we would like to be. Ron wants to be a seagull, another guest, Peter, wants to be an albatross – I said I wanted to be a young deer. I was scorned and pulled to pieces and analysed horribly, but still it was a wonderful conversation and someone was playing 'Claire de Lune' on the piano very beautifully. Then one of the 'Heavenly Twins' as we call those two young men guests wanted me to be in his bowls team. It's a queer set-up those two, they're not even brothers. They're good fun though and rather sweet and I did play bowls.

As this diary entry shows, I didn't know anything about homosexuality either. I didn't know I knew any 'homosexuals' — I know this sounds unbelievable but in 1956 I didn't even know the word. In 2019 in London thirty thousand people marched in the colourful and loud and happy Gay Pride Parade, and over a million people lined the London streets to see and cheer them. But in the 1950s — I didn't know this either, of course — homosexuality was a crime in both countries, for which the 'criminal' could be arrested and sent to prison. Soon after I arrived in London, at the very beginning of those 'swinging sixties', I met a friend from university and we walked along the newly trendy Kings Road in Chelsea one evening, me still so new to London, and he told me he was a homosexual and that it was illegal. 'But it's more —' he shrugged — 'anonymous here than at home,' and I just stopped in the street, mystified, and stared at him, as big red buses full of anonymous people squished past in the smoggy, foggy winter dusk.

WEDNESDAY 15 FEBRUARY 1956

Tonight in the Guests Bar Ron bought more drinks for everybody and talked more about Platonic Relationships.

He and Peter told me I was vivacious charming unaffected and could laugh at myself, and not to let University life change me. I'm not sure if it's good to be told these things.

It certainly wasn't. I became very self-conscious . . . caught myself being viv and ch – damn . . . Then one night that same Platonic expert tried to force me into his hotel room, which really shocked me — and perhaps him. I emerged unscathed but shaken and was confirmed in my thoughts that male people could be very, very unreliable.

But on the whole we had wonderful times: we called the kitchen 'Happy Hell', my friend Win was promoted to Second Cook, Tia continued to be — on the whole — a benign character; we swam and tried to fish and went for long walks across the hills . . . Win and Vanessa and I have just been laughing till we cried at life in the kitchen, today we walloped pots and cooked dinners till 8 o'clock. And we've managed to get that radio going again and it's playing some beaut music . . .

And then we went home to Wellington, waving goodbye, unsullied, clutching our earnings.

FRIDAY 2 MARCH 1956

I bought all my text books which are in stock second-hand – about £6 worth. There are some terribly interesting books for English – quite a few different English plays, books of poetry including Allen Curnow's 'Book of New Zealand Verse.' I still have £21 in the bank. Out of that I have to buy a few more books, a blazer and probably some winter shoes. It is nice to be spending my own money – money earned so enjoyably. But perhaps it was bad to be told that I was charming and vivacious. Went to Maria's Acting Club which is super but am getting an inferiority complex again because I cant be viv and ch without thinking about it. Damn it. But then just as I thought I couldn't act at all, I was suddenly, again, good in a part. Odd.

SUNDAY 4 MARCH 1956

10.15pm. I'm scared. University tomorrow. Thought I'd grown up but – ! At home everybody and everything including me gets flustered and worried and the same old tight feeling comes back and I worry – will I go to sleep, what will happen tomorrow, will it be all right, will people like me and so on. If only I could have that free and easy walloping-pots attitude I've just had. Mum growls because my frock isn't ready; everything is fussy . . . Still, tomorrow I will be a 'fresher', it will be fun and I must work.

And what did I think I was doing, that first year at university?

As my diaries have shown I had given absolutely no serious thought as to why I was studying full-time there. Just because I liked the library with all those books and the beautiful, tall window? I had enrolled for English, History and French, but as my school French mistress had foretold I lasted about a week in university French lectures . . . horrible French . . . I wrote, just as I'd once written in my diary so often . . . horrible Latin . . . I was obviously useless at languages. I dropped French and switched to — of all subjects — Economics. I'd read through somebody's notes, found them quite interesting, and then sat in on a lecture: next thing, there I was, one of the few girls in the evening Economics I lectures, grasping (and gasping) at matters like monetary policy and social credit. I recorded that the class was mostly full of old men (old to me was about twenty-five) and a lot of the 'old men' rushed up the hill after work to 5 p.m., 6 p.m. and 7 p.m. lectures. Causing such problems to them, as I record the boy who'd played Alexander the Great in that school play telling me, with the closing of all pubs at 6 p.m. (My diary tells me he also said he didn't like girls now because they didn't respond the way they used to; they were getting too intellectual, especially if they did Psychology.)

TUESDAY 13 MARCH 1956

It's queer how things happen terribly unexpected. Strangely, the first thing I thought of when I heard was my diary, it was in my bag thank goodness. Win and I were just coming out of 'Simon and Laura' – Googie Withers and John McCallum are touring here, and Dad met us and said I wasn't going home, our family was going to Auntie Mary's. Uncle Harry has escaped from the Mental Hospital and may come to our place so we have left. Last time I saw Uncle Harry I wasn't keeping a diary but – I cant ever forget. I am in Auntie's lounge now in a sleeping bag, Uncle Harry doesn't know where this place is. All this seems a kind of dream and soon I'll wake up and everything will be just as it was before . . . I expect the police will soon find him. Poor Uncle Harry I wonder where he is right now, it's quite cold.

WEDNESDAY 14 MARCH 1956

It does just seem like a bad dream now. The police found Uncle Harry this morning, he is back at the Hospital, we are back home. At Auntie Mary's this morning I noticed a photo of him as a young boy, inside the frame was a sprig of rosemary. Ophelia says it. For Remembrance.

It has been so cold and now I have weakened and gone to bed with a hot water bottle. Have done some more work on that history essay and I will do some more of it now, I've worked hard on it. 'The Wool Trade'. (No mention of New Zealand, this is the medieval English stuff!) . . . huh.

In both English I and Economics I we dealt, in some way at least, with some New Zealand matters; in History I we did not. The diaries mention Alfred the Great, Thomas Becket, the history of the British — our — monarchy: I have a very clear memory of sitting in an empty lecture room trying to push the Kings and Queens of England into my head and staring out over Wellington Harbour wondering why I was doing it.

And mostly that year it seems I ate fish and chips and grapes.

Looped through the entries for this first university year are various problems: how to study properly; difficulties with my mother; still blushing so much; fear of failure; and the same old wanting people to 'like' me — and this meant girls as well as boys. I was still trying to be friends with boys like I was friends with girls but so many boys wanted to 'go steady', that's what young people did. Wanting people to like me loomed so large that one girl I really liked complained that she could never talk to me properly at university because other people wanted to talk to me too, and interrupted. I was upset, because I knew it was true. So nice and more mature was this girl, Cath, that she understood she had hurt me and, my diary records, phoned me to say that she did still like me. All recorded, just as I recorded the complications with boys. I so wanted boys to like me. But sooner or later the same old pattern: I wanted to be free, to be *friends* with them, and that wasn't the custom.

SATURDAY 17 MARCH 1956

Apparently I have more of a reputation of a 'good time girl' than I thought. I like to be friendly but it looks as though as usual I cant, with boys, without people being frightfully rude or jealous or something. Then Stewart said to me tonight: 'Yes. But what happens when you're older?' Which I have been thinking about myself even at the age of seventeen. And I'm suddenly a bit tired of being ch and viv all day long. Flirting with everybody because I always have. So I told Win I would become a misojinist after Easter. (Of course she didn't believe me!)

But as usual I cant think of hardly anything nice about myself.

SUNDAY 25 MARCH 1956

11pm. I like to go to Church – especially at night when it seems more peaceful and religious somehow. But I'm not a true Christian am I: I cant cant cant feel that everything said is real, or believable. I try to pray. But my voice doesn't – it doesn't feel really real. I only know that, somewhere, there is a something. A God? That feeling I get sometimes when I'm acting? Oh I know it's not God when I'm acting! But what is it? And – things couldn't be so beautiful by themselves – even today, the mist over the Seatoun bay as I came through the tunnel. Finished my Economics essay.

As well as my not knowing how to spell misogynist, I'm not sure

Win and I had quite grasped the meaning of the word; anyway all the talk of misojiny after Easter got a huge boost *during* Easter, when the Universities Sports Tournament was held in Wellington. One of the guests at the Marlborough Sounds hotel, who with the platonic expert had told me I was viv and ch, and who wanted to be reincarnated as an albatross, had said he would be coming from another university and would take me to the Tournament Ball. He was drunk every time I saw him but he sobered up enough to pick me up for the ball, tell my parents it finished at 1 a.m. and then we were visiting a friend of his for coffee. Charmingly. My first sophisticated foray into University Social Life. I got home to the back door of our house at 5.20 a.m. where we were met by my father who had decided if we weren't back by 5.30 he would call the hospitals and the police; he had an important Education Department meeting that morning and Mum had to teach and neither of them had been to sleep. And by that time as well as numerous parties after the ball I had also had the most horrible, unpleasant experience in the front of a car (with two others doing the same in the back) of 'an attempt at intrusion into undergarments' as the notorious weekly scandal newspaper *Truth* might have put it (though of course we didn't ever have something as salacious as *Truth* in our house). In my diary (me, the 'good time girl'), I'd written quite primly . . . I do like boys putting their arms around me, or holding my hand etc – but I don't like the feeling of being kissed too much by most of them . . . I hated what was happening in the packed car and had finally extricated myself before any 'damage' was done, but as well as being in utter disgrace with Mum and Dad, I was in utter disgrace with myself for not somehow disentangling myself from the situation sooner. And who could I talk to? Ask about things?

TUESDAY 10 APRIL 1956

I have been promising to go and see Mrs Garland for ages now that Sally is away and haven't done, so I went this morning. I don't know how the conversation got on to 'sex' but it did. I could never say things to Mum that I said to her. I'm so very ignorant on such matters anyway. I only know that – well anyway even I know not much harm could come from – anything that happened at Easter – but I don't want anything like that to ever happen again. We talked about some odd – useful – things that I didn't know – which helped me. Mrs Garland is so lovely.

I had had my first, proper, simple lesson about sex.

I had short bursts of concentrated study, loved English literature, and to my surprise enjoyed Economics: for an essay on 'Social Credit' (briefly a political party in New Zealand) I write I got a really high mark. The poet Anton Vogt was in the class. I used to always sit next to Bryan Gould; later, in England, I knew him as a Labour MP who stood against Tony Blair for the party leadership; later again he became Vice-Chancellor at Waikato University. And one of the few other girls in the class — a pregnant married woman who seemed to actually manage to have her baby in the university holidays — was the New Zealand writer Marilyn Duckworth (and we laughed, remembering Economics I to each other years later).

But my diaries record, at length, a huge problem in another subject. Neither the History professor nor the History tutor liked my *essay style of writing*, and I got D minus for my second essay. *D minus?* I was, of course, mortified. I was writing my

History essays in the same style as my English essays that got 70 per cent or even higher, but over my whole university career I could never master the much more complicated academic style of writing that seemed to be required in some departments, and I was obviously never going to be an Academic. I got part-time work in the university cafeteria but was soon told I was too slow and spread too much butter on the bread. Not going to make it as a counter-hand either.

And yet years later (still spreading too much butter on bread) I write 'Historical Novels'. And I have been grateful for all the wonderful, so well-researched academic books about the subjects around which I have written the novels: I simply could not have written without them. Yet, as I've said earlier, I seem to have to touch a subject in another way, a different way, to feel confident to write about it. Reading scores of books on 'Art' — Rembrandt, Hogarth, Gainsborough — but shouting with frustration until the New Zealand painter Tony Lane explained fresco, showed me. I read books and books about Egypt and hieroglyphs, but having held the actual Rosetta Stone so helped; then being there, hearing the call of the muezzin echoing out across the mosques, and seeing the different, sharper blue of the Egyptian sky. Dr Bob Large of the Auckland Regional Pain Service, sitting with me in Auckland Hospital explaining that hypnotism and mindfulness are used for relieving pain — in Auckland, in this hospital, in the twenty-first century — and that his work, now, connects back to mesmerism in England in the nineteenth century.

And Alexandra Kollontai's grandson sleeping in my bed.

But in 1956 I was a failure at writing about history.

At this time Mum, now aged forty-six, started having — and reading the diary entries now makes me feel she was lonely — conversations with me, about herself.

THURSDAY 10 MAY 1956

I'm a bit worried about Mum. She's started moaning about Dad – doesn't see why she should entertain people who have been kind to him. Even to me she seems all wrong in that. But I can't argue with her any more: she just screams at me and tells me how hard she works and how lazy I am. I hope things will be all right. But she seems to take particular delight in nagging me – even Andrew and Ross notice now. I stay at Varsity as much as I can – unless I'm freezing.

MONDAY 14 MAY 1956

Rainy outside. Tonight Mum and I were sitting by the fire together. I suddenly felt that she likes to have someone swotting in the house – I'm not sure why: probably how she would have liked her own youth. How does she really feel about me being a university student I wonder. We can be good friends at times. Wish it was always. I asked her what she was like when she was 17: she said gauche, unsure of herself, gawky, inferiority complex . . .

FRIDAY 18 MAY 1956

Mum told me quite definitely tonight, just suddenly, that 'There is nothing when you die'. I cant cant quite believe that. She said when she had a nervous breakdown she decided that. She also said she nearly had a nervous breakdown when Dad went to America because it was so unfair. She

> said 'Why should he have gone without me when I helped him so much?' She said she had helped him ever since she married him, 'he couldn't have managed without me'.
>
> And now, tonight, Mum told me that she had only been in love once in her life – when she was about 18, with a commercial traveller – who 'breezed' in to her life. His name was Bob.

I asked her why she'd married Dad then. She said he had proposed, she'd refused, but one night she was on a tram and it was raining and she saw Dad walking in the rain by himself and felt sorry for him so had agreed to marry him.

But I had already understood — in my half-adolescent, half-instinctive way — something about my mother. She needed Dad. Was that what love was? And I lay awake in bed wondering if the 'love' that everyone sang and talked about really existed.

Of course it's not surprising that we all thought a lot about 'love' — young girls have always thought about love. In 1956, on the whole, girls 'fell in love', 'went steady' and many girls my age (seventeen) were hoping to soon 'get engaged to be married' — and indeed did so (and 'Love Is a Many-Splendored Thing' was still around on the jukeboxes). So far, so like young girls through time — but in the mid-1950s many of us were now more and more caught up and whirled about by that raucous explosion of loud, sexy pop music (still usually about love) — and Elvis Presley sang about 'Heartbreak Hotel' so that girls all over the world screamed that they loved *him*. (When I tried to think of just one song of the earlier 1950s that wasn't about love, I did come up with 'How Much Is That Doggie in the Window?'. Which turned out, when I studied the words, to be a love song really, if a slightly odd one for the time, with Patti Page singing that as she had to go to California her sweetheart needed a doggie to protect him.)

But 'love' still remained a mystery.

SATURDAY 26 MAY 1956

I wanted to go to the football at Athletic Park with the family but needed to work because of exams. It is a very crisp day but fine – just exactly right for football. I'm listening on the wireless at least. Bands playing. Winston McCarthy is well away with his commentary – I like listening to him getting all excited! They'll choose the next All Black team after today's North-South game. I bet, if I went for a walk, I'd hear radios going in backyards or out of open windows all listening to the game. Autumn crisp feeling and rugby. That's something Katherine Mansfield didn't write about!

Daddy turned 50 yesterday. Gosh that seems old but sometimes he doesn't seem old at all. He is a pretty wonderful Pop really and I'm very lucky.

MONDAY 4 JUNE 1956

Rehearsal for 'The Critic' for the Varsity Drama Club today which is fun. I am the maid and I have to pop in and out all the time – that'll keep me on my toes! Settled down to the history essay that I began to write in the middle of the night last night, finished it – and it's the best I've done – I think . . .

I got my Katherine Mansfield exam essay back. I thought I'd got everything <u>so wrong</u> – but I got 73%.

TUESDAY 12 JUNE 1956

Ye gods did I not have an awful interview with Mr Turnbull

for History! He said my essay was terrible. I had to fight very hard not to cry. I suppose he was helpful – but it's a bit depressing to see page after page of my essay crossed out – 'immaterial'. I thought it was the best essay I've done and I worked really hard on it. Oh – I don't know a thing and anyway Mr Turnbull will never give me a good mark. One of those older students saw me come out upset and invited me to his flat, he said he would help me with my essay. I went. Huh. I soon left again. And he seemed so kind and genuine. Ruth lent me some of her essays – Mr Turnbull told me to read them. But I hate the way I'm supposed to write. It's – peculiar.

All the boys went to the pub. Huh.

New Zealand licensing laws and all those hoses full of beer used to be famous! All government departmental offices (and there were a lot of them of course in the capital city) closed at exactly 4.35 p.m. — an odd time to down pens and paper, you might think, but it was imperative: the pubs closed at 6 p.m. And there was this rush of often be-suited (or, in summer, be-shorted, with formal shoes and long socks) men: hurrying along streets, down hills, across tram-lines, dodging tramcars and Morris cars and Austins to go to the pub for the very brief (they felt) after-work drinking time. And to deal with this tumultuous, noisy, late-afternoon invasion, pint beer glasses were lined up on counters and a hose was attached to the beer barrels and the man with the hose went up and down the counter filling glasses which were quickly emptied and banged down on the counter for a refill. The counters were wet; half-crowns and shillings and sixpences and pennies splashed. The only reason I (a female, not allowed in) can describe this so exactly is because in winter the roaring sounded like mad rugby games being played behind closed doors, but on hot summer days the doors and windows of the pubs would be wide open, horse-racing or cricket on the radio, and men's loud voices blared out — and we, the excluded females walking past, could see perfectly clearly the wet counters and the wet money and the huge quantity of big glasses full of brown foaming liquid, and the hoses. And smell the beer. A very vast number of women fluttered at the edges of this immovable ritual — and waited until 6 p.m.

MONDAY 18 JUNE 1956

I really honestly want to be an actress, surely it's more than just a schoolgirl's silly dream now. I've just been at the Dress Rehearsal for 'The Critic' in the Little Theatre. Dress Rehearsals are wonderfully heavenly mucky exasperating things and I love them. And I do do wish I could be an actress. But oh my make-up SPOTS. Spotty-face.

THURSDAY 21 JUNE 1956

I do love being in plays. Three costumes in 'The Critic'. It went over very well. All sorts of mad things happened – scenery fell down, sound effects didn't go etc etc. But fun! Then we all went to 'Frisco' for coffee – full of teddy boys and widgies and bodgies!

SUNDAY 24 JUNE 1956

I was worrying about boys as usual as the phone rang but it was Auntie Jean from Timaru – Granny died yesterday, nearly 103. I do so wish I had tried to talk to her about old

New Zealand. This is the first member of my family that has died in my lifetime. She used to put her clothes on at 2am and her hat and go walking round Timaru and Nana who's pretty old herself had to keep going out to find her in the middle of the night. I wonder what Nana will do now. She will feel funny maybe?

Irrepressible Ross thought about this news for a while. Then he suddenly erupted into a squeakily loud but quavering Glaswegian accent not unlike that of our very old, very deaf great-grandmother, *'Eh? Eh? John Ewing you say? Which John Ewing is this? Eh? Eh?'* (one of the last things we'd heard her say, not recognising Dad, her grandson), and even Mum and Dad laughed too.

Ross was always the funniest, and loved by many. We grew to believe in different things, but only ever had one really damaging disagreement: the Vietnam War. Ross flew there with the New Zealand Air Force, working with the Americans. I was protesting outside the American Embassy in London, being kicked by a police horse.

Later Ross also had the biggest Life Adventure of all of us. His flying career ended in his thirties due to ongoing health difficulties after a bad car crash while he was in the Air Force. So he decided to train as a doctor: 'I've been in hospital so often after the car crash, I reckon I know most of it!' So he (who'd left school without University Entrance) sat that exam, then trained as a GP, and was later an aviation medical specialist. He never lost his fascination with aeroplanes and became part of a group who bought old planes and lovingly put them on show in New Zealand. A few of this group, including Ross, travelled to America to inspect and then buy an old seaplane, a Catalina. While they were flying it home over the Pacific it malfunctioned in complete darkness, and started losing height. They were able to control it slightly but it finally fell into the night sea. 'You probably think water would be soft to fall into? It is as hard as concrete,' said Ross. The survival of everyone was probably because they were, after all, in a flying boat. The Catalina was badly damaged. And sinking. They had a life-raft and a radio; they all managed to get into the life-raft at dawn and got away from the still-sinking wreck; they drifted aimlessly, their shadowy treasure slowly disappearing into the Pacific Ocean. I was home at the time and we waited, terrified, hearts beating too fast, beside radios and telephones: at last we heard a ship had rescued all safely after nearly twelve hours on that life-raft. Ross wrote a book about the experience, and titled it, with a nod to the Mamas and the Papas, *Catalina Dreaming*.

In 2012, he was dying. He asked where I was: I flew home with a photograph album — black-and-white photos of these times when we were young. Ross making us laugh, Ross of the funny voices, Ross who could really sing and whose famous party piece was the song 'Speedy Gonzales' ('the fastest mouse in all Mexico'). And Ross who looked after me when I was ill. Now his wife Raewyn and his children and I looked at the old photographs with him, and although his mind was coming and going he nevertheless remembered things I had forgotten and he smiled his dear smile and we sort of sang 'Sad Movies'. He was sixty-eight.

At his funeral his son read a piece that Ross had written long after he'd left the Air Force. He had come to believe in his later life that going to war in other people's countries was wrong.

MONDAY 23 JULY 1956

Ross and I heard Tutti Frutti on the wireless when we were doing the dinner dishes, turned it up loud and started rocking and rolling round the kitchen and Mum started to go mad but a) about one second before that Dad had started laughing at us, I suppose we do look a bit funny, twelve and seventeen, and he took the tea-towel and started drying, and b) Andrew (he's a bit like Mum) was scrubbing the table clean with Old Dutch, so we were saved!

VII

I HAVE NO MEMORY HOW — my 1956 diaries don't explain, just describe — I hooked up with a group of Catholic students, mostly boys, but also a few girls I liked who told me stories about being taught by nuns. They seemed to spend a lot of time in the university cafeteria, discussing lectures and life and religion, but I was at least smart enough to realise they mostly worked extremely hard, never missed lectures — even the boy my other friends called a 'lout' because he was always going off to play pool downtown — and most of them were clever. We talked about many things but if we were discussing things intellectually they criticised my sloppy thinking, made me grasp a subject properly; to think before I spoke. Although there was a lot of teasing — and criticising, some of it patronising — and arguing, they were good for me and helped me start to work really properly. I really liked the 'lout' in particular, even though I knew he sometimes went to the pub in the daytime, but he had a very nice Catholic girlfriend, so the group disapproved — jealousies and displeasure came into play as well. But I did begin to really learn how to work harder. The Economics lecturer's notes were good and clear, and I used to type them up at home after lectures and read them over and over until I could properly understand them even though the subject was so new to me. But I still couldn't write the way my History lecturers wanted me to, so I would give up and go to a university party — or go to see the film of *Rock Around the Clock* again and then go to a party . . . I came home really late from that Varsity party and all the lights were blazing in our house and Mum screamed the house down and I'm not allowed out AT ALL. Luckily for me Win came over today. We were reading and quite enjoying poetry, old stuff. All those sentimental and romantic ancient love poems we have to study (we call them sent and rome). Win and I discussed maturity. She thinks it is having formulated ideas: I think it is knowing how people feel and think, understanding people. Win stayed for tea. Then we had a hilarious time reading plays we're studying with Andrew and Ross. Ross made us laugh till we nearly cried. I've got super brothers really. Andrew is talking in his sleep.

MONDAY 30 JULY 1956

On the way home I could smell daphne from the garden, a heavy scent in the night. I love it. Went to 'A Streetcar Named Desire' with Libby Gordon today. Maybe Vivien Leigh couldn't act in 'The Deep Blue Sea' but she was pretty magnificent as Blanche in 'A Streetcar Named Desire'. I was so weak I couldn't move when it was finished.

Years later I went back to New Zealand, to Wellington, to play Blanche in *A Streetcar Named Desire* at Downstage Theatre. I had by then played in, and knew a lot about, Tennessee Williams — and I had read also about the first Blanche DuBois,

Jessica Tandy, who wasn't at all like Vivien Leigh (and suspected that Mr Williams was really writing about himself when he wrote Blanche and was in love with Marlon Brando who played Stanley). When you're playing a huge, demanding part like that the best directors come on the journey with you, and the Downstage director Colin McColl came with me all the way in that production: the most precious gift an actor can be given by a director. And at the end of each performance I was, just as I describe I was when watching the film in 1956 . . . so weak I couldn't move when it was finished . . . mainly because of the emotional journey that Blanche DuBois travels in the play (and also because Jim Moriarty, the actor playing Stanley, broke two of my ribs in rehearsal!). The cast were told that we had broken all box-office records, the run was extended, and we all used to sit in one of the two (communal) dressing rooms after performances and consume immense amounts of brandy.

But that was thirty years later.

MONDAY 20 AUGUST 1956

It's university holidays but went in to swot at the library all day. Some of the Catholics there. We did crosswords and argued! Irv-the-lout seems to spend most of his time playing pool down town – but he's also doing Greek! I like him.

I don't think I've ever written in my diary about the trouble in the New Zealand Players. I don't want the NZ Players to disband but it sounds a horrible mess.

MONDAY 3 SEPTEMBER 1956

There's one Maori boy in the Catholic group, and I talked to him for a long time today, told him about Maungatapu – I thought he'd be interested, but he looked at me as if I was mad. He doesn't like Maoris, thinks people stare, and look down on him because he is a Maori, wants to get out into the backblocks of Australia and live there like a hermit forever. Isn't interested – I think because he's ashamed – in Maori culture of any kind, thinks Maoris are superstitious and tell awful stories.

Huh. One of the 'Natives of our country New Zealand who are proud of their heritage – basically untouched by the Pakeha' etc etc. He was almost crying at the end . . . Later from the tram, I saw him walking up Willis Street by himself eating a cream bun.

Final exams start in six weeks???!!! I am working, really hard, though maybe too late.

THURSDAY 4 OCTOBER 1956

How can I hurt the feelings of so many boys at Varsity? How can I be such a horrible person? Everything is horrible and I'm the most horrible part of it all. I have to work, and I cant. And why why do I tell everybody everything? I'm a human failure.

SATURDAY 20 OCTOBER 1956

8 and a half hours study today – didn't get me anywhere. My friend Irv took me to the pictures tonight. We stood in the rain. Irv-the-lout, who says he likes pool more than studying (but he's studying GREEK!), is such a 'rough' type somehow (and he calls me a ruffian) but what attracts me is the way he stands deep in thought with his head forward – like from some film I've seen I think and the shadow of a building sometimes half on his face. And he is so brainy, he

just hides it. Why? We had to come home in the tram and Mum was annoyed. She thinks every respectable boy has a car. Doesn't consider he has to get a tram and then a train, to go home again.

SUNDAY 21 OCTOBER 1956

The family have been pretty good to me with this final swotting, Mum has especially – It all starts tomorrow . . . Six three-hour papers . . . Sleep well . . .

SUNDAY 28 OCTOBER 1956

Nearly half exams over. I'll probably fail every single paper. Uncle Farmer John from Temuka is staying; he who puts chickens to sleep on his farm by whirling them about! Golly he's a character, he can always tell the wildest stories! He starts off with a small fact and then gets carried away by a wonderfully imaginative humour into a huge mad story! Rose time – red, red, fragrance and velvet – perfect shapes, Mum grows beautiful ones in our garden, she often puts some in my room, and I sometimes just carry one around with me at Varsity, the scent. I don't care if it's stupid. I get a sort of tight feeling inside, like when I read NZ poetry . . . Taken aspros.

WEDNESDAY 31 OCTOBER 1956

Ohhh. Ill and tired. I mucked things up terribly in the History exam – had to go out for a while, stood outside the door so the examiner could see, sick and dizzy, finished vaguely but I've definitely failed History. But Economics tomorrow – may fail that too. I'm listening to the radio – Israel attacking Egypt;

America and England have opposing viewpoints about the Suez Canal, and there is grave danger of a bad war.

WEDNESDAY 7 NOVEMBER 1956

Well. Waiting now for exam results . . . For the last time I've gone round with the 'Catholic gang': up the hill, down the hill, shoes off, fish and chips, and crosswords on the common-room couch, fights with Irv (then kissing him in the Botanical Gardens), talking with Mary about St Mary's College and the nuns, and Marguerite and Jim and Frank and George and Spiro and even Peter-who-doesn't-like-me. I wouldn't have come out of exams as well as I did, I mean, I would have done worse, I'm sure of it, without their brains, the way they made me think more clearly. Irv-the-lout is already working in the wool-store, Win and I going back to the Hotel next week for pot-walloping or waitressing. Oh golly there mustn't be a Third World War even if it would mean – as I now understand – an Economic Boom Period.

The father of Ruth Burton, one of our school friends, worked in the External Affairs Department, and after exams some of us were asked to their place to meet students from Indonesia and Borneo and Malaya and Burma: all studying in New Zealand under the Colombo Plan in which the Commonwealth agreed to help these countries with economic and social development. We danced and sang and enjoyed ourselves and I decided that if people from different countries met when they were young like this, and got to know each other, there wouldn't be any more wars.

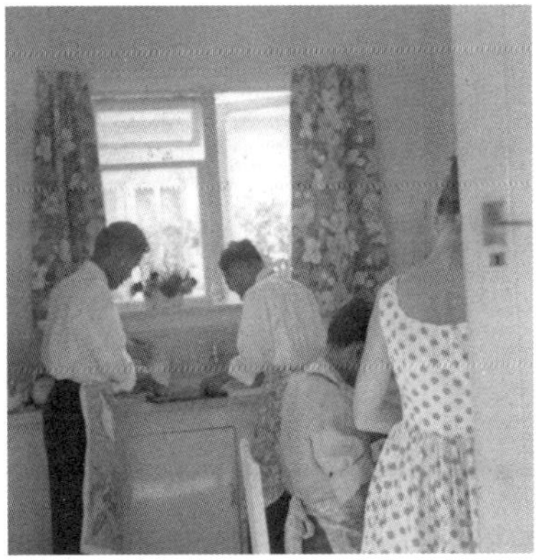

We all took a turn to ask some of these students to our homes — and sometimes the students cooked. They would arrive at our homes impeccably dressed in their best suits, but inside their neat satchels were aprons, and strange spices, and they got to work in our kitchens — and we had our very first taste of 'foreign food' and — cautiously at first — enjoyed it.

MONDAY 12 NOVEMBER 1956

Yippee!! 'B' pass in English I! Thank heavens I passed in one. If only I can pass Economics – I'm afraid it's silly to kid myself about History. And the 'lout', the pool-player, got an 'A' pass in Greek! My friends laugh at me disapprovingly about my various 'unsuitable' friends – and he got a higher mark than any of us!

Then Win and I and Vanessa and Ruth all went back to work in the hotel in the Marlborough Sounds again where we were greeted fondly by the owner. And this time met a young Māori girl, Violet, who was related to Tia the Cook. She had dark eyes and curly black hair and a huge, huge smile. I think she was still fifteen when we first met her; she had left school and Tia got her the job at the hotel. Violet, I soon got to realise, was a very intelligent young girl who shouldn't have been scrubbing pots and making beds for a living. But she first charmed me by having two radios on different stations in two rooms while she was cleaning them, so that she wouldn't miss Elvis singing 'Heartbreak Hotel' or Little Richard singing 'Tutti Frutti' if the two songs came on together. Sometimes we all piled into Tia's room after the pots were walloped in the evening to catch the Hit Parade on her radio. Often we went into the Guests' Bar and drank a lot of alcohol and I flirted with the guests, as usual.

FRIDAY 16 NOVEMBER 1956

I've failed History. We just got a telegram: Win Pass, Barbara Fail. So I've been lying on my bed weeping my eyes out, even though I knew I'd failed. And Economics . . .?

SATURDAY 17 NOVEMBER 1956

I rang home just to be sure Economics wasn't out but Mum says I mustn't ring, that it costs too much. True. But I'd rather ring home at a certain time than feel physically sick every single time the hotel telephone rings. I should prepare myself for the worst. But it was cheering tonight, sitting round the big kitchen table after work while Violet plays the guitar. She's a character, and giggles a lot!

The dairies remind me how much Violet loved dancing — especially with a boy called Wally. Her cousin Hemi, a deckhand, a kind boy with a limp, seemed to look after everybody in Picton *and* Violet, and he would sometimes book an old wooden launch to come and get us all, including Tia the Cook; we'd speed through the pots and the dishes after dinner and jump on the arriving launch as night fell. We saw phosphorescence dancing in the waves that we made as we approached the funny little town of Picton that was full of sailors and wharfies and deckhands and had palm trees growing on the beach. Various other cousins would meet us and either go dancing in the town or, if there was a car, out to their old family home in Waikawa . . . with a washing machine and only two cups it seemed and some grown ups who we were introduced to . . . and the boys would drink beer and play steel guitars and sing 'Your Cheating Heart' and 'Blue Smoke', and then we would have to speed back to Picton to catch the very last launch at midnight. Sometimes some of the cousins escorted us back on the launch so that we could keep singing . . . with guitars and lots of beer. Could Mum – and maybe even Win's Mum! – have seen us: drinking beer out of a bottle singing in the middle of the night in the middle of the sea . . .

Then up early and into the kitchen, earning our wages.

TUESDAY 20 NOVEMBER 1956

I've got it!!!!! I got Economics: 54% and 50% – Whew!!!!!! Everything is ka pai. I'm feeling a very contented wahine – actually I'm just showing off my Maori words that Violet has been teaching me, 'I know how to speak Maori, even if my mother was a bloody white man' she says! But Win didn't get French – I was so so sorry, my heart actually jumped for her like it does for myself, I know how horrible and failing it feels. Then later on I caught myself thinking: At least Mum cant compare me unfavourably with Win, as she always always does. But that's a horrible, selfish way to think. I wrote it down right here right now so that I know how horrible I am.

THURSDAY 22 NOVEMBER 1956

I've been reading tonight a highly immoral book of Tia's or Violet's and it's set me thinking seriously . . . about a couple of those things that happened – or I should say didn't happen – at Varsity with men – who want things I don't, I don't even like writing about it. They seem so nice at first and then – they, oh they always say they're 'in love' with me but it's, it must be – desire they feel which is quite different – and desire we learn is wrong – whatever it actually is. I have dreams of another kind of love but I'm now wondering if perhaps that's only in books? One of them called me immature and puritanical – and I found out later he was married and his wife was away having a baby! Huh. Me immature? At least I've woken up to the world but it's hard to know how to think rightly about all this.

SATURDAY 24 NOVEMBER 1956

How it all comes back. Sitting in the same Hotel lounge with that peculiar feeling that sometimes comes after a few Pimms or dry sherries – that feeling, and someone playing the piano . . . only unfortunately this woman tonight played abominably.

Mum sent me a biscuit tin full of my favourite biscuits. Maybe her letters and phone calls aren't lovely and loving like Win's Mum but she is a wonderful cook and knows my favourite biscuits all right.

I'm learning Maori from Violet – who, like Tia, also sings the same songs the girls down the road at Maungatapu taught me '. . . you'll never find another wahine like me'. Isn't that weird, particular party songs jumping from Maori village to Maori village? It's hard to get the Maori grammar right BUT I suddenly have the wonderful idea of taking it for my degree foreign language. I guess it must be taught at Vic?

One day I heard Violet use the word wairua about one of the old army huts that were used to house the hotel staff. This particular hut was never used — I think it had no electricity. But Violet said it had a peculiar wairua and not to go in there. And I remembered wairua was the word the girls down the Maungatapu road had used, about their ancestors, and asked Violet what it meant . . . and she said it meant 'spirit' and I said dead people might have spirits but not army huts and she just looked at me. 'Everything has a wairua, e hoa' she said. 'That tree there has a wairua and you have a wairua.'

A word for me to ponder on.

MONDAY 26 NOVEMBER 1956

Writing in my diary by torchlight. The last guests went this morning (only the family to waitress on, hurrah) so Mr H. has turned off the generator – so: no electricity, no radio, no music! We don't care, we just sing 'Blue Suede Shoes' loudly! Taffy Evans, the old Welshman who helps here, sings 'If You're Irish, Come into the Parlour'!

He told us the best way to see the last of rats: this is what you do. Catch one. Paint it with whitewash. Let it free again. All the other rats will run away because they'll think they're seeing a ghost! And Win and I were following it all quite seriously!

WEDNESDAY 5 DECEMBER 1956

O My God! Sometimes the world can be a ghastly mixed-up place full of horrible people making life unpleasant. Tia is just a 'bloody bitch' and the kitchen has got a bit horrible – she seems to have her knife into me suddenly – but why? What did I do? She has become so unpleasant. And Mrs H. is, as Win calls it, 'a humourless martyr'. We'll be glad to be home and out of the kitchen for a while but we're coming back after Christmas and Violet says she will teach me some more Maori, yippee. Maybe I COULD, seriously, take it at Varsity as my language paper?

When we got back to Wellington, Win's family decided it was their turn to entertain the Colombo Plan students; I went to her house to help before everyone arrived; we ran out of pots, so Ross volunteered to bike over with some of ours. Just as he arrived we were battling to open a pressure cooker and asked him to help: he heroically tried and the whole thing exploded and hot food burst all over his face and all over the ceiling. Ross was badly burnt and had to go to hospital where his face was wrapped in white bandages; we tried to clean the ceiling; the Colombo Plan students and other guests arrived; the party went on. But our family never used a pressure cooker, and Ross always and forever had to try to keep his face out of the sun.

THURSDAY 20 DECEMBER 1956

Ross much much better at last – thank goodness. How horrible that was, and he was brave. And all our fault, for being so dumb.

FRIDAY 21 DECEMBER 1956

Ross cheerful and laughing again. He really was brave, my brother. I hope I'd be like that. I'm going to buy him extra Christmas presents.

Something funny. I say goodnight, and close my door, and get into bed to write my diary – preferably with the radio going. I've done it for 6 years continuously – must've helped me become whatever sort of person I've become.

Only sometimes – in the middle of anything – there's just a – sudden panic and I wonder who am I? And there is no answer. Like, sort of looking at myself from the outside: perhaps I am seeing things in perspective for the only time . . . Don't know why I wrote that but I suddenly felt it again. I'm allowed to go for a brief break in Maungatapu before we go back to work.

Maungatapu: where the sun shone and where mānuka trees covered in dust stood silent in the heat. But: that rumoured motorway was going to be built through Maungatapu. The unpaved, dusty road was indeed to become a main road, hooking up to a motorway bridge across the water to that popular holiday island, Mount Maunganui. Which would of course change the shoreline where the Māori children swam and played and where I, clinging on to a Māori boy, galloped on a horse when the tide was out, and from where the Māori men still went out fishing. We watched Pākehā men surveying the dusty road with funny instruments in preparation, and the children taught me to sing *Me he manu rere*: *if I was a bird*, and what their parents or their grandparents felt about the coming changes I never knew, or thought to enquire, but I wandered into the small school yard once again, breathing in the warm dust, and the macrocarpa trees, and the school.

And I pondered on my plan to take Māori as my language for my degree. When I got up the courage I tried out the Māori words that Violet had taught me on some of the children, brown heads in the blue sea, but either they spoke English or said 'What?' but politely. And I wryly record that down on the beach a new Pākehā Maungatapu resident was so surprised because '. . . look! the Maoris are wearing swimming togs just like us!'

SUNDAY 30 DECEMBER 1956

Almost the end of another year . . . I love the long conversations with Auntie Ellie at night: the others are gone to bed, and I'm just going, and I sit down for a minute to talk, and minutes last for hours as we talk about so many things. Tonight we talked mostly about Uncle Harry, her brother. I would want to look after my brothers too – but I don't like remembering those days. Again at Auntie Mary's on Christmas Night I saw that photo of Uncle Harry and that sprig of rosemary, for remembrance . . .

MONDAY 31 DECEMBER 1956

New Year's Eve. Well?

I like University. But I need to work harder. I've changed a lot – I've sort of become a bit daft in a way – barefoot, carrying a flower, trying to get away from that 'big-word' way of talking and writing, that 'intellectualism' of words that makes me feel so ill. Why cant things be written simply? I know I failed History because from the very beginning I hated that way of using words that seemed – I dunno, big and complicated on purpose, and I couldn't do it. Irv calls me a ruffian – he understands me almost too well though he mightn't know it himself. It was a good year at Maria's, and being in plays, and she says I am much better again. But . . . even if I've got the acting ability which she keeps saying I have, I haven't got the stamina, I don't think, for the life that would follow. This blessed eternal non-sleeping wouldn't be any good for a real Actress. Shall I really, seriously try to enrol in Maori language for my degree?

My diary advises me that after these ruminations I went to a Tauranga New Year's Eve party of young people who were all dancing to 'Rock Around the Clock' and 'Don't be Cruel' and 'Blue Suede Shoes' all night. I LOVE rock and roll . . . says the entry for 1 January 1957 . . . I simply LOVE it and couldn't stop dancing.

Back in Wellington many of the boys we knew had turned eighteen and in the New Year were all off doing the fourteen weeks' Compulsory Military Training that eighteen-year-old men were required to do. We were packing to go back to the hotel to work for another six weeks before the university year started. Just before we left, Maria Dronke's beautiful daughter, Marei, who had married Con Bollinger, a journalist, asked us to a party at their place . . . Win and I went to Marei and Con Bollinger's. They've made their little place so lovely – lots and lots of interesting books, modern curtains, straw mats on the floor, coloured cushions – and a picture of Lenin over their bed . . . (I had obviously got to grips with 'communism' in some ways at least.) I also faithfully record a conversation I had that evening with one of the guests . . . He said: 'The difference between males and females is so easy. The boy is simple, has only one thing on his mind, the girl lets so many other things come into any relationship and I'm saying this to you because I have to paw someone and you're the nearest.' Huh. I declined to be 'pawed' thank you.

I decided that back at the hotel I would talk to Violet seriously about my plan to study the Māori language as a university subject, whether she thought I would really be able to do it. And if it seems odd to be wanting the advice of a fifteen-year-old it was because while the university was closed I couldn't think of anyone else to ask.

VIII

VIOLET HOLDER. THE YOUNG HOUSEMAID and kitchen-hand at the hotel in the Marlborough Sounds who said, *'I know how to speak Maori even if my mother was a bloody white man.'* Who when she was room-cleaning kept the wirelesses on separate stations in separate rooms so that she wouldn't miss any Hit Parade songs, and believed army huts had spirits inside. Violet had already, before Christmas, taken over, in a practical manner, what the girls along the unpaved road at Maungatapu had started. She was articulate and clever and helped me; now I picked up, as well as more words, some very basic rules. Adjectives came after nouns. Plurals: she knew there was no 's' in Māori (though she used it) but explained that for plurals the definitive article (that's not what she called it) changed from 'te' to 'nga'. She used the language every day mixed with English and laughed at me if I pronounced a word wrongly. She was such a good, clear teacher I kept thinking she should have had the chance to be a school teacher, instead of a kitchen-hand. Often she and Tia the Cook spoke to each other in Māori, and when her cousin Hemi and his brothers came over on the launch with their guitars they all spoke to one another in both languages, so I heard it: a language being used. I loved the sound of the Māori words — all of which end in a vowel so they can sing: no wonder Māori soldiers got on so well with the Italians during the war. I had escaped from Latin, I had escaped from French. Because they weren't real to me. But now I had heard another language being casually spoken in a kitchen. I hadn't told anyone, including my parents, of my plan, but a Bachelor of Arts degree had to have some language element: could mine be Māori? Surely it was a subject? Surely.

That was the plan: six weeks back in the Marlborough Sounds, pot-walloping, singing and laughing — and learning more about the language from Violet.

FRIDAY 25 JANUARY 1957

I really so enjoy singing with Violet again, 'Blue Smoke' then 'Blue Hawaii' then 'Blue Moon', then 'Blue Suede Shoes'. We're working in the kitchen, have all our meals there, Violet makes me talk Maori to her, I'm learning quite a lot of words and rules and so the kitchen is mostly fun, though Tia is still a bit horrible sometimes. We went down to the lounge after dinner (they like us to mix with the guests). They asked Violet to bring her guitar, and guests and staff all sat around and sang. They made Violet and me sing our kitchen songs, 'such perfect harmony they keep' but I know it's Violet who has the harmony, it is just completely natural to her to do it, '. . . you'll never find another wahine like me . . .' – from the Maungatapu road to a hotel lounge in the Marlborough Sounds (where all the guests are Pakeha of course!) 'What's that pretty song?' asked one of the men playing the piano, 'I've never heard it before' and Violet grinned at me.

SUNDAY 3 FEBRUARY 1957

Ohhhhh. I'm just so weary I can hardly write. Except to say Tia has changed even more than before Xmas. She is a lazy bitch – everyone else has worked hours overtime with the hotel full to bursting, while she has done, say, three hours all day. Pots, pots, pots and her shouting at Violet. And oh God I've been in with Violet now, trying to stop her crying, and I've just taken away her aspros because she took four at once which isn't a very good idea. She's leaving. Her Wally has gone out with someone else and left Violet unhappy and crying. It's not like her at all, tears falling down her face, and quiet, and Tia so horrible to her. I love Violet and hate to see her so terribly unhappy. I thought I'd talked her to sleep but now I can hear her and Sophie talking in the hut next door. And I'm so bloody tired and I hate the smell of bad meat and old fat and vegetables in a bucket, things floating in it.

To put it mildly, the Happy Hell as we had called the kitchen turned into purgatory and Tia had suddenly reported Violet for being 'lazy', which Violet certainly wasn't, so Violet just gave a week's notice and left. The hotel was completely full, and I can only think — I don't know why everything smelt so awful — that that generator was playing up: anyway, the kitchen became a nightmare and Tia turned (in my diary) into a witch, with none of us quite knowing why. We all worked so hard but this time Tia didn't: she used to lean back on the kitchen bench and watch us and laugh at us . . . o hell I hate this work when it just about kills you in the process, hot, hot, greasy, smelly kitchen, ugh, trying to serve entrees for nearly 60 and Tia going off laughing, just disappearing, leaving me to it . . .

MONDAY 11 FEBRUARY 1957

A request on the radio for Elvis Presley and 'Heartbreak Hotel' – and no Violet next door to get excited with me. I just feel lonely for her singing and vowed to myself I wouldn't sing in the horrible unhappy kitchen all day. And no more Maori lessons, so much for my plan: Violet has been replaced by a girl from England.

This afternoon some guests and I went for a swim, played tennis, and then sat on the verandah, drank ginger ale before I went back to work. I enjoyed it. But on the tennis court I suddenly got that feeling again, that horrible, scary feeling. 'Who am I?' I question and question and there's never any answer and for a moment I panic.

SATURDAY 23 FEBRUARY 1957

3.15am. I am writing this in the Terminus Hotel in Picton

where Violet now works! First time I have ever stayed in a hotel AND by myself, it's a funny old cold place but I don't care except I wish I had a hottie! Hemi and Violet asked me did I want to go to the Rangatira Ball with them and the family so I went across in the launch after work, Violet booked me this room. And I had a super evening! I really am too weary to describe things properly but I'd just like to remember for a minute how super their family were to me. Hemi's Mum gave me her lovely necklace of shells that I'd admired, and his Dad kept rocking and rolling for me because that's hard for Hemi because he's lame but Hemi's not too bad a dancer at all and I had one absolutely glorious jive with some really really old chap – it was fun! Funny how you always see people you know wherever you go – there was a girl who used to go to Miramar South Primary School at the Ball! Tia was there of course, laughing and singing. But Violet was lonely, no sign of her Wally, and she is somehow changed and different, but what can I – or anyone – do? She refuses to come back to the hotel. I saw that no-one took much notice of her – yet she told me she'd had 13 invitations to the Ball. Just like Tia, and kind Hemi – they all – I dunno – just like our Uncle John from Temuka who is not a Maori – take a small story and embroider it till it's bigger and bigger! Sign of a good imagination! But Violet is so sad. And it's cold in this funny little room in the old Terminus Hotel. I've wrapped my cardigan around my feet.

SUNDAY 24 FEBRUARY 1957

Very weary back at work again tonight! Tia still off hurrah, poor Violet had to start work at 6am at the Terminus. But –

I did have a marvellous time. I even had breakfast with Tia who was at the Terminus too and we were a bit friendly at least and the last I heard of her she was the only woman among the Rangatira firemen having a party on board this morning . . . the talk of the town is a 13-year-old girl Lucy who didn't arrive home last night at all and was found on the Rangatira and a young boy is now in jail.

Hemi and all the family came in from Waikawa to see me off on the launch – the older men went into the bar of the Terminus Hotel (only place they can drink, it's Sunday, pubs closed) – I had to work so caught the 2.15 launch, we all waved. I wish I was better at recording feelings to make memories clearer. In the warm, warm sun this morning, just sitting by the Memorial – no shoes, me and Hemi and Hemi's Mum and Aunties, them chatting in English and Maori, me yawning on Hemi's shoulder, so content – and peaceful. I couldn't help thinking I feel more – I don't know what word – so relaxed in a new way for me. No one was fussing about, just peaceful.

FRIDAY 1 MARCH 1957

The 'Tamahine' is on strike so we will have to fly home. I've never been on a plane . . . I'm glad to be finishing work, sorry to finish this freedom, NOT looking forward to flying, and this army hut is in an absolute mess!

TUESDAY 5 MARCH 1957

Although we're in Wellington again, as the launch went over the water and as the Hotel and the mad generator disappeared I wondered if I'd be back again. Funny old

> Picton with its happy memories looked lovely again in warm morning sun as I left it and I hoped to be just as happy and relaxed in the sun there again some time. Briefly saw Violet at the wharf: gave her a big hug. I don't suppose she'll write to me, but I hope things go well for the small one.
> And I have been in an aeroplane and flown. Quite an experience which is hard to explain – going up, and not coming down, oh it's peculiar. And noisy. But ok, sort of, when I got used to it, and quicker certainly.

Next day in our non-stop lives we all enrolled at university. I said I wanted to study English II (my diary reminds me I gulped a bit when I learnt that Stage II included studying old Anglo-Saxon English), Philosophy I, Education I — 'and Māori Language Stage I,' I said. I was advised there was no Māori department at Victoria University. But I could enrol as an extramural student with Auckland University as several people had done previously — and teach myself. I must have looked a bit crestfallen; one of the staff directed me to the students' noticeboard. On the noticeboard a piece of paper advertised a weekly evening Adult Education class in the Māori language, to be held in a university lecture room.

Professor Ian Gordon, head of the English Department, stopped me after our first English lecture and told me that I had taken on too much, that my workload was too heavy. Which made me even more determined to work really hard . . . and I talked to someone who has done Maori extramurally: 'hard but interesting'. I know how to work hard now and I love English, and Education and Philosophy are going to be really interesting and I will soon be recovered from the Happy Hell kitchen ha! I can do four subjects, I can. It means I will catch up from failing History last year, and still have my degree next year as planned. And I deposited a £45 cheque! I've bought clothes and make-up and heaps of books – how money flies . . .

The term started: my first Adult Education Māori class, to be taught by a 'Mrs Ranapia', was in a few days' time, but I still hadn't told my parents because I instinctively knew — although I didn't know how violently — my mother would disapprove of my unconventional decision.

THURSDAY 21 MARCH 1957

Lectures lectures lectures! A headful! I haven't quite recovered yet from the Hotel and have big dark circles under my eyes and I cant go to sleep properly and I often feel a bit sick and I think I don't eat enough. And I do get worried about all the work.

And yet – underneath, deep underneath, I am very content and happy! I don't understand? – is it because I had one peaceful Sunday morning, tired in the sun in Picton and feeling I'd learnt that you don't have to worry and fuss about everything?

I'm so glad to see Irv the lout back from Military Training, working hard too – and this afternoon he and I went down to the Casa Fontana and sat there, exchanging our news, coffee and cigarettes for 2 hours. That place – or is it Irv? – a different Irv from Irv in the crowd at Varsity – has a wonderful soothing effect on me, I love it. We talk about so many things. I told him all about Violet and Hemi and the Rangatira Ball and doing the Maori language for my degree! 'You can do anything, I can do anything, just work hard!' he said. Irv the Lout. Irv the pool-player and drinker! Irv who turns out to be cleverer than any of us! He told me all about the Army which he hated. He was going to meet his girlfriend and I know and he knows that is best, we are friends, that is different. At Varsity with the Catholic Gang he's horrible – at Casa Fontana, just us, I really really like him. And this time we're both working hard already.

AND: SAVED TILL LAST!!!!: Here we go: YES! Tonight I have had my first, really super Adult Education Maori lecture – two hours. And the teacher, this Mrs Ranapia, isn't a Maori at all, she's Scottish! But she seems very good and nice and knowledgeable. It's hard of course but I did enjoy the first class tonight – had to read aloud and made a lot of mistakes but maybe out of nervousness. Quite a lot of strange-looking people in the class, about – fifteen maybe, I don't know if anyone else is doing it for University. I am in better 'accent' than a lot of them and I knew the grammar we did tonight, all thanks to when clever Violet helped me, I feel so pleased! I think the teacher, Mrs Ranapia was a bit surprised . . .

Beth Ranapia had come from Scotland to New Zealand with her McGregor family when she was a young girl; she still had a slight Scots accent. She trained as a teacher, went to teach on the East Coast in the 1940s, married Patu Ranapia and learnt the Māori language while they were living in his tribal area. She was remembered there always as an excellent teacher, and she had helped many Māori pupils and their parents to open their horizons: *'Keep going, keep going, don't leave education, stay on into the sixth form, go to Teachers' Training College; go to university.'* She also at that time got to know and worked for Sir Āpirana Ngata, the hugely influential Māori MP and leader who played such a significant role in understanding that the Māori language could be lost if work was not done. His endorsement of Beth, a Pākehā, must have been pivotal. Later she was appointed the Māori editor for School Publications in the Department of Education.

Beth. What an extraordinary woman she was — as some of today's older Māori academics know so well, because she had a big influence on them and their careers and on the beginning of the real work to save their language. And, lucky, lucky me, it was Beth Ranapia — teaching then at the Correspondence School in Wellington, where Patu had a job as a bus driver — who was the Adult Education teacher of Māori for two hours a week in those evening classes at the university. She was a wonderful, wonderful teacher (I was amazed to discover that some sounds — vowel sounds in particular — in the Scots accent lend themselves to the Māori language), and I remember she always wore bright red lipstick.

And so I had begun.

Next day I told my parents that I had decided to do an extra subject. My father showed initial interest but my mother totally disapproved of such a 'ludicrous' decision, and trouble really started. At one stage I thought she was actually going to go up to the university herself and un-enrol me. If I tried to discuss it with her she — literally — wouldn't speak to me.

TUESDAY 26 MARCH 1957

Varsity and home are just two different lives – they don't

merge at all. Mum says it's 'dangerous' learning Maori, whatever she means by that – but I have to have a language and she knows that, and even Win failed French last year.

So it's you and me diary. Something really important today – I was sitting in the library working so hard at my Maori grammar. At first I could do it, and the work that's been set – and I just love it, I really do, it's beautiful and I love sitting in that old, quiet library and working hard and learning. Then something suddenly cropped up that I just couldn't understand or work out – and no class or lecturer to tell me. Luckily someone introduced me to a Maori student studying Geography, everyone calls him J-J, who could really speak Maori well and in frustration I thrust my Maori grammar book at him, nearly crying! Result – he explained it, I understood – so now I also have a Maori tutor one hour a week to correct my exercises which I hand in each week!

I am going to work so hard in all four subjects and I am going to pass.

WEDNESDAY 27 MARCH 1957

Relations with Mum are just as bad as they can be. She domineers the house – and tries to run people's lives for them until I wanted to scream and go anywhere away away. She says over and over I shouldn't be taking Maori, it is a terrible, wasteful mistake. She rules me. And – again – that funny feeling, Who am I? as if I am on the ceiling.

I went to see Mrs Garland today – she wants to let part of the house now that Sally has gone to England as well, and would rent it to me. It would be a good solution, if only we could talk about it, but Mum is unapproachable. It is not good to be so frustrated as she is – and if I frustrate her, well, wouldn't it be best to go away and preserve any good relations that are here? I thank God for Irv suddenly. We went for a walk today and he made me feel saner than I have. He tried to make me see Mum's point of view and I do. But I have a point of view too.

Andrew and Ross began to support me at home as things got worse (and, observing many things, they both left home as soon as they left school). I found myself in an increasingly stressful situation — it is true I had a huge workload, but I knew I could do it if I worked. But I quite literally couldn't mention my Māori course at home without causing a row. To try and keep the peace I set myself a fairly impossible task of being one person at home and another at university.

SATURDAY 30 MARCH 1957

I have an idea. The root of all Mum's actions towards me I guess at last. She is scared I'm becoming 'common' and sexy and provocative etc etc etc in fact anything concerned with rock and roll and tight skirts etc etc etc, let alone Maoris. Could I be two people – demure and sweet and unjive-ish at home? I'd like to try.

So: Mum has been particularly nice tonight – me home, eighteen years old, sewing a new frock, on a Saturday night, me talking about Decartes (I don't think she was very interested!) I wonder if my 'sweet old-fashioned' girl would work? It's worth trying, might lead to peace in two worlds, as long as those two worlds don't meet.

And a letter from Violet – 6 and a half pages!! I didn't think she would ever write – but there it was. Tia has left the Hotel!!!! So Violet's back there. Come back at Easter, she says. Should I? Go back and work there over Easter and speak Maori? Shall I?

SUNDAY 31 MARCH 1957

Mum and I are on good terms at the moment – it's nice. It's pretty good while it lasts, my solution. Let her be the one to get sulky and moody – the others of the family are with me – and just, as much as possible, go ahead my own way – but be sweet to her. It'll be good for me to curb my horrible moods anyway. My April resolution.

Mrs Ranapia told the class about a friendly meeting place called Ngati Poneke, which had been started before the war when there were so few Māori in Wellington and it was a lonely city for Māori people who came to find work. She said that we too would be welcome there, especially if we at least tried to speak Māori, and that it would be an important part of our learning to hear Māori being spoken as a used language. One of the boys in my English class offered to go with me but of course I knew my mother wouldn't 'allow' me to go to such a 'dangerous' place, so one Saturday night when I knew Mum and Dad were going out to a party . . . I said I'd be home a bit late because 'Marguerite and I are going to the Casa Fontana after seeing "Sabrina Fair".' So: I've now started telling actual lies . . . It still bothered me, lying to my parents.

In 1957 Ngati Poneke was the name of a big friendly hall where there was music and dancing, a strictly enforced no-alcohol rule, and I think food made by volunteers. We were indeed made welcome and I really enjoyed going there, hearing people speak Māori and — this was really exciting for me — understanding some of it, and of course dancing to the usual music of our time, and a woman with a beautiful voice sang 'Blue Smoke'. I caught the last tram home, relaxed, knowing Mum and Dad would be out — and then saw our car was there . . . my heart fell but I plucked up courage, pinched and scratched my arm very hard, I can see the marks now, to try and stop myself blushing and went in: there were Mum and Dad sitting in the dining room – 'waiting' for me? my heart nearly dropped out. But because of something to do with Ross which I wasn't allowed to know (?) they had stayed home. But then Mum asked me if I'd been smoking. So I said the truth, yes. Mum thinks smoking is 'cheap' behaviour. So she told me off anyway. God. Help!

WEDNESDAY 10 APRIL 1957

Right. I've done it. I know I'm a bit tired but I'm off to work at the hotel again next week to work over the holidays. Good thing for all concerned especially me – Violet will be there to speak Maori to and no Tia, hurrah!! Another long letter from Violet today – I never thought she'd write. She thinks I'm funny doing Maori as an exam! But I'll be able to practice the language with her the whole time I'm there. Once the English and Philosophy tests were over today, and my Education essay was in, and the next Philosophy essay was in, I could go back to Maori properly. I'm getting there. Joan Stevens, the English lecturer, helped me today – I was asking about applying English grammar to the Maori language because she's done it too. She was very clear in explaining. But I mustn't neglect other hard things like

Philosophy which I am enjoying but battling with. Wish I could sleep better.

I was very, very lucky in Philosophy. An older student, Bede Rundle — who ended up at Trinity College, Oxford, and was described in his obituaries very many years later as one of the finest philosophers of his generation — was fond of me, I think, and saw that I was really trying, and all through this difficult year sort of tutored me sometimes, making this new subject so much more alive, and truly interesting and thought-provoking.

THURSDAY 11 APRIL 1957

If only I could sleep. I had a wonderful lesson with Maria today, wonderful. What a lot she has influenced me in my life. I have been very lucky. And Maori class tonight was so cheering it frightens me. Our teacher Mrs Ranapia is so good – and she's Scottish! And Bede helped me with philosophy at lunchtime. All these interesting things to think about and all these good teachers! But yet another row with Mum.
So. Who am I?

The 'who am I?' feeling, the dividedness, and seeming sometimes to see myself watching myself — sometimes from the ceiling — began to happen more, frighten me more, but I knew if I told my mother she would stop me going back to the hotel. Walking among the old Wellington wharves, which I loved, I tried to explain all this to Irv, who listened carefully, and I think understood, and put his arm round me caringly and said, 'We all probably feel confused about who we really are.'

But in the Catholic group next day we fought, as usual.

A few days later, I set out for the opening of Maria's new Acting Group, which I was very excited about. But I had to come home again because I felt so dizzy . . . I must pull myself together and get back to the Hotel. My legs sort of feel unsteady underneath and I keep feeling sick and giddy. I am so tired, I almost fainted again and I've been vaguely packing for going to the Hotel and it's raining, all my clothes are wet . . . I'm NOT getting aa..xx.. hh again.

What was I doing? What did I think I was doing? My diary entries tell, I think, that I believed that if I could just get back to the hotel, and Violet and Hemi and the sea and singing in the kitchen again with no Tia, and walloping pots, and being able to actually speak the language I was learning, and getting away from the difficulties at home, then — I seemed to think — the dizziness and the insomnia and the odd things happening in my head, like seeing myself on the ceiling, would just — go away. I have included the messy account of the next few days as I tried to describe them: it seems to me a record of a teenager suffering from a kind of 'anxiety' which wasn't recognised in those days. Seeing yourself on the ceiling instead of . . . inside yourself . . . is very scary but the account shows I tried and tried to work it all out by myself . . . what is happening to me?

I got off the overnight ferry from Wellington — the cheapest fare was as a deck passenger and of course I hadn't slept, though I had my sleeping bag — into chilly early-morning Picton: everywhere yawning deckhands, drunk sailors. I got the launch down the misty Sound, arrived at the hotel, gave everyone a hug and started work . . . and suddenly with Violet and me singing and Mike the handyman giving me a cigarette I was back. I thought that the dizziness would go away then, it didn't but I still kept going till lunch for the guests was finished . . .

Everything is described in a disjointed entry of a Thursday, Friday and Saturday:

> . . . but after lunch everything went sort of tight and weird and really peculiar and Violet was still talking or singing – I tried to have an afternoon sleep but I couldn't at all everything was fuzzy and tight inside my head I don't know where I went then I was on a hill, I was wandering around the place and crying and crying and lost and really crazy-mixed up is this what a nervous breakdown is or going mad? I didn't know what time it was or quite where I was I got more scared because of the dizziness and everything and in the end I did the only thing, I went to find Mrs H and I didn't even get a chance to explain, she just took one look at me and she was so absolutely wonderful and – and really motherly, she put her arms around me and kissed me and told me to go off duty altogether and to go to bed and they would get me home as soon as they could.
>
> I was in bed and I was crying but I was more peaceful, then Violet came up, I was sharing her army hut and we talked and for a moment she seemed to – understand something deep I was trying to say. That it's so different in Wellington and I cant join it all together. She listened then. And then she said 'We never join things together e hoa!' And oh – how I was at peace as it got darker and we talked. Then she went away to work and then later came up with my dinner. Mike the handyman came up later and we ate miles of chocolate and he told me how things had gone since I last left, Tia

leaving and everything. Then I tried to sleep, later Violet came up. I was peaceful and sort of asleep, but not exactly because I could hear the night all night and vaguely I heard them work this morning, now it was today. At 10am Mrs H came in with some breakfast and said I was flying home this afternoon and I was leaving on the 11.30 transport launch. People were so kind. I wish Violet will come to Wellington but she probably wont, but anyway what's the use, Wellington is so different, I wouldn't even be able to bring her home. She rang Hemi to meet me, I said goodbye to everyone and I was sad mostly for Violet, and I went away on the launch. At Picton there was Hemi, with some of his brothers, and he'd borrowed a car and they took my bag, there were a couple of Maori girls too – and they all took me to the Air Centre in Blenheim, Hemi and I walked in the rain and he put me and my case on the airbus.

When she met me off the plane Mum at once asked me worried questions that I couldn't answer — how could I answer when some of my answers would hurt her? But: if this was a famous 'Nervous Breakdown', well, that mad little determined, resistant piece of myself that had saved me before wasn't having any of it. Because over those wandering days I had at least begun to understand what was happening to me: I didn't need to have a nervous breakdown about it. I wrote that down too:

. . . of course – I realise now, it wasn't just tiredness. It's the other thing. Of being between two worlds. It's something tied up with Mum's strictness and the not being allowed to mention Maori things yet it is one of my degree papers and also as well this strange restlessness thing that wont go. How can I explain all that to Mum? It's something about this – peace I seem to get when I'm in the other life but of course I'm not that stupid, I'm not in that other life, not really, I pretend I can just join other people's lives and be just like them and happy – but I know I'm not really and then I start to cry again and my head goes funny oh I don't know what I'm writing, I don't feel like sleeping even after all this time which is why I've been writing and writing and trying to work it all out but I am NOT having a nervous breakdown whatever it is, I'm NOT, you don't have one I bet, if you catch it . . . and surely that means I'm not MAD, I'm not suddenly going to go mad.

But if I look back in derision, ever, at this time, I hope I hate myself.

MONDAY 22 APRIL 1957

I'm ok. I'm not sick. I AM NOT MAD. I'm not letting myself be sick. I'm just – odd.

But I gotta come back to this world. Today I got up. And when I went into town with Dad tonight, to meet Andy from a Bible Class camp, I know that I love Wellington.

THURSDAY 25 APRIL 1957

Anzac Day. Andy and I went. I saw a band leading 10 or so old old old men – survivors of the Boer War – marching, marching along as best they could, limping and yellow parched faces and medals. War. I AM NOT SICK. I must've done hours of swot today, finishing another Education essay. And I see a pattern of interest emerging in my mind between two of my subjects – Maori and Education. What if Violet had had a really good education? Mum would hate it of course. The Maori part I mean. I look haggard in the mirror. Will I see them all again I wonder? I don't know that I'll be back there, well of course I cant after this trouble I caused, yet for the people I want to be. I'm sorry I was so troublesome and couldn't take it all, this tiredness and funniness that had been coming. I pretended it wasn't. But I'm so glad I saw them all.

FRIDAY 26 APRIL 1957

I wont write too much. I dont want to think about everything. Back at Varsity. But I've backed out of a play at Maria's. A talk with Mum about what's wrong with me – but it's all something I must work out myself, though she was really kind. But I think I've learnt something, over this strange time.

I know now I have to begin to learn to deal with the difficult things by myself.

MONDAY 29 APRIL 1957

When I practice speaking Maori I love it – and I know I get better and better – but I feel funny again, I don't know who I am. I'm not like a Maori but I'm not like any other Pakeha I know. I feel lonely.

TUESDAY 30 APRIL 1957

I was allowed to go out to Irv's place tonight to stay the night, so I met his mother at last, who likes Irv's girlfriend. I wish she will see I'm not a 'threat' to that. She is really

really sweet and kind and his dad is nice too. We took fish and chips home in a taxi from the train station because his parents were out till later – oh – the warmth of their kitchen, and the heater, and the light left on for us and this sweet note about a hot water bottle for me if I was cold. And his parents were so welcoming and nice when they came home, and we all had cocoa together. And I think they saw it: that Irv and me, despite being a girl and a boy, are real, real friends. We know each other very well. I am so lucky to have been able to talk to him about – all what's happened. We are careful of each other because we know we cant be good friends really any other way. I think he accepts what I am like, loves his girlfriend, but still wants to be my friend, and I so want that too. But he said something strange to me tonight. 'I'm different from your family. We live in a State house.' I asked him what he meant? – lots of my friends live in State houses. 'But you don't,' he said. 'But it doesn't matter,' I said. 'It does,' he said. Funny old Irv. He knows I really care about him and I know he really cares about me and it's nothing to do with State houses.

THURSDAY 2 MAY 1957

We had the weekly Maori class tonight and I'm keeping up quite nicely except the Maori Bible which is very very hard but Mrs Ranapia is so good at explaining and I love, love working and working and trying to put it all together. 'Ko Ihowa toku hepara, e kore ahau e hapa. The Lord is my shepherd I shall not want.' Mikaere Rangi has joined the class this week. He was in Economics last year.

IX

THE DICTIONARY SAYS SIMPLY: 'Narrative: a continued account of any series of events.'

And as I have written earlier, I believe we can only know the real plot of the story of a life, how one event led to another (the thread as the dictionary says), in retrospect — and even then only perhaps if we have a clear enough record.

It is the diaries that make it clear to me now (of course I did not understand then, and would never have understood without reading the diaries all these years later) that when Mikaere Rangi, who I thought was the most beautiful man I'd ever seen, walked that night in 1957 into the once-a-week Adult Education Māori class, in his grey suit (with waistcoat), I was a Perfect Storm.

For all my seeming *joie de vivre* in public, always — always — laughing in the university common-room, I still felt insecure, I still wanted people to 'like' me — and I still felt uneasy every time someone talked about 'going steady', though other girls were able to do it. Was 'falling in love' something real or was it a ridiculous story people made up, and wrote about in books and songs? Was it even perhaps something really to do with oneself, not the other person?

But something else had happened.

I understood that something bewilderingly life changing had woven itself around me . . . I don't know who I am . . . I feel as if I am looking at myself from the ceiling . . . As if I had lost myself. As if I had somehow . . . fractured my psyche. And perhaps I had, as I ran back to the old hotel to solve myself, and then wept and came home again. And perhaps that's what happens when people wander from — or are forced from — their own familiar culture, and willingly (or not) find themselves entwined by another culture? A fractured psyche?

And then, Mikaere Rangi walked into the Māori class.

Mikaere Rangi was, unusually 'for a Māori', already highly promoted in the international shipping and tourist company where he worked full-time. He had been at university longer than me, and had suddenly decided to enrol in stage I Māori extramurally so that he could, with his other subjects, finish his degree that year. He also, with a passion, played rugby for one of the university rugby teams. He was extremely clever, hard-working and ambitious. And I thought he was beautiful. And so for all sorts of reasons (I know, I know, including my own longings and confusions), for the only time in my life I fell in love instinctively and absolutely. It does exist; it is not a lie or a dream or sex, or a figment of pop music. I know — now — that there are all kinds of love, many much happier and ultimately more fulfilling than 'falling in love'.

But it exists, that falling. And I fell.

Memory again: this . . . *thing*, this part of the brain by which we are the person we are, and without which — although our bodies may still be living — the person who we are dies. That dreaded word, dementia — from the Latin word meaning 'out of one's mind': the *loss* of who we are.

Over our lives we must forget so many things: life changes, can be so busy, so varied, so different — I don't see how our heads can hold it all! And perhaps sometimes we remember as we prefer to, not quite as it was. And yet, and yet . . . once again my day-by-day-by-day accounts — the 'bloody diaries' — show that memory can be so *right* — even deep down to that moment, that room, that song. And the light in the sky.

There were three of us in that Adult Education class who were taking Māori I as a subject extramurally from Auckland University. This new person, Mikaere Rangi. A boy called Sam Karetu who seemed very fluent in Māori, *and* who I had already heard talking German to a German woman in the classroom! And me. Beth Ranapia was familiar with the university syllabus, knew what we had to learn and understand, she believed in us — and seemed at once determined that these three particular students would pass Stage I Māori if she had anything to do with it.

It was 1957.

And so much, then, was so, so different.

And so much, then, was the same as it is now, and as it has always been.

TUESDAY 14 MAY 1957

On my way home from working in the library all day even

though it's holidays I walked past Kelburn Park to the cablecar. And just knew I'd see Mikaere Rangi and his rugby team practising there, and I did.

And – I saw him – see me.

THURSDAY 16 MAY 1957

I'm not sure how to write it.

I – think – something has happened.

Mrs Ranapia has been giving extra Maori classes at her house over the holidays to Sam Karetu and Mikaere Rangi and me, and tonight Mikaere brought me right home here – 'Would you like a ride on my bike?' And we talked. I was rude. I had to be or else he would've guessed and – he obviously has his way with girls.

I had to be rude.

I don't want to write about it.

I'm glad I'm going to Maungatapu tomorrow.

FRIDAY 17 MAY 1957

Cold – 'makariri' – stormy windy day to leave Wellington – 105 miles per hour gale – the wind tried to blow me down Lambton Quay and I had to hold on to a lamp-post. But it's really comfortable and warm on the train, have a whole seat to myself with a shilling pillow and my coat, and outside rain and wind and cold. I am immersed in 'True Romance' and dozing. I'm not thinking about anyone, not even about myself.

SATURDAY 18 MAY 1957

Maungatapu. My favourite place, before they changed it.

Lucky me to have known it. Been in bed most of the time since I got here – rotten cough, that cough I always get. Lovely to be with my dear Auntie Ellie – only I bet Mum told her to 'talk to me'. But I cant bring myself to talk properly even to her about – some things. And I'm certainly not thinking about Mikaere Rangi. What would that all lead to??? I'm just so immature and childish.

SUNDAY 19 MAY 1957

Was at the vineyard – lovely evening, people doing a reading of 'The Cocktail Party' by T.S. Eliot. I love these evenings at the vineyard – in the nice outside room, fire roaring, lamps, intellectuals too but I still enjoyed it. I'd like to have lots of evenings like this one day, some day . . .
It was suddenly dark before I realised. Like Katherine Mansfield said.

But Maungatapu was changing fast. And the family had decided to leave in a few months' time.

Now the old, dusty road was covered in little stones and red flags; a battered bulldozer was parked up, and small boys swarmed all over it. Expensive modern homes were already being built all along the coastal side of this suddenly very 'desirable' place, except at the peninsula, where most of the local Māori community lived . . . today some of the kids from the school and I were remembering paddocks with cows and the rooster – or a goose was it? we're not sure! – that bit people. Of course I tried to say it in Maori ha! Bite? Rooster? But – I suppose I wont see them much more – but why did I begin to learn Maori but for them? It all feels funny now.

SUNDAY 26 MAY 1957

It was cold and terribly windy when I walked down the road early today to say goodbye and it blew all my thoughts away for a moment. The girls sang and laughed and I took a photo. Muddy puddles all over the stony road and only shafts of sunlight, and the wind. They sing as usual, and lots of little boys swearing proudly on a bulldozer. Me trying to speak Maori. Will they remember? Myra and Maketu and I jived on the stony road and sang Pokarekare Ana. It rained. We ran. Night train and shilling pillow now. Varsity tomorrow and swotting. And – what else?

WEDNESDAY 29 MAY 1957

I have to write it down. But how – useless – words are sometimes even though this is something I have been thinking about for years. They say – an arrow.

I saw Mikaere tonight. He was standing at the top of the steps by the main door and the ivy was shadowy and he was looking for me and he saw me and his eyes – saw me and sort of went bright and he looked so – beautiful. And I felt – no point in writing hundreds of soppy words – all I mean is I knew that my feelings are real. Even though I don't know what I mean.

He was so nice while we were together – even while telling big stories like they all do! He – smoothed my hair for a moment. But I came straight home, only – I did very little swot despite Friday's Philosophy terms exam. Funny. I spring-cleaned instead even though it's autumn, and played with cut-out dolls, and my little koala bear.

THURSDAY 30 MAY 1957

Thursday means our university Adult Education Maori class. But – will I have to content myself with Thursdays and a few more glimpses of him, usually at rugby practise with his team, and nothing else? Am I just a little girl to him? after all he hasn't given me any indication really. Yet I sort of sense – I saw him, looking for me, and then seeing me – oh I don't know. He is so handsome. Anyway what's the use. Pakeha. Maori. Family. And yet – I haven't ever felt this feeling before and I'm not sure how it got here. But – it's here.

FRIDAY 31 MAY 1957

Philosophy exam ok. I like thinking about Socrates.

Cath heard Mikaere asking someone in the common-room where I was. Later we found each other and we wandered about town – there was hail – and I went with him to his office of all places, to get his stick – he has sprained his ankle at rugby. Lifts and corridors and keys, this empty shipping office with desks, files, big travel posters.

I keep smiling to myself. Andrew caught me. 'What's cooking, Sis?'

THURSDAY 6 JUNE 1957

1. Another Philosophy exam today. I'd worked really hard. Bede helped me. Passable.

2. My good friend Irv worries me very much, drinking and playing pool and then sitting exams. Why does he? We still talk about everything though. But I worry.

3. Had lunch with my dear Maria. She was so sorry I didn't audition for Sally Bowles in 'I am a Camera' and I WANTED

to – but I have to get all this study for four subjects under my belt first.

4. Maori class. If I'm not careful I'll fail. I let myself go too much tonight and Mikaere hurt me. But not again. I am going to be grown up and never again let him see that I care at all. He said: 'I don't want to see you around – I'm a working man. I'll see you next Thursday.'

TUESDAY 11 JUNE 1957

'E mahi ana ahau i tenei ra i taku mahi Maori' – I've done two hours non-stop. People like J-J help me if they can but it is SO SO hard without regular classes. He mea taumaha. See – I am 'grass-hopping' – that is what Sir Apirana Ngata called it (disapprovingly) – jumping between Maori and English – and they all do it! Violet and Hemi in Picton did it all the time, and children at Maungatapu – at the school, and still. And today I find – ha – Mikaere was looking for me again in the common-room – which I was certainly keeping away from. After what he SAID. He wont find me.

Of course he found me. Of course we met.

And so begins, in day-by-day-by-day entries, a record of a teenage girl who started off falling in love with love perhaps, as the old song says, but really falling and falling in love with a real person. Entry after entry about love: teenage diaries. But some of the entries give such immediacy to that time also — when boarding houses really did have notices in their windows saying **NO CHILDREN MAORIS OR DOGS**. But at first I didn't notice things. We weren't walking around holding hands yet, of course, or kissing in the street. But we did walk around Wellington's winding streets in the evenings, talking and laughing. We followed an alley, arguing all the way about where it led because he was sure it turned one way and I was sure it turned another. (It had a fork in it and went both ways!) We often went to record stores to hear the latest: Elvis Presley sang 'All Shook Up' and Johnnie Ray was still singing about the little white cloud that cried. I became very familiar with that night-empty shipping office and the big posters on the walls of ships and far-away places, and finally Mikaere kissed me beside his file-covered desk . . . the world says I'm looking better at last, after my illness at Easter, etc. I am. And – I can tell – Mum knows there is something – suddenly she knows I am happy and so much better than I have been. But her theories on life could make things go all wrong again. But not – this time, though I don't know where this road is leading . . .

Mrs Ranapia told everyone in the evening class that we needed to attend a Māori funeral, called a 'tangi', when we got the chance; part of learning a language, she said, was learning about the culture of that language. This was one of the very few things that I, foolishly, mentioned at home to Mum and Dad — I remembered how our French teachers looked excited when they spoke to us (with many pictures) of seeing the Arc de Triomphe and the Eiffel Tower and the Notre-Dame Cathedral. My mother said (I wrote it down of course), 'It is hard for me to reconcile that you could actually go to somebody's funeral simply because it's interesting.' Mrs Ranapia (and Mikaere and Sam) often talked about 'Pakeha hypocrisy'.

One Saturday morning Mikaere rang to ask me to come and watch his team play rugby. I said I was 'busy' (busy sewing at home with my mother on a Saturday). Really I was scared to arrange anything that might arouse Mum's suspicions: I wasn't used — yet — to lying.

But in the weekday evenings we started going to one or other of the exciting, sophisticated new 'coffee shops' that had begun appearing all over Wellington, serving that 'real' coffee. Lit with flickering candles in empty chianti bottles, wax spilling slowly downwards, music playing. And exotic names like *Casa Fontana, Mexicali, Man Friday, La Scala.* We must've consumed immense amounts of caffeine.

TUESDAY 18 JUNE 1957

Well. It's happened.

Mikaere has asked me out, properly. To go to the Tourist Association Ball with him on Friday. Dad was on the back porch when I came home and I told him first and luckily he was super and actually interested but Mum heard and came out and made such a fuss of disapproval. But already tonight I was walking with my head in the stars. Win said she saw me talking to him on the stairs – she said my eyes gave me away.

Oh yes, I did 4 and a half hours swot in the library today – even more than I'd planned and Mikaere said 'doesn't it give you a good feeling?' And it does.

WEDNESDAY 19 JUNE 1957

Couldn't help telling Maria about Mikaere – she was so terribly shocked – because she thought I'd said <u>'married'</u> not <u>'Maori'</u> – she didn't seem to think 'Maori' was shocking at all!!!

Win is in a very depressed state – things at home are pretty

ghastly, with her grandmother who lives with them very ill. I went home with her. I'm not a good enough friend to Win. Talking to her grandmother there is a lovely smell of apples. I think there is a box of Golden Delicious stored under her bed.
Win and I each bought a black polo neck jersey, all the rage.

THURSDAY 20 JUNE 1957

I am so excited about the Ball tomorrow. And then when we sat on that seat to wait for my tram after class he moved so that I wouldn't be so cold. And then he told me – or rather dogmated at me – how he abhors 'jealousy' and 'women's stupid ways' re this girl he knows who he is taking to the Anglican Ball next Friday. Well, at least I know about it, that was his way of telling me I suppose ha ha. (I know all those manoeuvres of course!) So I said 'Oh, that Friday I'm going to the pictures with some of the Catholic boys I know from Varsity' (not). He looked furious!

FRIDAY 21 JUNE 1957

Ohhh – Mikaere. The Ball was wonderful fun. Nobody's ever bought me flowers like this before to pin on my frock. An orchid. If only I could believe that he's sincere – but I'm so scared that perhaps he's not – at least not in any real way. I'm so scared I'm going to get hurt . . .
First of all we had to meet lots of old people, shipping people, but I saw it was important for him and I know how to do all that. And then the wonderfulness of being together at the Ball, meeting some of his friends, knowing some of the people there. And dancing with Mikaere . . . I didn't know

men could be beautiful but he is.

I wonder what was Mother's opinion when he came to collect me, not that she would have any except anti, he only stood in the hall, I made sure I was ready. Nothing can come of all this: it's a very hopeless sort of position to get into and all the time I know it – yet I keep on GOING. I know I know I know I know I know.

No matter what: it's a wonderful night to remember.

My orchid is squashed now. Must be from when we stood outside our back door to say goodnight . . .

TUESDAY 25 JUNE 1957

Mikaere found me in the empty lecture-room, so that we were both late for lectures.

My parents were used now to me being at the university for long hours during the week, often 'working in the library' at night, and they could see by my frequent test results that I was working very much harder this year: I record 81 per cent for an Old English paper and 70 per cent for a Philosophy essay. Ironically, the disapproved-of Māori was a very good influence: he got me to spend less time in the common-room (I wasn't stupid: I already saw he didn't like me being in the company of other boys) and more time swotting in an empty lecture room to which he came more and more often as soon as he came up the hill for lectures after work. Andrew had reported to me (and I had then reported to my diary) that when we left for the ball he heard Mum say, 'I can see why she likes him', but straight after the ball she had made it very clear to me that my permission to go was a one-off; my Māori studies did not mean I could go out with a Māori boy again under any circumstances. She watched me like a hawk and listened to every phone call. Perhaps he knew so early on; perhaps he didn't: at first we didn't discuss such things, Mikaere and I. But now I really did begin lying to my parents. I lied about where I'd been, what I'd been doing. My ability to 'feel' the energy in a room developed further: I learned to breathe and prepare myself and my story before I even came into the house in the evenings (my arms, which I sometimes hid, got covered in pinch and scratch marks to stop my blushing) and then to discuss the day casually. One of my education books said 'late adolescence is a time for intimacies — not least intimacies with oneself'. I was learning that, certainly.

At first Mikaere still went home to his family and his village most weekends (or at least straight after Saturday rugby), even though it was more than a three-hour drive over the Rimutaka hills. He had built up very many safety barriers so as not to get involved in any way with anything — or anyone — that might interfere with his ambitions and plans, and did not want anything to change. So I often went out to parties and dances as usual — but I sometimes just stayed home and worked: more Saturday nights (when girls always went out with their boyfriends) with my mother.

THURSDAY 27 JUNE 1957

I DON'T KNOW! I wonder what is right? I have to tell lies now, and it makes me feel funny and guilty. Only – I think I really do love him . . . that word. Tonight we went to that coffee bar, La Scala, and talked for such a long time about – Maori and Pakeha differences. Pay attention to this diary – Mrs Ranapia thinks my Maori accent excellent, surprisingly so, and introduced me to Bill Parker from Broadcasting as 'one of my outstanding pupils'!

I loved the Māori language. I loved the sound. In the 1950s there were no macrons to help with pronunciation, so you just had to remember. I was fascinated by Māori pronouns — for instance, the number of words for 'we' — and I wondered if it was because it was an oral language, so had its own way of making things clear. You could say tāua, just us two, or you could say tātou, us including everybody. But you could also say māua: us two but not you. Or mātou: all of us but not you. I worked and worked by myself in empty lecture rooms, then used the language with Mikaere, and in class.

TUESDAY 2 JULY 1957

I am more sure of Mikaere now. We wander arm in arm, or hand in hand, or with his arm round my shoulders, along in the rain, 'Grass-hopping' it is true. Some people look away, disapproving. I see them. (I'm sure he does too.) DIS-APPROVE-ING. What business is it of people we don't even know passing us in the street? I don't care. They know nothing about us.

And something very, very important. Even before Easter and what happened I often 'lost' myself; suddenly felt apart from the world, not belonging to it and – looking from somewhere else at myself and everyone and everything around me. Now I think I can assure myself that things are real. I cant explain properly but – I am myself again.

What a wealth of material I have, in these diaries, in my head, about so many people – as well as about myself. Perhaps one day I <u>will</u> write – and it will always be about people. Everyone – all the people I know – have problems to face as well as me.

I suppose really this diary has seen the most important thing in my life. I became frightened of my mind – I must be stronger than that and rather <u>understand</u> my mind. To do that now is to prepare myself for the life that lies, excitingly, frighteningly, ahead of me. More than anything I want – where did I read it? is it a prayer? – 'the grace of courage, gaiety, and a quiet mind'.

Courage for my convictions is important to me, courage to stand for them. Gaiety has always been something precious to me – and now I realise that a quiet mind is perhaps the most precious thing of all but – am I a person ever – ever – to have it?

Sometimes I was allowed to stay with one of my friends for the weekend, often to 'revise' together — and then at last I too could go out with my boyfriend on a Saturday night. Other mothers didn't seem to 'wait up'. On Saturdays, there were occasionally parties at the Māori hostel where Mikaere and J-J lived; I was amazed at how many other Pākehā girls were there too, as well as Pākehā rugby players — just another party to their mothers, presumably, or perhaps they didn't have to 'account' for themselves in the way that I did. At the hostel Mikaere was always in charge somehow; if there was a problem, or a fight, it was always Mikaere who talked quietly, sorted it out, took J-J outside when he got a bit rumbustious. We danced and sang and the hostel boys sang 'Cindy' to me, one of the pop songs around, making a fuss of me because of Mikaere. The hostel managers were a very dignified Māori man, who took my learning of the language very seriously, and his wife, who used to get somewhat inebriated and talk to me across the room in a very loud voice so that others could hear her too — 'Don't get serious Cindy', 'You're not mature enough Cindy'— and then always said to Mikaere, still in a **very** loud voice, 'Promise me you won't make a habit of her' as everyone danced and sang and drank beer. One Saturday night Mikaere walked me back to my friend Cath's house in the midnight air and told me he wanted to get a Māori scholarship to travel to connected shipping offices . . . with or without me . . . and we finally told each other we loved each other, but then Mikaere said how was he to know I didn't say that to all the boys, and I wasn't certain if he loved me at all . . . his life is planned out and it doesn't really include me . . .

TUESDAY 9 JULY 1957

Swotting at home for bloody Old English exam, hours and hours and hours. More exams next week: I am so determined to prove I can pass four subjects.

Have just read Mikaere's name in the newspaper putting forward a motion at a meeting. That'll please him, it will get him known. People will know about it – and that's what he wants – more than anything. I see that. He doesn't need me. I curse myself one hundred thousand times for opening my big stupid mouth on Saturday night ie Sunday morning and saying I loved him which I have never ever said to anybody ever. He's scared, I know, that I'll lose the sparkle that he's fond of and get 'sentimental' (his word). How strange: me, the good-time girl – being too sincere – and 'going steady'.

FRIDAY 12 JULY 1957

Something has happened.

I cant write about it.

We were in Mikaere's office . . . If I thought we would get married it would be all right. Yet – we didn't do anything to be ashamed of: yet even this – intimacy – is wrong if Mikaere doesn't feel as strongly as I do. Oh how can I explain it with pen and paper. It's – something that I feel couldn't happen with anybody else I've ever known. And that I suppose – is love. Is it?

Now he's feeling – what? I almost – I don't want to see him.

MONDAY 15 JULY 1957

I tried not to see him. But tonight he was waiting for me. And never so tender.

TUESDAY 16 JULY 1957

We laughed in the street before I came home – a whole lot of his friends, or relations (mostly female) came out of Ngati Poneke and saw us walking together down the road hand in hand. He was <u>so</u> embarrassed, his face was a picture which was so funny that we – him too finally, realising – just laughed and laughed!

But – I cant write properly about us now.

What happened between us in his office – it wasn't anything huge at all. Just – if we could get married it wouldn't be wrong.

I have never – been in any way like that – with anyone.

TUESDAY 23 JULY 1957

I must write now. I know it's important to write now, this particular moment, because things get so difficult so easily. But there are days full of happiness and contentment – that's what love does, and I know now he loves me too. It means that I don't mind – in fact I enjoy – spending most of my day in an empty lecture room working – and to pass four subjects I must work. Everything fits in – everything seems to have some purpose – the days, the pattern of days. Later it might be too late and I wont be able to catch the goldenness of the pattern of time, as it is today.

Now, for today, I think I have never been happy like this and I'm so glad to write it down now, whatever else may happen.

It was as if I had a premonition.

A few days later I would stop writing a day-by-day diary forever and it's not very easy to decipher some of the words of the last entry.

SATURDAY 27 JULY 1957

Saturday night. At home.

Saturday night and suddenly everything is so depressing and hopeless and useless.

I'm not allowed to go out with Mikaere. Forbidden. I cant go out with my boyfriend on a Saturday night like everyone else. I'm eighteen and a half years old and I'm 'not allowed' to go out with 'any Maori and that is definite Barbara'. It was so hopeless talking to him on the phone tonight, him wanting to see me, Mum all ears standing in the hall listening to every word, of course he knows. And of course he minds.

And then – he puts the phone down in the middle of me speaking. And was gone.

Everything is gone.

This diary is – vaguey. I cant. I cant write. I cant. My mind is all muddled again like Easter.

Sentences muddle. Scrambled egg colour.

I cant.

I'm not going to write a diary any more

Maybe I'll start a new one sometime.

Maybe.

Two thousand four hundred days faithfully recorded.

X

AFTER A WEEK OR SO of course I wrote entry 2401. But I never wrote a day-by-day diary again.

I couldn't, yet, survive without writing things down sometimes: I suppose it was a kind of addiction. Sometimes I wrote for days at a time like I used to. But slowly it becomes a journal, often one entry covering lots of days and events: something quite different. Without the day-by-day-by-day entries, huge swathes of the past are gone. I had already filled two and a half small Collins diaries and twenty-one big notebooks in the six and a half years since 1 January 1951. (And to write this account I've had to read every single bloody day of them!) But from now until the night I left New Zealand, the number of notebooks is three.

The narrative went on, of course, and the characters — and the plot.

FRIDAY 9 AUGUST 1957

I cant keep away from writing. Perhaps not very good writing but I seem to have to.

A journal, because a diary is not good in that it inclines me towards myself all the time. Introverted or – introspected – too self-involved. I don't know that's it good to write all the things. Exams are getting close now. I must work so hard. And I do.

Dad has just broken a milk bottle outside in the dark. I can hear him patiently picking up the pieces of glass. He is a patient and kind man. I am very lucky.

Is it so much more difficult to go out with a Maori than a Pakeha – or is it just that being in love brings the happiest moments, but also the very saddest? He can hurt me so easily. Sometimes I'm sure that things will work out for the two of us together. At other times I can just feel the casualness he deliberately uses, like a sort of numbness. It is his way of protecting himself, I understand that now. Underneath he is insecure in his world of neither one thing or the other.

We were in the 'Man Friday' coffee bar tonight, talking and talking in the half-darkness with the candles. We've made it our place. He finds parts of the Maori class hard, tonight he cursed his parents for not giving him a Maori education. 'Why couldn't they have sent me away to an old Maori, to learn the language and the culture?' But – he says that with a firm Pakeha education behind him where he did so well. I cant – solve his problems but I can listen. I met him on the common ground of his culture and his language, that's important too. And – it's hard being a woman, I – understand that. I always wanted to 'do' something when I was younger. To have a 'career', like boys do. An 'actress' of all things – it was just a dream wasn't it. If I marry Mikaere I will have to subserve (is that the word I want?) my personality even – and my aims and ambitions – to him. To be quietly there all the time to help him along without him quite realising it. Because – his battle is harder. But – do I want to give up all the hopes I've had? – because I know that what he wants from the world will have to come first. And of course he wants to have lots of children but – of course I think this (but don't say it of course) – what say I – turn out like Mum?

I was becoming more and more aware of many things. I saw now how many of the boarding houses that had rooms to let had **NO CHILDREN MAORIS OR DOGS** in the window. I certainly by now knew that many people looked disapprovingly at us as we passed them, hand in hand now, and people sometimes even made rude comments loud enough for us to hear. We just held hands tighter and kept on walking. I saw that if Mikaere had to get a taxi, he waited till he found a Māori driver on the rank to be sure he wouldn't be turned away — and he was a businessman in a suit. I overheard someone in the common-room call me a 'hori-girl'. I was learning.

Every Wednesday evening Beth Ranapia was now giving Sam, Mikaere and me extra Māori classes, based on the exam requirements from Auckland. There weren't a lot of Māori-language texts for us to work from in 1957. We studied very carefully the old Māori of the Bible. We studied old Māori proverbs, whakataukī; luckily a book of them by Reweti T. Kohere had already been published by A.H. and A.W. Reed. We studied the Māori poem-songs from *Ngā Mōteatea* that Sir Āpirana Ngata had long collected from tribal records and memories, and that Pei Te Hurinui Jones had helped translate.

We had a set text for the exam of one of these old poems — in this case anonymous — that I never forgot:

> . . . In this great longing,
> Is there no one who will share it?
> For there is no one more melancholy
> Than he who yearns for his native land.

Again, it's only when I read these old diaries that I catch a pattern, a thread, of something else. Something connected to these special classes. And this thread is that after a while Mikaere and I began having regular, upsetting arguments. Almost always ending up about Māori–Pākehā relations. On a Wednesday night.

In class it was so clear that Sam Karetu, so immersed in their language, would easily pass the university exam; Mikaere knew the language, but nothing like the way Sam and Beth Ranapia talked together. And he resented it, as the previous diary entry shows: resented that he was having, in some ways at least, to learn his own language. And the dates in the diaries make it absolutely plain that it was particularly on a Wednesday night — after these special Māori classes — we had these bad times.

The rows made me very unhappy, as entry after entry shows. In between there are very happy, loving days. And we never saw the pattern, never saw the threads which are there so clearly.

WEDNESDAY 21 AUGUST 1957

What will happen? Things don't just go on and on indefinitely. Something happens in the end? But what? Tonight Mikaere and Sam Karetu and I had a really, really special Maori class

up at the Ranapias' lovely old house overlooking the harbour, their daughters were sitting on the verandah laughing with their father in the gentle rain – te marangai – and watching the sky when we arrived, stars shining, the fountain playing different colours, and sometimes the monastery bell rang through the rain. How lucky are we that Beth Ranapia ('call me Beth' she told us) really does believe in us. Sam of course is so miles and miles ahead of us – he spoke only Maori till he was about seven I think and now speaks French and German as well!! He must be the most brilliant linguist in New Zealand! Tonight we talked Maori only – no English – there were some Maori friends there to help us – gosh it was fun. Three groups scattered over the room, one for each of us pupils; then later a whole lot of them laughing uproariously at a huge Maori man telling a story in Maori. (I couldn't follow it all though). And Mr Ranapia teaching us 'Haere ra, e haere ra, e taku reta' an old song I'd never heard. It was wonderful. So what if afterwards Mikaere was in such a terrible, cruel mood and everything went wrong and he was horrible. I cried by myself on the tram home. Not for him to see. The rest of the evening was wonderful.
It's cold now. A storm came up. I look so hard into the future. But I cant see things properly.

FRIDAY 23 AUGUST 1957

So: I'm 'going steady' after all . . . Me who never would. Most of all I hate the lies and deceiving at home. I can take so much of that, but then I cry by myself in the toilets at Varsity. But I'll tell you something diary, after a while you don't blush when you tell lies, they just come out glibly. Don't even have to pinch and scratch my arm. Huh.

We often walk on the wharves if it's not freezing, and we both know people stare, and so what? We don't care – we both just look at each other and don't care – because we have each other. Much rugby talk, and many rugby games! And the coffee shops, our own coffee shop, Man Friday, where we've talked about the biggest thing of all – the Maori and the Pakeha – and the endless arguments . . . Going to his office in the evenings, meeting the caretaker – and once one of the Shipping bosses! Of course there's the bad moments. When we've both been tired. When he hurts me more than I thought it was possible for anyone to be hurt. Win's disapproval. The lies at home, Mum still phone-hovering and, either silently or loudly, disapproving. And all the time: working, studying, working. I know I can get all four subjects and I will – but ohhh if all this could just be a bit less stressful.

Final Exams coming so soon! 8 hours Philosophy swot today, and that clever Bede Rundle patient enough to go over some thoughts again with me in a corner of the caf at lunch-time – he is so clear, and makes me understand. Last Education essay in. So surely I can read a magazine with an easy conscience now – 'True Life' magazine which is much more jocular than real true life! So, so tired and thinking too much and worrying about exams.

And Mikaere. And Mum.

And so the diary went on recording, even if not each day: working really hard for end-of-year exams; still laughing and dancing at parties occasionally; difficulties at home; Wellington losing the Ranfurly Shield to Otago — and both wonderful and terrible times with this complicated man I had fallen in love with. Who, I knew now, had fallen in love with complicated me. We sat in the freezing cold at the Basin Reserve cricket ground late one night when I was 'at a party with Cath', and Mikaere said he thought we should stop seeing each other or he would miss his exams and I (sort of) . . . *has he stopped loving me?* . . . did understand, and I agreed. Only two nights later my diary says we were in 'our' coffee bar, Man Friday, needing one another, sitting in the half-darkness where the candles flickered and Harry Belafonte sang 'Island in the Sun', talking about our relationship seriously, both exhausted, both in love, both so glad to be with one another.

And then he was gone . . . *so casually – a football trip for the weekend and will he miss me very much? . . . oh – just sometimes I wish I didn't have to work so hard, and lie so hard, and could loll about with the old gang and books just left lying there so that the pages turned up in the sun . . . But to pass four subjects will mean so much for everything and I can. I WILL . . .*

We continued to take turns to invite Colombo Plan students to our homes, where they cooked Indonesian food, Burmese food, Malaysian food with those strange spices they somehow acquired. They were mostly male students but there were several nurses also. We all asked our friends to these gatherings, and there was much singing and dancing and flirting and laughing and starting to enjoy the strange, exotic food: young people from foreign countries getting to know one another. But Mikaere wasn't interested in coming, wherever these evenings were held.

Then spring came, and Mikaere and I laughed at our difficulties when it was so good to be alive . . . I giggled when I heard, on the phone to his office, someone telling Mikaere: 'Mr Rangi, it's Sweetie,' too near the receiver! He sometimes made me tea and toast at the hostel and then he would walk me down to the tram stop and . . . we laughed most of the way. I was talking about saying 'cross my heart and hope to die if I tell a lie' when we were young: no-one would dare say that if it wasn't true. Mikaere laughed and said he used to! He often told so many big stories that I found myself . . . telling fantastical stories back without blinking!

And although we talked sometimes of eloping to Taupō (I don't know now why we chose Taupō), all throughout this time we made our plans. He would have his degree at the end of the year if he passed his exams, and now knew he would be promoted at work. I would have my degree at the end of next year. We were ready to get married but legally we couldn't: in 1957 you needed your parents' permission to marry before the age of twenty-one. Mikaere had already planned on going overseas to study on some sort of scholarship, his firm encouraged him, and he now wanted me to somehow go too.

MONDAY 23 SEPTEMBER 1957

A sense of belonging and – loving.

I see more and more into him. And I find out more and more what love is. It is starry-eyed like in the songs and passion too, but it is more. It is tenderness, understanding, a realisation that it all wouldn't be easy, but it would be worth it. A realisation that I would be making sacrifices for his life. That that is how it would have to be.

At Cath's place on Saturday they said I looked radiant and beautiful when Mikaere and I arrived at her super-fun party. If I did it was because I am in love and very proud of him. And oh – how good to be staying at her place and not having to worry about being home early or what Mum will say and how she will – stare at me. And then when everyone had gone, including my darling, Cath and I went and sat in her Mum's room and drank hot milk and we talked about it all. Not quite like my house . . .

TUESDAY 24 SEPTEMBER 1957

I had lunch 3 times today: 1. Irv and his Mum. 2. Mikaere. 3. Maria.

Tonight I started worrying about the Colombo Plan students who are too small a group to be fighting among themselves – fighting amongst themselves – in New Zealand? Indonesians, Burmese. Malaysians. Fighting. So my idea that if we meet when we're young there will be no more wars is just rubbish? I felt that, tonight. But some of them know they wont get terms for anything at all, poor things. I tried to comfort them but of course how can anyone? Will they go home, failed? What will happen to them all? What will their governments say to them?

And I've had my philosophy terms exam – it's no use me swearing any more and saying I've failed. People just don't believe me because I keep getting good marks.

I think (thanks to Bede Rundle, who is so clever and goes over and over things with me) therefore I am. Cogito ergo sum, ha, Latin useful after all.

FRIDAY 27 SEPTEMBER 1957

Win, and J-J my sulky tutor, and Mikaere and I all had lunch together. And, o hallelujah, Mikaere and Win took to each other at once. I knew they would, hurrah!

And tonight after swotting for hours and hours in the library he and I sat on a seat on the wharves and watched the sea and boats in the dark. He said to me 'He aha te huarahi i muri i a taua inaianei?' What is the road in front of us now? I don't know. All I know is that I love him and I know now, even when he gets mad and criticises me, that he loves me. I know I have to change myself. I have to realise that people settle down and change, that girls have to be realistic. That's how it is. I love Mikaere.

THURSDAY 3 OCTOBER 1957

I have passed my Oral Maori Exam – a fabulous fluke because I was terrible, and tired.

But it is Mikaere really that I cant keep out of my thoughts. It has taken me ages to get undressed tonight: I find myself standing and staring at nothing, miles away.

Things have been bad and getting worse: exams I suppose and Mikaere scared of missing his, because of me. Came to a head last night after our Maori class – he was a bloody child, sulking, in one of his moods – why, I literally did not know, oh he was so absolutely hateful, I was crying again on the tram coming home. I couldn't sleep, what with him and the Oral Exam so I was tired and depressed this morning when I saw him. He was sorry by then but it was too late, I was really horrible to him this time, and by the time I got to the Maori Affairs Department where the Exam was held

> I was absolutely in a terrific state – I still don't know how I even passed. I couldn't even feel elated when they said, yes, I had passed, 'Kia ora.' And then I came out of the place. And there stood Mikaere, who should have been at work, waiting for me. We went away and had a good talk in a car he has borrowed. And for the first time Mikaere actually spoke for a long time about being in love with me and what it means. Actual words are hard for him but when they come they mean more just for that reason.

All of us, I and so many of my student friends, were getting more and more fraught over the looming exam Finals, so, as a break, someone arranged for us to go to Wellington's Skyline, a sort of nightclub with a strict 'no alcohol' policy which the police had lately been very strict about. Mikaere insisted he wanted to pick me up in his borrowed car; I told Mum he was picking up a lot of us. 'Is it that same Māori?' said my mother at once, and then, just as immediately, 'We won't be here to meet him.' But they did stay home, and I wasn't quite ready when Mikaere arrived (my diary explains I had just done seven hours' Education swot in my bedroom), and so they talked to him briefly and asked him to sit down in an armchair in the lounge (no doubt to 'look him over').

At the Skyline with its big windows there were little candle-lamps everywhere, and boys brought in discreet brown paper parcels and the girls all drank Pimms, and Mikaere introduced me to someone as his fiancée . . . And I felt how I loved him with all my heart.

SUNDAY 6 OCTOBER 1957

> HERE IT IS. The crisis from which there is no turning back.

Mum and I have actually been talking about Mikaere – she says if I really care about 'that Maori who came here again'. I am just grasping out for problems – her final words: 'If you are in love with trouble – go to it.' She says all my friends would only say nice things to me, and not the truth. That isn't my idea of friends. And it wasn't my idea of marriage either, her pessimistic, hopeless view. She says – really awful things. And she says she will never accept him – and she says I must realise that now. That there will be many barriers besides her so I may as well accept her for a start. Mikaere rang just after this – he knew there was something wrong – what can I say to him? My mother doesn't want me to see you because you are black and Maoris smell different.

WEDNESDAY 9 OCTOBER 1957

Sometimes I lie on my bed and cry and cry – like tonight. Oh – I performed well at Maori class, and made Beth laugh. But as soon as we left Mikaere was hateful and sulky and cruel. In the good moments he apologises for the moods, but there are always more. Oh, it's not just him – it's exams and work and tiredness too, and everything at home, I know. He is tired too, I know – and I try to help him – and he is horrible. Then I come home like tonight and Mum wonders why I 'look at her' as I do. I am 'mean' – why should I hurt her just because she does what she 'thinks is right'?
Between them they'll smash my head.

FRIDAY 11 OCTOBER 1957

There were so many things I promised Mikaere I would write in here tonight. He now has time off from his office to study at Varsity all day with exams near. And: what will we be doing on October 11th 1960 we wonder . . .? He told me to write about Jock Fowler and his girlfriend who sit swotting in the library and holding hands lovingly. (I suppose one of them, in that case, must be left-handed.) And how someone said that now, with the Russians' satellite launched, going round the earth at some fabulous speed, we cant even hold on to the fact that after a war there'll still be something left . . . write it, he said. I love the old parts of Thorndon, we went there for fresh air. Katherine Mansfield's memorial – Mikaere likes to compare us – he has just finished lectures on her. But – maybe I've lost writing, as well as acting. Oh gosh we work!!!! But we've both passed terms exams in everything. We keep talking of eloping to Taupo . . . and tonight we watched the sea round Shelley Bay and the wind rattled and whipped around outside the car but we were warm. And very much in love.

MONDAY 14 OCTOBER 1957

Because we have so many Maori-Pakeha arguments I sometimes don't write that we are just people also, like tonight. I am lucky to have a person like Mikaere. He has always said to me it was hard for him to be sympathetic, and there were times I thought I could never tell him about Uncle Harry and fainting and all my secret fears that I don't tell people except Win sometimes. But tonight I did – and he couldn't have been more comforting and wonderful. Somehow things must work out for us.

Today after slaving at Philology, sigh, in the library, he and I went to the Botanical Gardens and read poetry and

Katherine Mansfield. There was warm warm sun and children played 'Thrippenny Run' on the grass: 'I'm hot of bowling.' 'Good chuck.'

At the Turnbull Library the other day where we were working Mikaere and I met 82 year old AH Reed, the publisher. One of the Old World gentlemen – white, white hair and upright, in a suit, and making notes from a Hawkes Bay newspaper 100 years ago. He gave me a little card with a poem on because I gave him a piece of chocolate.

SUNDAY 20 OCTOBER 1957

I've just heard on the Request Session a request for 'Blueberry Hill for Violet Holder of Picton'! The song that Wally sang on the guitar, her Wally, and maybe she had a baby? She stopped writing to me after a while but I think Wally had come back by then. She used to talk and talk about him but where the truth and fancy was – she hardly knew herself. How we sang, me and Violet . . .

I've made myself out a work timetable from now to the end of exams which I simply must stick to. And tomorrow is so rosy with TEN hours Middle English revision to be done! Never again THANK GOD! But I've discovered Hazlitt really properly and read and read, an exciting discovery, I love that very clear, concise way he writes.

WEDNESDAY 23 OCTOBER 1957

Last Maori class. ANOTHER BIG ROW after class with Mikaere about Pakeha hypocrisy. And then came home to yet ANOTHER BIG ROW with Mum about 'that Maori'. On and on and on and on. If it's not one of them being bloody

horrible it's the other one. WHY DON'T THEY JUST GO AND BE BLOODY HORRIBLE TO EACH OTHER. O God.
Or cant we at least have all these bloody rows AFTER EXAMS.

FRIDAY 1 NOVEMBER 1957

Brainwashed: 5 three-hour Finals Exams in 4 days. And in today's Maori exam – and at the last moment – Irv walked in to the extramural exam room for his Greek II exam and sat right in front of me – pale as newsprint and he'd been to the pub.
And I so love Mikaere – but feel guilty too, he would have passed everything easily if it wasn't for me – he knows it.
I don't know for sure of course – but I think I have passed everything so far. I felt all the papers were ok. I'm just so, so tired and I'll be glad when everything is over. But I will have caught up from failing History and have my BA degree in one more year!!!
What a year 1957 has been in my life!

FRIDAY 8 NOVEMBER 1957

I shall just put it in Hazlitt's plain style, clear and concise.
The last English II paper, my very last exam, was this morning and I had thought it was this afternoon – I turned up for it and it was over. The Registrar is very sorry but says there is nothing that can be done. They will have to fail me in English II.

XI

PICKING AT THE SILENCES, I have to piece the remainder of this story together. Partly from a couple of journals that contain sometimes very enigmatic entries months apart; partly from entries that suddenly again cover days at a time; partly from old letters still dustily taped at the back of the journals.

And partly from memory, though now I have learnt that memory, so very clear sometimes, can also forget and distort.

Mikaere passed all his subjects while working full-time and playing much rugby and having a girlfriend: he had his degree. I passed Philosophy and Education and Māori, but mistaking the time of the final English Stage II paper — my best subject — meant they had to fail me and that I would not be able to finish university next year as I had planned: as we had planned. Now it would take another two years minimum to get my degree.

The phone kept ringing, people asking me out, but I didn't want to go where people were discussing exams and degrees. One of the professors saw me on Lambton Quay and stopped me . . . He told me I must forget what happened, put it out of my mind, for there's nothing at all to be done . . . I got a job at the

California Coffee Shop, £9 per week if I did overtime, but it wasn't a romantic 'coffee bar' with candles — it was just a café, open in the daytime, that served sandwiches and scones.

MONDAY 18 NOVEMBER 1957

Write something at least . . .

I would like to write sensibly of at last going after exams finished to Mikaere's home but I get very tired when I write – even a few words get muddled up since I muddled the exam time . . . all I can remember is that I dreamed Win's grandmother died that night. And next afternoon she did.

Being finally 'allowed' to go to home with him at last was so odd – only happened after exams because everything was so – mixed-up. Long, long, long drive, over the Rimutakas, up to his village, over three hours. Everybody kissed me and accepted me but I felt – lonely because Mikaere was busy with the party and I didn't know anyone at all. It was the housewarming of Mikaere's brother, and his new (Pakeha) wife. Mikaere's mother is so nice and was very welcoming to me (not like at my house). She hugged me. But she immediately made me go and sit with a group of women who talked about babies and I did feel a bit funny. (But if he ever came to my place ha, he'd be with the men wouldn't he.) There was lovely singing, everyone did action songs. Someone sang 'You'll Never Find Another Wahine Like Me', those same party songs – I haven't heard that song since Violet and I used to sing it in the hotel kitchen. And it was a long, long, love journey home (I had to come home of course, Mum and Dad said no matter how long and how late I must come home, poor Mikaere driving and driving). We stopped on the hills somewhere, maybe near where I was born I thought afterwards, and lay there together in the warm night with the trees and the stars and our love. We know perfectly well what is happening to us and how my missing the exam has messed everything up. He has been amazing about it all and he said, as we lay near the stars: 'Whatever happens between us, now and the future, whatever it is, you know that you can always rely on me and trust me.' And I do know that. And I love him for saying it so strongly and loyally.

He has now had to go to Auckland for three weeks to the shipping office up there.

FRIDAY 15 NOVEMBER 1957

I didn't go to the University end-of-year 'Hop'. I ushered instead for Maria's poetry reading. Her voice – it's something I've known for so long – it sort of washed over me. The Shakespeare sonnets were wonderful. Her T.S. Eliot was wonderful too, 'time future contained in time past' – she makes it understandable somehow. I had to give her flowers on stage and she gave me a big theatrical embrace after which I fell down several stairs in the dark making a mess of my stockings, my shoe, and me!

THURSDAY 12 DECEMBER 1957

A waitress hasn't much time for writing, I enjoy the work, I do all the overtime I can get. But cant sleep. Mikaere's back from Auckland and there is trouble with him and me – talk of finishing and – oh I cant . . . just trouble.

Write it.

He says we can sleep together properly from now on without

harm because he has bought a sheath. I know what one is, Mrs Garland told me. But something holds me back – I'm scared.

Huge rows at home, and the big simmering one brewed and brewed, I knew it was coming of course, and it burst at last. Last Saturday just as I was going to Mrs Ranapia's 'Christmas Party and Celebration' for us, her three Maori I students who all passed, Sam and Mikaere and me, Mum talked about me missing the English exam and said it was the fault of 'all this foolish Maori business' and I lost complete and entire control of myself and screamed everything at her, what she says about Mikaere who is a person just like she is, and how hard she'd made it for months and months, 'He's a PERSON,' I screamed at her, and had she considered me missing the exam could be partly her fault too. I shouldn't have said that, it was my fault I missed the exam not hers, and I got a fright that I'd said it and so did they I think, awful awful, awful, the outcome was a promise from Mum never to complain about him again – only to 'hope and pray things go right'. But my mother doesn't pray does she.

The next time I write, some weeks later, I am back in Tauranga on New Year's Eve — but not in Maungatapu. My Norwegian uncle, that sailor caught in New Zealand when the war began and then Germany occupied Norway, started many and various enterprises after he married my Auntie Ellie and settled in New Zealand. They had sold the house he built, and left Maungatapu. He had now built another house in Tauranga, in another new and burgeoning suburb of modern houses near another old Māori settlement by the sea.

And I read, now, something in an old journal with utter amazement: I have absolutely no recollection of this and yet — wouldn't you think I would so clearly remember it? . . . Mikaere was at our house on Christmas night, with Mum's cousins looking him over, poor thing, how brave of him, and he kissed me goodbye at the train station, which must have meant too much to Mum. But she has tried hard. Have I for her . . .?

FRIDAY 10 JANUARY 1958

Judea it's called, this new Tauranga place. Not magic – and the house not so near the sea. A long way away from where I stare out of the window four little children playing in the low tide are like tiny insects. For a moment they all sat down in the shallow water and looked like a tree trunk. Mum and Dad have been and gone. I had a long talk with Mum about Mikaere, she says I should wait for three years, and then she will support me. Three years huh. She suggested I write to Nana about it all.

This was a very manipulative move on my mother's part. We didn't see a lot of my grandmother, although I was fond of her, and wrote her letters sometimes, and she wrote to me — and I certainly still knew nothing about the disaster of her own marriage.

But my mother — and presumably my father, who would have had to put everything in motion — had putative plans for me.

That I didn't yet know about.

SATURDAY 18 JANUARY 1958

Somehow, today, even Maungatapu didn't work its usual

> charm of peace. I went over there today and I suddenly felt a bit of a fool with all the kids, as well as the ones I know, there were lots of other little kids, some of them are about six – what am I doing with them all? I am odd, just like people probably think. But I didn't want to get to the stage where I would think it too.
>
> It's partly that cursed drunken letter from Irv – my private life and my 'unusual Maori connections' are apparently now being discussed in the Woolshed where he is working. So many boys I know working there. I know I was meant to appreciate his letter which was supportive, written in the warm glow of happiness with the aid of something a little extra, well I didn't . . .
>
> Back to Wellington next week and all its problems and my mother. Back to the Californian Coffee Shop. Back to my friends. Back to the man I love who – wants things I am scared of.

When it came to writing about sex in the privacy of my own diary: as I've said—I couldn't. Write it . . . I ordered myself. I tried, but I didn't know how. My friends and I never talked openly about sex, not really in words; at least sensible Mrs Garland had told me some rudiments, and about 'sheaths'. My total inability to express anything openly is scattered all through the diaries where I had always tried to be truthful . . . is this wrong? . . . we didn't do anything really wrong. And . . . I am scared . . . If we were married it would be all right . . . I had no idea how to write about it, let alone deal with it.

Yet it is all there, stated but not stated. It was 1958 and I only knew how to write nothing. But everything.

SATURDAY 25 JANUARY 1958

And Wellington is very bleak and dreary even though it's summer and there is a foghorn moaning and mourning but – oh oh it's been good to see Mikaere again. But difficult now.

Well – I'm back in Wellington, I'm starting work at the California Coffee Shop again and I'm going back to University and I'm going to make the best of things. I am.

THURSDAY 13 FEBRUARY 1958

I suppose I better pick up my pen and write a note of today. It is the day Mikaere and I have made an end to – to Us.

The reasons are varied – he cant and wont share me, doesn't like me even being in the company of other boys at all, just talking to others for god's sake – and I am me.

And. This other – disagreement goes on. I'm scared. We cant get married for a long time and he says a passion, a feeling, cant lie dormant for a year, two years – maybe more. But I am scared. 'No,' I said.

FRIDAY. For one whole day it lasted like a knife twisting my insides. That is a real hurting actual feeling not a literary phrase. And then late at night I didn't have any pride left and I rang him. He answered the hostel phone, he said he knew it was me.

SATURDAY 22 FEBRUARY 1958

People going away, parties, the Colombo Plan students who have been all our friends. Parties. Clever, kind Bede Rundle to whom I owe so much for all that philosophy help, made remarks at a party about my 'coloured friends' and even though I know he didn't mean to hurt – he did. Mum starting again now . . . o God.

But I am in love with Mikaere. And all the rows and all the endings cant change that anymore.

We were all at a party last night: Pimms – and life was wonderful, and Mikaere and Win laughed at me and brought me home.

But – it was the time of loving before we went to the party that I cant forget. I did – make him happy. And I wanted to make him happy. Even though I am scared.

WEDNESDAY 5 MARCH 1958

Today was university enrolment – the outlook of another year at this place and dreary old OLD ENGLISH and MIDDLE ENGLISH all over AGAIN is horribly bleak – but that is my fault not the university's fault. And Maria is also enrolling! She is going to do a degree, majoring in German. She asked me to look after her and help her and take her about, which as anyone who knows Maria will know was exhausting and a bit dramatic and theatrical! But I love her and it was fun in a way.

Now of course, I know I will, in the end, marry Mikaere.

I had to repeat English II. I now enrolled to do Māori II, again extramurally from Auckland — a Herculean task even with Beth Ranapia's backing. And I also enrolled for Political Science.

Lectures started.

But my parents' plan must have slowly been hatching. The next entry from my journal, not until a month later, on Easter Sunday, doesn't make sense otherwise. They had been busy making arrangements, and finally, when everything was completed, advised me of my immediate future on Easter Sunday afternoon.

They had arranged that I was to leave Wellington.

Next term I would be sent to my father's old university in Dunedin to live in a hostel (which they had already found and booked), taking — they had ascertained it would be made possible — my university subjects with me. (Dunedin. No doubt an excellent choice for doing Māori II extramurally, away from that Mrs Ranapia person . . .) And I could visit my grandmother in Timaru for the weekend sometimes.

I was advised of the 'New Arrangements for my Studies'.

Then they went out.

I phoned Mikaere and told him.

SUNDAY 6 APRIL 1958

And in the end the person who has given more joy, and more sadness too, than any other person ever, lets you down just in the very, very, very moment when you need him not to. In a way it is not his fault. How hurtful – and a shock – all this is for <u>him</u>. I of all people should understand what this does to him, his trying to join two worlds and – maybe even seeing the ceiling . . . and my 'news'. But – he had <u>me</u>, and he knows how much I love him. I'm not my mother. I AM NOT MY MOTHER. He – hung up when I told him they are sending me away.

So you have to face the trouble suddenly alone and must do this thing by yourself. It is Easter Sunday but I don't go to

Church. And I forget to pray and I am too scared to answer the question: what is it all for? I have only ever prayed to God when I wanted something.

Down the street, after hearing Mikaere's angry voice before he hung up on me, I passed a neighbour's house and I saw the lights where they prepared for a family wedding party. Brightness and warmth it seemed like.

And I couldn't even cry.

So I kept on walking and went to a party and laughed and didn't tell a single person.

There is a black-and-white photo from this time of me and some friends, taken by one of those freelance street photographers who took photos of people as they were passing and then handed them a card showing where the photographs could be seen in two days' time. I am laughing of course. I usually laughed in photos. But in this old photo it's a sort of . . . false laughing, with lines and dark circles under my eyes. In photographs of this time Mikaere looks — always — beautiful. But photos do not show what this situation was doing to him: to his spirit, or his soul: his sense of himself, and his identity.

I write about Mikaere angry, my mother looking old, me feeling guilty — everything was somehow all my fault . . . I saw my mother's face, sad – and old because I have made her that way . . .

SUNDAY 13 APRIL 1958

Last night I stayed at Mikaere's home for the night – in their friendly house, that gets so much sunshine, or that's how it seems to me, yet our house gets sun too. I was only allowed

of course to go once more because I am going away.
Football first, and then the team all <u>running</u> to the pub till 6 o'clock.
So that another girl Sophie, and me, and Mikaere's two younger brothers, poor boys, had to wander around with 10/- of fish and chips for one and a half hours: I spose it's the sort of thing that I'd have to live with and bear cheerfully. Then there was a 21st at the marae in the evening with Mikaere as usual rushing around helping everyone and me with the wives, we cooked kumara and cabbage and things on a huge stove. One lady said to me: 'Mikaere must have a very, very good girl to look after him. He is going to do great things.' Next morning the sun was shining and I lay on the sand as the boys – oh my God – did more rugby training after about two hours sleep!! Aue!
I like all the family: what a difference in reception from vice versa. His mother has a beautiful singing voice, they always ask her to sing.
And. All the time, in Mikaere's home, hearing him and his friends laughing and enthusiastically planning the new football season, I've had an odd strange glimmer, like a chill ghost: the ghost is . . . I'm not sure what it is.
Why do I write that? I don't know why I write that. I don't even know what I mean.
I only know that, after everything, I love him I love him.

Any young person reading this now could feel so exasperated: Why doesn't she just leave home, for God's sake? Why don't they take their lives into their own hands now?

Mikaere and I didn't at any stage think we could alter the

situation. I was nineteen, too young to marry without my parents' permission. There was all sorts of overt and underlying racial prejudice, and there were also unspoken, conformist conventions to contend with. In 1958 New Zealand, on the whole, young people didn't run away from home, break all the rules, live 'in sin', follow their hearts. It would have been a much-disapproved-of scandal — disapproved of by Mikaere's family as much as by mine.

Because Mikaere was carving a new path, and an example to encourage others. The Māori university students of the 1950s were early warriors for the Māori renaissance of the 1970s and 1980s, and they knew they were role models — it was a responsibility they had to carry. Like some of Mikaere's and my 1950s university contemporaries: Eddie Durie (later Sir Edward Taihakurei Durie, Justice of the High Court), Mason Durie (later Sir Mason Harold Durie, psychiatrist, involved all his life in a different approach to Māori health) and Sam Karetu (later Sir Tīmoti Samuel Kāretu, knighted for services to the Māori language). Today there are a large number of articulate, powerful Māori women role models who have fought for their rights too. Members of Parliament, government ministers, doctors, teachers, business leaders. There are also wonderful and talented Māori women artists, novelists, poets, historians, directors — and actresses. But in 1958 Violet Holder in Picton, who taught me so well, would never have even thought she had the chance of training as a teacher (and hadn't stayed at school long enough to begin).

And I, a Pākehā, may have had plans to somehow make something of myself — but I too was a girl all the same.

In 1958 there was a conventional, recognisable path for girls.

And now I, 'silly girl', already criticised to my face and behind my back for my choices by many people, as well as by my own parents, had messed up everything by so ridiculously missing an exam I would have passed, which put me back me a whole year.

MONDAY 21 APRIL 1958

The people who know things, the people of experience – tell me it is for the best, my going away. In my deepest heart I know that, because I cant live at home any more – but – there is that other thing, that ghost at Mikaere's house, the chill feeling as I heard him making excited plans for the rugby with his friends while I am supposed to make plans to go away from him and from everybody. I think that . . . never again will things be – like this.

Last Wellington afternoons in the cold autumn, watching the rugby. The world friendly and happy and critical and encouraging and the cold whipping through your bones.

And cold whipping through your laughter too.

MONDAY 2 JUNE 1958

Tonight I leave Wellington.

To live in Dunedin, to go to Varsity there for the rest of the year.

Perhaps it is a good idea? Once I get used to it? But when you love someone . . .

There are things I want to remember. Mikaere's home and the kindness of people there and sitting in the still of the night on the verandah in his warm arms before we had to go to bed.

Mikaere's terrible jealousy sometimes if I pay any other boy any attention. Tears and heartbreak and fear, and then Mikaere: arms and words comforting and loving and making the hard times seem – solvable . . .

Extrav Varsity show at the big Opera House I remembered acting in – but I don't ever act now, now I was helping with some backstage work. Will I ever act again like I once vowed to do . . . wasn't I once going to be an actress?

The people I find who are real friends. Win most of all. And Irv, who comforted me so much and told me to love Mikaere above all things and people. And Vanessa. And Irv's Mum kissing me goodbye. And Beth Ranapia, my wonderful teacher, kissing me goodbye. And Maria Dronke my other wonderful teacher kissing me goodbye.

And utter fear of losing my nerve – the middle of the night is worst of all. But stern resolve that it is all worthwhile. I'm leaving home anyway. Someone from Church gave me a prayerbook, god help me. As much as I can pray I want to pray that God, if there is a god, will help me to help myself.

And tonight at least I wont be alone.

My family came down to the wharf — those so known, so loved Wellington wharves — to wave me goodbye.

I waved goodbye.

Mikaere had boarded much earlier. We spent the night on the bottom bunk of a two-bunk cabin — a kind, youngish man above us, to whom we must have, I think, given some inkling of our story. Because although — he told us — he had an important meeting next morning, he was kind and not disapproving and we were very quiet.

The first whole night we ever spent in each other's arms was in a shared cabin on the inter-island ferry.

From Christchurch Mikaere saw me onto the train south to Dunedin, and we kissed goodbye.

XII

TUESDAY 5 AUGUST 1958

Dunedin.

I don't write any more. I have been here nine weeks, haven't written here once.

I'm in bed in this university hostel, with one of those hacking coughs I always get. Shall I describe Carrington Hall – in case I ever forget and want to remember? Straight away a tiny student's room of my own in a hostel was all right because life here was infinitely preferable to what went before. I was never homesick – only so lonely for my friends. As for loneliness for Mikaere . . . it hurt like an actual pain in my actual heart, it was unbearable – and still hits me hard often.

But.

He has let me down here. He hasn't written very much after the first almost overpowering loneliness that I think was hard for him too. But it costs too much to ring, unless I ask him and unless one of those overseas telephone operators is on duty that Sam Karetu knows, who give us some free minutes if they can. Football took over. And work in the shipping firm where, promoted, he now has so much more responsibility. And I became a nuisance because I 'demanded attention' – his words – especially I wanted regular letters at least – and he cant understand why I mind. Why I mind? Why am I here? That I love him still is a certain thing in my mind. But even in the University holidays when I'm coming back to Wellington, except for one week guess what, he will be away from Wellington playing rugby. I am glad he is doing well – but I can't bear this. I dream a lot – but the reality of what I dream is very doubtful. Formal-sounding letters that I wait so long for but somehow aren't – real.

I've got to make something of myself. If only I could still act. Or write . . . those things I used to do, and used to have hopes about . . . that word I never use: a 'career'.

Of course a hostel is a terrible place for privacy. Especially for me – used to yakking my head off. For the first time in my life I've realised that if you want to keep something private you just must not talk about it. What a hard lesson that was. I have fitted in and made friends. One of the girls, Lynley Orbell, I really like – she laughs like a horse and that makes me laugh! I went one weekend to visit her family's bach at Lake Wanaka and I had to climb out the window in the middle of the night to go to the lav because I couldn't find the door in the dark! Her father Doctor Orbell is a really eccentric loud chap. He has re-discovered the takahe bird, which they thought was extinct.

People know me now – well I knew so many anyway, quite a few people from Victoria, old boyfriends even! There was trouble at first. 'The girl with the kink who knows all these coloured students' – at least six of the Colombo Plan students from Wellington are here also! But – after all – people accepted me – and found they liked the Colombo Plan students too!

Once there was real snow – just a little bit – and it was lovely and soft and peaceful.

Apart from Mikaere, mail has been fantastic. Win and I have had the most wonderful long correspondence. And all sorts of other people have written lots to me – I get LOTS of letters. I am so lucky in my friends.

And it's been really nice getting to know Nana a bit more in the little old house, going to Timaru some weekends. With the oven to keep our feet warm and flowers on the wallpaper of the little hut which is the lavatory, down the garden path. She is a wonderful, straight, person and makes me laugh, and she told me she occasionally puts a little bet on a horse-race if she's been given a 'tip'! I would like to be like her if I must be old. I showed her a photo of Mikaere. She told me not to get married yet – not 'don't get married to a Maori' but 'don't get married yet. See the world.'

Work isn't very good. I'm in the throes of term exams. Huh. Hei aha.

'Tahi Nei Taru Kino' has just started on the radio as I am writing. 'And now we have a short programme of Maori music.' (In a posh voice.) Those songs I began to learn down the dusty road so long ago. I have just started to really understand my Friday night Maori class I found here but they will soon be finished so: I'm dropping Maori II (how convenient for my parents) because it is far too difficult to do it almost completely on my own, no Beth Ranapia, it's not just the language now, there's lots of anthropology which I know nothing about. To do Maori II I'd <u>have</u> to go to Auckland where it is a proper university subject and proper lecturers. But it has been nice in the funny little class here – dear old kuia, and crazy Rua Bristow, and Mason Durie, Eddie's brother, is such a nice person, and one afternoon a Pakeha who knows a lot about things Maori took Mason and me for a drive all round Dunedin – Lanarch Castle and a fake Maori carved church – stone impressions of carving and mistakes in the Maori. But I know I have to drop Maori II all the same, I simply don't know enough, and I'm not clever enough, I need teachers. Political Science ok. And English II repeated: huh.

I like my small student's room. I had photos of Mikaere everywhere but it didn't help as I waited and waited and waited and waited just to hear from the photographed person so now I have only the 'one' of us from his Graduation Ball that everybody seems to find so fascinating. Mikaere's favourite too.

The Matron is a twerp often but she has a kind heart if she thinks you are sweet and somehow I appear sweet. She has wee chats with me about the Colombo Plan students – how good it is that I am friendly with them etc etc and 'if you want to go to their quarters' (they were mostly put in a house across the road) just to 'ask' her. As if, because they are 'coloured' God I hate that word and she will use it, they have no designs on me. 'I know who I can trust' she tells me. I could laugh in her face and tell her that the other night Djoemardi from Indonesia who is much older than me explained to me, because I really wanted to know scientifically, exactly how a contraceptive sheath works. Could it spill out? I asked him.

I used to think that the expression about a hard knot inside was just a literary touch, like all those other 'literary' expressions, until now. It's a real, physical feeling. It happens to me when I read one of Mikaere's letters. I wait so eagerly – hope springs eternal and all that soppy stuff . . . and then a letter comes at last, lots about football mainly, and it only pushes the knife in a bit deeper and – I feel my actual heart getting a little tighter and harder.

I cried and cried and cried at last when I finally got here, a bit scary. But I had stopped myself the whole time before I left Wellington. And I don't cry here now.

Why should I cry?

Nine weeks. I'm changed.

❀

WEDNESDAY 12 NOVEMBER 1958

I really have changed. Over five months in Dunedin.

I have only ever felt a visitor at Otago University. But I know how Dad must feel about Dunedin. Blossoms by the Leith. And when I arrived the students' walk was covered in brown and yellow leaves, and then bare, skeleton trees. Then blossom and greenness coming. I've never been so aware of the seasons before.

After that first scary crying I only ever cried once: when Irv sat the wrong paper for his Greek III finals. Oh – how I understood what he must be feeling.

I'm in the middle of finals exams too. I'll pass. English II all over again. Huh. Middle English AGAIN. Luckily I've really enjoyed Political Science. A man came from South Africa and told us about the Apartheid Government there. And 'coloureds' as a category as well as 'blacks'. And Indians. All separated – by law. But I dropped Maori II – till next year . . . Half way through this term I went to Christchurch to meet Mikaere for the weekend. In a way it was – wonderful. We stayed in a hotel and I wore a sort of curtain ring. That afternoon we read NZ poetry – and just as it was getting dark that old song came in through the window from nowhere '. . . Night and day . . .' There were tiny baby ducklings swimming on the Avon. And we had a wonderful meal with a Maori relation of Mikaere's, and his wife. And the two deepest, most perfect hours sleep I ever remember, waking up in the morning, in a bed, with Mikaere's arms around me. But . . . oh it's hard for me to write now. I fully understand if I marry Mikaere I will have altered a lot from someone who – might have done something.

I suppose I will burn all my diaries soon too.

He has been good about writing ever since that weekend. And he prays for me in my exams. And what are prayers to me? I would rather have had letters . . . Yet I will always be in love with him, something jumps in my heart when I see him. In the holidays I went home with him again (that one weekend when he wasn't away from Wellington, playing rugby) and at the marae I helped cook a meal again, with all the married ladies . . . Of course physical nearness changes things, of course I love him, but I have learnt a lesson also.

You have to – keep a bit of yourself.

You musn't need somebody that much. You have to be a person.

TUESDAY 18 NOVEMBER 1958

Exams finished. Amid a ghastly mess I sit wondering, among goodbyes, with a terrible hangover (I was revoltingly sick all over a forest), whether I'll ever get the train from Dunedin.

Five and a half months.

Goodbye funny little room.

When I left Dunedin, a tiny splinter of concrete had lodged itself somewhere in my heart.

XIII

I HAD — INDEED — CHANGED.

I passed my exams.

No more entries at all this year, nothing. But by December I had somehow — helped by Beth Ranapia and contacts she had — made a plan.

Which I had determined for myself.

As soon as I got back to Wellington I began work at once, in the Department of Maori Affairs, with the District Welfare Officer, Kara Puketapu. And it had been arranged that in January I would move to the Maori Affairs Department in Auckland, where I had checked that I could also attend lectures, part-time. At last I would support myself financially. And finally get my BA degree.

What my parents thought about this I have no record and no memory.

But Mikaere asked me to marry him.

TUESDAY 13 JANUARY 1959

Packing for Auckland on my last day as a teenager. Once I

would have written pages on such a 'significant' occasion. Huh. Well – wont be living off (or with) my parents any more. Good.

Maori Welfare with Kara Puketapu as my boss has been hard but really interesting work – hope I'll be as lucky in Auckland.

Mikaere has 'formally' proposed to me – he asked me to marry him. I have accepted but: I'm still going to Auckland to work, and at the same time to do Maori II and English III, and finish my degree. I must do that at least. So what do I really want?

It's a question I cant answer any more.

He gave me the most beautiful engagement necklace. Greenstone and jewels.

I do love him. Can I also say to him: 'I love you but, just like you do, I want to make something else of myself as a person also.' But: huh – the things I want to do are dreams anyway aren't they.

I couldn't live at home any more. I am going to share a flat in Auckland with Win and Esther.

I made the decision.

Wisdom teeth out, they didn't do me much good did they ha.

Motor license acquired.

It is from this time that I found the photograph I couldn't 'believe'. It is a photograph of my mother and my father and Andrew and Ross and me just before I go to Auckland. And Mikaere. At a picnic somewhere, a deserted beach. It's a sort of uncomfortable photo. I am laughing, of course.

I have no recollection of this at all.

XIV

IT SEEMS TO ME THAT acting and writing use, in some way, the same part of the brain.

In 1999 Virago Press published my novel *A Dangerous Vine* in the UK.

The publishing world has since changed fast because of the internet, and Amazon in particular, and huge global conglomerates stepping in and taking over. But in 1999 Virago was an imprint under the umbrella of the publishers Little, Brown who several years earlier had accepted my second novel *The Actresses* — written, as I have told often, after I heard the actress Glenda Jackson say she was going to become an MP. Male colleagues of her age and older were still finding plenty of big, satisfying acting parts, she said: 'But **not** middle-aged women. And I'm **not** waiting around to play "the wife" or "the mother".' (She didn't wait around: she was Parliamentary Under-secretary for the Department of Environment in Tony Blair's Labour government; later Shadow Minister for Transport; and she eschewed show business completely. And then, at the age of eighty, she returned to the stage: as King Lear — in both Britain and America.) But in the 1990s I had decided that if Glenda Jackson wasn't waiting around, nor certainly should I, and I wrote *The Actresses* while still acting: parts of it were written in theatre dressing-rooms all over England. I was actually putting the final draft together in the Number One Dressing Room at the Bristol Old Vic Theatre during a run of *She Stoops to Conquer* — scissors and glue and cut up pieces of paper all over the dressing-room floor. (Then I would very unprofessionally hurry on stage before I had time to switch professions properly in my head: one horrible night I looked at the other actors on stage in amazement — luckily only for a split second — in that 'actors' nightmare', when you don't know who you are, or where you, or what to say.)

The Actresses was a commercially successful 'bonk-buster' set in London, and full of sex and scandal (and about middle-aged women, a subject usually considered to be commercial suicide). And — ironically in these later times — about actresses having to put up with 'attentions' from male employers as part of their lives. So it was reprinted in 2018.

I had already had my first novel, *Strangers*, published in the UK and the US in 1978. I wrote it when I was Judi Dench's 'standby' (just a posh form of understudy) after she found she was pregnant just before the play *London Assurance* starring her and Donald Sinden opened in London. I had special rehearsals and wig fittings and costume fittings — obviously Judi wouldn't be able to do eight shows a week . . . What a lot I learned from her. She was a professional to her fingertips: once she cried because she was so tired, occasionally she was sick in a paint-tin on the side of the stage — but she never missed a performance. So — whew! — I never had to go on stage instead of Judi Dench (I kept imagining the audience booing with disappointment), but I was bored. So: apart from playing Scrabble sometimes, I wrote my first novel while being paid as an actress.

Strangers was the book I wrote when I was still . . . what do I mean? . . . unable to write *A Dangerous Vine.* I had become interested in South African politics when I was at Otago University, I knew about rugby problems with South Africa, I was a member of the Anti-Apartheid Movement in London, and so I wrote a novel about 'legal' apartheid instead, and about a foreign young actress in London. And about loneliness. Not a hint of another story, another country. (Except in the dedication.) *A Dangerous Vine* lay there, dangerously perhaps, waiting.

Twenty years later *The Actresses* — which had earned me a two-book deal — sold many thousands of copies. And as the second book of this deal, a deal 'given in good faith' as Little, Brown said to me angrily now (i.e. in good faith that I'd write another commercial bonk-buster, hopefully not about middle-aged women this time), I was offering the publishers a novel about '***race relations in New Zealand in the 1950s? WHAT?***' What in heaven's name, they asked me, were they supposed to do with it?

I inserted some political chicanery and scandal and finally a murder . . .

And I was rescued by Lennie Goodings, the publisher at Virago — who had in fact discovered *The Actresses* for the umbrella company in the first place.

A Dangerous Vine was then, to my total astonishment, subsequently long-listed for the Orange Prize for Women's Fiction, as it was called then.

A Dangerous Vine used many of the complicated and painful problems covered in my diaries, but I had written it without even thinking about — remembering even — those old, unopened exercise books. It never occurred to me to consult them. And I had no memory at all of the way my mother constantly used the word *dangerous* about my Māori studies (as my diaries have shown): I wanted to use for the title a line from one of the old Māori party songs. 'A dangerous vine' is a free translation by a Māori scholar with whom I discussed my thinking, from the first line of the song 'Tahi Nei Taru Kino'. I kept thinking of the entwining, gnarled roots and branches of old, old pōhutukawa trees, which often — instead of dying, or snapping off — dig deeper, wider, entwine more, will, perhaps dangerously, not let go. Novelists — sometimes — do of course use real life, but almost always they will change it. And indeed I changed the true story enormously. I also inserted events in a government department I called The Bureau. Not a thousand million miles away from one of the offices run by the New Zealand government where I had worked myself.

TUESDAY 31 MARCH 1959

I am settled in Auckland. I go to work every day. I go to lectures every day. I love the studying in both English III and Maori II and I am happy working in the Maori Affairs Department, will be moved to Welfare as soon as I've learnt more about the other offices. At the moment I am working in the Maori Land Records and filling in so, so many huge piles

> of land files so so meticulously, which can get very boring! (And oh! I attend the big wonderful drunken parties in that big dark Courtroom! Dancing and singing nearly all night!)

The old Department of Maori Affairs is now, often rightly, criticised for its paternalistic attitude and its employment of so many Pākehā civil servants, including me (signing in daily to the office — there was a signing-in book — after an 8 a.m. English III lecture; signing out to attend my Māori II lectures just before the men ran to the pub). I found an old 'staff photograph' taken under those gnarled old pōhutukawa trees in Emily Place in Auckland, so I am sure of my statistics. Less than a quarter of the Auckland staff were Māori; two of them were Heads of Department, and one was a typist who, though blind, was the fastest typist there and used a dictaphone. And less than a quarter of the staff were women: the typists, the 'machinists' (who used huge adding machines) and the clerks. I was a clerk.

But. A positive thing that cannot actually be counted in statistics, or official staff photographs: in the 1950s a large proportion of the staff, Māori and Pākehā, were middle-aged men back from World War II, and that shared war experience tied them together in a very particular way and, paternal or not, my observation was that not all but many of the Pākehā staff were genuinely dedicated to their work with Māori. And many of those middle-aged men — unusually for the time — socialised with one another in a shared way that we younger staff, Māori and Pākehā, simply joined; I never sang so much and laughed so much at so many parties in my life, before or after. Always at parties as the evening wore on these old soldiers would at some stage give a (usually inebriated) shout and all get up and sing the old war song 'Pa Mai', and the Pākehā soldiers knew all the words and actions too, and so, in the end, did we. Quite a lot of the men in the office, both Māori and Pākehā, had war-wounds of one kind or another: big scars, or limps, or even wooden legs, or hook hands, or — in particular — something I already knew about: what we would call now post-traumatic stress disorders. Oddnesses. And damage.

War damage. We used to go to the Anzac Day dawn parades and see our bosses, marching.

Nineteen-fifties New Zealand boasted, often, of its fine race relations . . . well, I already knew something about that. And of course New Zealand was crazy about its rugby. My journals tell that in 1959 there were ongoing rumblings of anger about leaving Māori players out of the teams sent to South Africa, anger which had been rumbling (in some quarters) since 1921 when a South African journalist sent a telegram home to say that the Springboks were 'disgusted' that white New Zealanders cheered on a Māori team playing against white men. (The operator who leaked this message in 1921 was fired.) In 1981 — when the Springboks came to play, welcomed by the New Zealand government, and the rumblings erupted into something like civil war — some New Zealanders were surprised to be made aware of some of the realities of their own 'fine race relations'.

Realities we were already only too aware of in 1959, in the Department of Maori Affairs.

I wrote occasionally in my journals of what I saw. We lived of course under British/New Zealand law, not Māori law, and this caused many problems, especially, still, involving land —

although Sir Āpirana Ngata had worked so long and tirelessly for redress on behalf of Māori owners. I saw the tortuous Māori land records being meticulously kept, day after day, in the Records Office — including for weeks and weeks and weeks by me, by hand, in huge volumes with leather covers, no computers or internet. When parents died, so very often without a formal will (karanga mate?), their share of their tribal land was divided up among their children, fragmenting it, and then in another generation fragmenting it again — into 'uneconomic units', to the Pākehā eye — but in the Māori eye retaining it as a tūrangawaewae, literally 'a place to put the feet': a psychological safety net, a homeland to return to. Which means that, to this day, very many blocks of land still have many owners who, if they want to make individual decisions about their share, must make special arrangements with the other owners.

I saw traditional Māori informal adoptions being legitimised, which again caused cultural difficulties but helped complicated legacy problems that could arise when parents died.

For years now Māori young people and families had been arriving, wave after wave, into the big cities to find work: I saw Māori apprentices (one of them I knew from Maungatapu!) trained by the department, building houses for Māori families who would never have been able to afford a house otherwise. All this was set up by the Maori Affairs Housing Office; deposits on mortgages were arranged, very often by the capitalisation of family benefit. Māori hostels had to be set up for the apprentices (I knew about Māori hostels: . . . *don't get serious Cindy . . . You're not mature enough Cindy . . .*) because so many Māori people — Māori students and those Māori apprentices were the lucky ones — found it hard to find any accommodation in Auckland at all. Where so many flats and boarding houses — many more than in Wellington — had those same notices in the window: **NO CHILDREN MAORIS OR DOGS.**

There was a Māori Land Court, which was the largest room in the department: an internal room which was so dark it had to have an electric light on even in the daytime, and where those big land files and land records were stored, piled high on shelves all the way round the walls. This court was where people brought old and new grievances about land ownership (and where we, very unofficially, had those wild office parties). And although there was very much discussion — we talked about it in Māori II classes all the time — about how the language was dying, Māori interpreters were still sometimes required in court at this time. All the judges were Pākehā — although to my surprise and interest a couple of the older ones did speak Māori — and some of the older Māori people who came to the courtroom with land issues still spoke their own language. (I used to go in quietly sometimes, and sit at the back to listen. And sometimes, in the almost-dark, usually almost-empty room — maybe five people, and the interpreter, and the judge poring over papers in the bad light, but with the beautiful language going on and on — I used to imagine the big land files that I knew so well listening there also, their wairua whispering, waiting . . .)

I also saw somewhat dubious matters. It seemed that very small landholdings, seen to be useless and uneconomic, could be legally taken from Māori owners and joined together as an economic entity, no matter how the owners felt: this part of the department was actually called — how ironic it sounds to me now — the Alienations Office. I saw the unofficial process of 'pepper-potting': not building too many Maori Affairs houses together in one place, but sprinkling them around the suburbs of the city so that not too many Māori people would congregate together in one place where (it was automatically assumed) they would get drunk and sing loudly and disturb the neighbours. I later understood that some Māori families (they thought they might have to live among too many Pākehā) decided they didn't want a Maori Affairs mortgage after all. I also saw a Māori employee in the Housing Office stealing the mortgage money from the Māori savers.

Later I also observed in particular my extraordinary boss in the Welfare Office where I finally ended up: Lieutenant-Colonel Arapeta Awatere who had served with the Maori Battalion. (How could I not put a fictional version of this charismatic man into a novel?) Dealing, like all the Maori Welfare officers, with so many lost souls in the city. Visiting prisons so disproportionately full of Māori prisoners; helping people find somewhere to live; arranging job interviews which included visiting many firms to encourage them (and in his case sometimes bully them) to employ young Māori people. For there was (as I now knew only too well) so much unspoken prejudice. Job interviews, or accommodation appointments, would be set up for properly qualified Māori people who happened to have Pākehā names who found, when they got to the interview, or the accommodation office, that the job, or the room, was suddenly 'not available'. Arapeta sometimes decided to just send young people home again, away from the city on the late-night or early-morning 'paper bus', if life became too difficult for them. And sometimes Arapeta (Peta, as everyone in the office called him) would go into the small airless interview room where there was some privacy and say he was not to be disturbed under any circumstances. Strange human sounds emerged: I later understood he was composing, just with his voice, various pieces of Māori music — an oratorio, he told me, to be sung by a choir — of which later a long-playing record was made: I have it still. And there I am on one piece, as the narrator.

Peta also collected mortgage money from Māori wharfies on payday before they might go to the pub. He would come back from the wharves, pulling notes and coins out of his pockets along with a list of names, instructing me, the Welfare Office clerk, to sort it out, which I did, and then I carefully carried the sorted and counted mortgage money, and the list, in a brown paper bag along the corridors to the Housing Office.

It is also true (this is also in *A Dangerous Vine*) that I, the Welfare clerk, was locked into the Maori Community Centre in Auckland with Arapeta and with a young Mormon trainee Maori Welfare officer, Wally Tukukino, by the (Pākehā) second-in-command of the Maori Affairs Department. He, tight-lipped, drove us there in a government car one early morning: we would not be let out of the Centre until we had rung him to say we had finished the yearly Maori Welfare statistics for the department's Annual Report. I took papers and files and pens and pencils and various notes: as the clerk I was supposed to collect the statistics, but they were a half-hearted mess . . . it is so hard to keep the office statistics as I am supposed to . . . nobody will ever give any statistics or numbers to me no matter how often I ask: 'too busy' they always say . . .

And indeed a Maori Welfare officer certainly wasn't a 'statistical' kind of job: there wasn't time; from the early morning till the office closed the phone never stopped ringing, calling urgently for help of one kind or another. In that office it sometimes felt like we were a piece of sticking plaster on a — sometimes violent — whirlpool. Apart from Arapeta, for the whole of the wider Auckland area, stretching, I think, almost to the Bombay Hills, there were only three Māori women welfare officers (one of whom later became Dr Ngapare Hopa, the first Māori woman to receive a doctorate — from Oxford University). And three male officers (one of whom became Sir Ian Hugh Kawharu ONZ, of Ngāti Whātua, who received a doctorate from Oxford University). And there was Wally the trainee, also locked in the Maori Community Centre that day, and me the clerk, who answered that telephone all day long, and tried — often helplessly and often completely on my own — to assist people who just arrived in the office because it was just somewhere to come. And one of the clerk's jobs seemed to be to keep the kettle boiling and to wash and re-wash the cups (and purchase tea and milk and sugar) for the many, many cups of tea that were dispensed all day. Sometimes a few old Māori ladies would arrive, puffing through the door; they came and sat by the reception counter, 'two sugars please dear' . . . they listen openly at the counter to the problems that people come in with, but they do give advice, sometimes they can really help, they mention a useful name I can sometimes contact thank goodness, they roll their tobacco, they give me a phone number, or sometimes they themselves ring a relation on the office phone . . .

So even I learnt to help somehow, working out what to do, or who to ring, how to try and stem the deluge of problems. A burglar briefly out of prison came in sometimes, and after a while I thought, Well, he may be a burglar — which he told me about quite openly, even describing some of his work methods — but he was also clever and articulate, and spoke Māori fluently. One day I told him about extramural university classes, and how he could take the Māori language as a degree paper. And when he went back to prison, as he inevitably did, he enrolled to do a BA degree.

How many 'Welfare' statistics did Peta himself cover when he went on one of his day trips round Auckland? He probably, in one day, talked to a number of Māori prisoners in Mount Eden Prison; collected mortgage money from the Māori wharfies on payday; helped a Māori buy a decent second-hand car which he needed for his job; went to a boarding house where an unemployed Māori had smashed a door down; went to the hospital after a Māori had been badly injured in an accident and no one in the hospital knew who to contact; collected — barefoot — some mussels down at the beach while sorting out a family problem and brought them, the mussels in a sack (and possibly the family), back into the office. (And missed a Heads of Department meeting.) So the day we were locked into the Auckland Maori Community Centre the lame Māori caretaker pushed a big broom slowly around the floor and we three sat on the stage while The Platters sang 'The Great Pretender' on the jukebox, and we made up the statistics. And were let out at the end of the day.

The Department of Maori Affairs was a product of its time: that place — of hurt and hilarity and parties in the Land Court, but also much hard work and goodwill, always a guitar playing somewhere — is long gone. Replaced by a government-supported Māori institution with Māori employees dealing with Māori matters (and maybe the guitars play still).

And those old, old land files that I somctimes used to imagine whispering together in the dark as they lay heaped up in piles on dusty shelves in the Land Court room, waited.

And when the Waitangi Tribunal began to enquire into historical land claims also: there they were. Evidence.

So very many things have changed since 1959.

While writing this, I heard Warren Gatland, the New Zealand coach of the British and Irish Lions rugby team for their tour of New Zealand in 2017, explaining to the BBC why he had hired a choir master for the Lions when he first took over the job. 'They knew about the haka of course. But they had to learn to sing if they were going to New Zealand,' he said. 'I told them they would be officially welcomed in lots of places with a Māori welcome, a speech followed by a song — and they had to return the honour, and bloody sing properly.'

And now of course there are Māori immersion kindergartens, Māori primary schools, Māori secondary schools. Māori tertiary institutions. Māori political parties. Māori radio stations. Māori television stations. The work of the Waitangi Tribunal has meant Treaty settlements. Land reparations. Big Māori conglomerates. Those Māori students I was with at university, and many, many other younger people, including now many women, changing our country. I observe that many — not all — New Zealanders and institutions respect the Māori language, try to pronounce the Māori place names correctly. There are still arguments about whether the language is dying or not: in the meantime, there are Māori language classes all over the country which Māori, Pākehā and even Asians queue to attend. And: I was in New Zealand in March 2019 and felt so proud of, and moved by, the grace and inclusivity with which our country and the Prime Minister — and the Muslim community — dealt with the terrible events in Christchurch. It seems clear that the Māori culture is as embedded now, in New Zealand's approach to any major national event, as absolutely as the monarchy, the pageantry, the red-uniformed horse-guards, are embedded in Britain.

There are extremely good books and accounts of all these things, written by Māori writers.

I have been writing about the past.

And yet.

My life has worked out in such an odd way that not only do I know about the huge positive changes but I also know about ongoing problems and unacceptable statistics of the present day. And I know them not just as statistics.

And a man I loved long ago said to his children: 'My children shall not marry Pākehā.'

SUNDAY 5 APRIL 1959

Most of the writing in these diaries when I do write is painfully squelchy. Because this is important I hope it wont be.

Win and Esther and I are domestic in our Mt Eden flat – a funny old unfurnished one that we've made friendly and nice. We get on fairly well: Win and I admirably even sharing a room and she has just kissed me on the top of my head as she passed me writing – something she will be most embarrassed about one of these days if I remind her. Esther lights candles every Friday night – I love the flickering light on the blinds.

I have been away from the office for a few days with the

same old, same old – hacking cough, tonsillitis – penicillin injections, pills – the usual.
There are some nice people in Auckland but it's big and impersonal, not like Wellington. I quite like funny old Queen Street with its broken wooden verandahs and the little streets running off it – I am a first-class window-shopper and would love some nice clothes. Some people are beautifully dressed and make one feel dowdy, but some Auckland city streets are sleazy and dark. It is very seldom windy – and yet I find I notice the wind as soon as it comes, because it – reminds me of Wellington.
Dunedin is just – a memory.
Main arguments here revolve around Esther's and my different musical tastes!

Come on come on, write the main thing. Stop putting it off.
So – time progressed. Mikaere again didn't write much, again I was miserable, but this time I had made the choice: even though we were supposed to be getting married I came to Auckland, I could never live at home again, and at last I am doing Maori Studies II and loving it. Then it was Easter – and the University tournament was in Auckland. So we had a house full of visitors – hectic! Including Peter Campbell who loves Win, and Mikaere who combined business with pleasure and arrived for 3 weeks. He is still here.
We knew, both of us, that this was the deciding time.
And two things have happened. We have both understood, truly and openly, that we really do love one another – whatever this thing called love is, we have it deeply for one another and are not certain how it will go away. We actually

ponder on the word. Love – what is it?

But we have realised the other thing. We must stop knowing each other and we will not marry, because falling in love which we know has happened to us, is not enough for marriage. All the times – just look back through this journal alone to find just a few of them – when I loved and didn't love him; when I said I couldn't marry him and then said I couldn't live without him. And he has felt the same. I know – I have known for so long – I do love him in a way that I am – lucky I think, to have known.

But it was as I felt somewhere deep inside – we couldn't make each other happy: we are too, too different (or alike perhaps) and we could only break the other person, yet loving all the time. A kind of fatal mix. Mikaere is leaving Auckland next week and with that leaving we have agreed we are leaving each other for good. I think it is the hardest, emptiest thing I have ever done – though I know it is right and so does he. We have been too much to each other. We know also it must be a complete break – we will just drive each other crazy and we must stop.

There is no use writing any more – everything is written and my room is dark with autumn evening.

SATURDAY 18 APRIL 1959

Cant write really. Just – numb. Mikaere has really gone, left when his work finished, as we agreed. It is for the best.

We had done the right thing, the sensible thing, but I remember the crickets outside sounded sharp, like scissors cutting as they sang outside in the Mount Eden night, and I stopped writing.

The next entries, a month later, written in Wellington, say I was down there for a wedding to which Mikaere and I had both been invited; that my parents had sold our house and moved to Brooklyn where huge picture windows stared down at the city I had so loved; and that Mikaere had kissed me in the street when we met, just as he always had.

SUNDAY 24 MAY 1959

Mikaere and me? We did have a nice time, as well as the wedding. I never once felt that old hurt feeling: whether he was being particularly nice or whether I really have changed I don't know. We went to the Boulevard and a Charlie Chaplin film. And the loveliest bit – Mikaere and I not fighting, it was such a relief. I think it is because he hasn't the power to hurt me any more. Even so busy talking to some All Blacks at the railway station he forgot to even wave me goodbye when the train left!

I'll never, ever, love with all of me again. But it's hard.

MONDAY 1 JUNE 1959

It isn't that I want to write. It's just that – it's a year ago that I went down to Dunedin.

To and fro our love zig-zagged, all that New Zealand winter. He would come to Auckland for a few days, I would go to Wellington for a long weekend; we agreed we must not do this, but then we would go to a ball together, or our old coffee shop with the melting candles and the music. We would talk and talk, and not quite be able to make the final break, either of us.

My diary entries, and Mikaere's letters at the back of the diary or still dustily taped beside my entries, show us both knowing what to do — just not able to do it . . . he and I are both – too alive to play second fiddle to anyone. We talk a lot, try and sort out our difficulties honestly. We are good at that. And we do love each other. But . . . oh I have one big, huge, huge wish. How I wish we'd been left alone to work it out for ourselves . . .

Mikaere sends me a letter: . . . *and we know Barb that it isn't because I'm a Maori and you're a Pakeha that's the problem but because I'm Mikaere Rangi and you're Barbara Ewing . . .*

And then I suddenly write in French for one brief entry.

MONDAY 29 JUNE 1959

. . . l'on n'aime qu'un seul: c'est le premier. Les amours qui suivent sont moins involontaires.

Loves that follow after are less — involuntary.

I went out with other boys: he would still get jealous. He had met another girl: I still got jealous. Meeting sometimes still — but my very few entries keep saying things like . . . why is everything so unanswerable?. . . All this – life's untidiness. What do people do? And most of all . . . oh for God's sake just get on with your life NOW! I had already walked barefoot in city streets, carrying a flower, spitting grape pips. Now I became wilder, drank more, didn't care who I kissed. I didn't care about anybody — especially about myself.

But: I enjoyed working at the Maori Affairs Department — and I enjoyed both my English and my Māori studies. Wordsworth, Coleridge, Byron, Pope — and in Māori II we had to make a linguistic comparison of Māori with some other Polynesian language and I chose the island of Mangaia because someone introduced me to a man from there and I was fascinated to compare words and language structure. So, luckily, I may have been spitting grape pips and drinking too much and not caring about myself or what I did — but I also worked hard.

MONDAY 28 JUNE 1959

I never thought I could be so completely without morals of any kind, and all the time I despise myself for it. Why am I so much harder and uncaring? Am I the same person who wrote so passionately day by day in my diary – with all that feeling and aspiration and – realness? And now what am I? Harder and harder and having a stupid 'relationship' that doesn't even mean anything. What am I doing?

TUESDAY 6 JULY 1959

The face of a woman in a milk bar through the glass of a big orange-drink holder; the juke-box music; Mr Lover-Boy and I sitting there, arguing a little. It all seems so unreal. The public library, where I sometimes work, its alcoves, the funny old snuffling men there and the old lady in the torn coat with a packet of cheese . . . nowhere else warm to go except the library I expect – it's all part of an unreality, a pattern of unreal things that tries to engulf me. I don't even like having this relationship. But I just – do.

I don't care about anything at all really now, except my work and my studies.

MONDAY 20 JULY 1959

On Friday I got very drunk at an office party in the Maori Land Courtroom at a farewell for Brownie Puriri and fell down some hill! Where? A letter from Mikaere saying he is now going to apply for a grant or a scholarship to travel which he would have done earlier, if not for us. He's right. We are right. Me coming to Auckland was only half a decision, and he will do it this way.

I seem to have had so little sleep. Huh. I never could sleep anyway so what's new.

TUESDAY 11 AUGUST 1959

To Tauranga briefly on my way home to Wellington, study leave, over the Varsity holidays. Needed to get out of all the mess in Auckland – the stupid mess and madness of my stupid 'love' life. Huh. I have only despised myself – and done nothing about it. Till now. That's finished.

And Maungatapu is utterly changed. I went over there for one last look. The dusty road is an asphalt highway, a smart looking bridge at the end. The vineyard is gone, the orchards are gone, the tracks down to the beach where we got prickles in our feet are gone. Just posh houses and lots more neat, cleared, sections, with paved roads leading to them. And letters to the paper complaining about 'the terrible old Maori houses by the bridge that disgrace our new road'.

It was a beautiful spring day . . . still the same smell of those manuka trees, and the sea. As I walked along the shiny road to the marae today, hating all the changes, some children called out 'Are you still Barbara?' Ha. Am I still Barbara?

SUNDAY 16 AUGUST 1959

I am at our new house in Brooklyn again, with its huge, huge, many windows overlooking Wellington that isn't really home at all. The view is – too much, too huge. It's exhausting. One day I want to live where there is a view, but smaller, of the sea and trees – peaceful like Maungatapu used to be.

Win is in Wellington too and this morning she asked me if at the end of this year we should make a tentative booking to go overseas. Ohhhh . . . I do want to travel I suppose – only I don't want to leave for too long, New Zealand. So many people go to England – Peter Campbell is going, and Win wants to go too. Vanessa wants to go. Sally has long gone. Of course it's a matter of money which I haven't got. Most sensible would be to live at home next year and save, as Win will do. No.

What am I going to do about a lot of things?

One day, perhaps tomorrow, or one day, I should ring Mikaere I suppose, I didn't even tell him I was coming to Wellington this time. Sometimes, when I think clearly of things, I realise we progressed an enormous lot in two years, to an understanding of each other. (And of ourselves maybe?) But I don't know that another two – or twenty-two – could make much difference again. Is it possible to be able to remain friends with someone who was – so important?

What a train journey down on the Limited on Friday – everyone coming to Wellington for the rugby test. People drunk everywhere – girls being sick, lights flashing on and off the whole night through. Refreshment stops resounding with the sound of breaking glass and bouncing Railway cups which are about six inches thick!!

Mum wants so terribly for me to come home. She has just told me she is sure we will not disagree any more about things and that I should not blame her for her 'perfectly natural reaction to the problem that confronted me'.

I'm just going to visit Beth Ranapia in her old house by the monastery.

MONDAY 24 AUGUST 1959

Sun shining (Wellington mid-winter!) Saw Ruth, looking forward to the baby, Win and Peter together, Cath planning to go to England, Vanessa wants to go also. Still that wonderful friendship with Irv, his letters are always good to wait for and when we are occasionally together we fight – with dishcloths! But real friends – talking, listening, telling each other the truth about ourselves, laughing. I had a lovely time at his place the other night, I always do. His Mum is one of the goodest, kindest people I know.

Mikaere. He sounded so thrown when I phoned him and told him I was here. Suddenly it is he who doesn't need me at all, who wants a 'clean final break' but who likes us to be 'good friends' and he will always think of me 'with affection'. Well, isn't that what we agreed? But he was quite suddenly very hard to me, that's really new – and yet he was still jealous that I went to Irv's place . . . he told me he took somebody else to a Ball on Saturday night – and I hated that – though I was at the pictures with laughing Fred who's left Maori Affairs and is training as a cop.

Mikaere has so much of me, and I of him – too much to just forget easily, although what is happening is the only right thing and we know it. How ghastly divorce must be. I am seeing him tonight and I expect we will be able to say a final goodbye at last in the right way, as we must.

I want to go back now, to Auckland, and pass those exams. Been studying and reading here, I so enjoy doing it, learning, English studies and Maori studies, both.

Sixty — sixty — years later I will just 'narrate' from the diary that we did not say goodbye in the right way. We had a terrible fight, like a nightmare, with terrible things said, and I remember the dark of the night and the walk up the path from the Māori hostel to the road, where a taxi waited for me, rung at my request by J-J. I wasn't crying but I couldn't stop shaking. Mikaere put his hand on my shoulder, trying to say something, but we couldn't, either of us. And the taxi came and I got in. And when I got home, not crying in the least, I just wanted to go to bed. I said goodnight. But Mum and Dad began asking and asking me what I'd been doing.

. . . just like the bloody old days. For some reason they wouldn't leave it alone: 'Where have you been?' 'What have you been doing?' and so I suddenly told them – their dearest wish of more than two years had come true, and I threw it at them which wasn't fair really, but was remembering back to what had happened in those two long years of so many things. And cried – cried till I actually vomited, from crying. Mum tried to come to me, 'I'm sorry. I'm sorry that you've been hurt,' she kept saying but I only screamed at her to go away, to leave me alone. I must have hurt her so much – but I kept remembering all the times she hurt me because of Mikaere, and how she hurt him and I wanted to hurt her too. Then Dad came into my room with a hot water bottle and I stopped crying at last. And just when I was almost asleep I felt one solitary tear going down my face. And then this morning J-J rang me and said 'are you sure you've broken up properly because Mikaere was singing really very loudly and happily this morning as he shaved and dressed?' That didn't hurt me at all because I knew that was how he would be. Too proud to show his feelings to anyone, perhaps even to himself. He is hurt too but it is a different hurt. But we had to make that final break.

'I'm sure we've broken up properly,' I said to J-J.

TUESDAY 29 SEPTEMBER 1959

Tonight, in Auckland, that girl who lived in our old house in Wellington seems only someone to remember hazily. Often late at night I'd walk home from the tram-stop, and down our path, past small pink roses on the prickly rose tree by the front door, and the hose to trip over in the dark and a bucket by the dripping tap under the bathroom window by the back door.

And that famous blossom tree by the gate, planted when I was little for me to 'say goodnight under', to my boyfriend. Ha. Anyway the tree didn't grow very high but stayed kind of stunted.

And I lived in my small room and worked at my desk and lay on my bed and was lazy often and read lots and wrote in my diary, and always vaguely afraid of my mother and was so desperate at the end and so truly in love with Mikaere.

And was it really me, who is now?

I only remembered all this suddenly because I thought tonight, in Auckland, of those times. Mikaere has written to me, rather formally – our first correspondence since that – night. To say he has won a scholarship to travel overseas, to visit several countries to discuss improving NZ tourism. I am trying to find words to write him a really pleased, proper friendly, not formal, letter back, and so the memory of – a different me – came back.

XV

SATURDAY 10 OCTOBER 1959

I am at the kitchen table in our Auckland flat immersed in Coleridge, and Wordsworth – who Peter Dronke called Pie-Face – and in Dorothy Wordsworth's lovely journals, and in the sadness of the story of Swift – and Stella who waited in Ireland and how he would write to her just before he went to sleep at night, and Hazlitt who describes Coleridge and Wordsworth so wonderfully and Pope who was nice underneath and needed to be loved, and opium-taking Coleridge reproved in his writing sometimes and Byron was an odd one, but I like some of his poetry and old Defoe trading away in the goods of the world.

I am wondering (if there's still people) how they will describe the twentieth century in a hundred years. The age of atom bombs and rock and roll and racial tensions and stern T.S. Eliot, and Dylan Thomas whose life is reminiscent of the 18th-19th century Romantics, and jazz and angry young men being angry all over the place, and psychology. Perhaps they'll use the term human sympathy, no, human understanding. Everyone is so busy trying to understand themselves these days (what else have I been doing in my diaries for years!), I suppose it was always so (but nowadays there's more textbooks to tell you how to do it!). At least it means that we look back to other ages and don't condemn out-of-hand people like Pope or Byron or Swift or Coleridge or Hazlitt, but rather look to the reason for them being that way.

Out of the window, everyone coming home drunk after football, and that's what they always do on a Saturday.

The exams finished: plans had to be made. Whatever the exam results, we would give up this Auckland flat at the end of the year. Esther was going to go back to Wellington to train to be a social worker. Win was not going to finish her degree or her teacher-training yet; she and Peter had decided to get married and go to England together, so our tentative travelling plan was dropped . . . I am so – I have lost her, but I am so, so glad for her with the real part of my heart. And I meant to say before about Win – how wonderful she is, trying not to hurt me now, now that she loves someone else besides me, not wanting me to feel left out, but wanting to go with Peter terribly, to be married to him and go to London with him, in the middle of next year. Yet she was so wonderful when it was me and Mikaere and her a third one, and I am sure I was not nearly so considerate.

We had last parties in the flat (and I doubt Esther or Win ever missed them!): guitars and beer, singing all the old songs and dancing, the cleaning up on Saturday mornings of dozens of brown beer bottles and cigarette butts and fish and chip papers.

I had stopped using the term 'pseudo-intellectuals' because

I had become friends with a number of people in the English Department who weren't all 'pseudo' after all. I went to different sorts of parties: once on a moored boat lit with candles, with a string quartet playing Mozart. Little groups in the candlelight, a full moon and stars . . . the poets's son – Wystan – who is now my friend and a real intellectual – talking earnestly and quietly to Mike (who called me a wog-lover once) and Max (who told me he was writing a poem about me). Wystan gesticulating with his pipe and his hair in his eyes and at one end of the boat a couple slowly rocking and rolling – to Mozart . . .

FRIDAY 11 DECEMBER 1959

And so. After everything: I have my Bachelor of Arts degree. This has been such a – year – funny to think I passed English III and Maori II <u>and</u> was employed <u>as well</u>! How much I enjoyed the study this year. There is no Maori III or I would have gone on. When the Maori results came out kind, lovely John Waititi came puffing in to the Welfare Department, he'd found out I had got a B pass and he – and Arapeta, and everyone – they were so pleased and – proud of me. I was so <u>glad</u>. My job as a clerk in the Welfare Department is pretty good but really hectic, I should write much more about my crazy boss, Arapeta Awatere – I really admire him. He was a Lieutenant-Colonel in the Maori Battalion, he has a bayonet scar right across his stomach, and says yes, he killed lots of Japanese but always gave them a feed first. He has lots of flaws that I can see so clearly (he's a bit mad actually!) but he is enthusiastic and dynamic and forthright and hard-working – though it is so hard to keep the office statistics because he goes about things in such funny ways (and composes music in the interview room). But he is fantastic and I feel really lucky to work with him. Interesting Welfare Officers' conference a few weeks ago and I learnt a lot – simply had to concentrate because I was minute-taking! I like the Welfare Officers all around this northern district, and here Connie Smith especially, she helps me with my Maori sometimes. But I sure don't want to be a welfare officer now – must be Maori welfare officers. Now Peta wants me and Wally Tukukino to train as Interpreters for the Courts. We stay after work, he has set up a blackboard to teach us some of the legal terms. It's interesting but I know I'm not nearly good enough for all this legal stuff, and already we had to cancel some of the lessons because Peta is so busy with so many things, there's always people wanting him, phoning or calling in, or shouting 'Where IS he?' as if he had an ordinary job and ordinary hours, poor man!

Arapeta Awatere, this extraordinary, energy-expending, charismatic, war-damaged man from whom I learnt a great deal, was, some years later and ill, convicted of murder, a 'crime of passion' against a rival. He died in prison where, for years, he had worked with prisoners so dedicatedly. And still did, I bet, until the day he died.

. . . Good party the other night in the Courtroom – farewell for one of the old bosses, Mr Sullivan. All the bosses got tight, and then sentimental about the War as usual – Peta led the haka and we finished up singing old war songs – 'Tipperary', 'Pa mai', then I sang 'A Nightingale Sang in Berkeley Square' (where there were never nightingales apparently!)

Mum and Dad want me to be capped in Wellington. But I've decided to myself I would only go if Mikaere goes with me as I did to his. We are friendly now in the proper way and I will ask him. Otherwise I will just be capped, 'in absentia' as it is called, for getting a degree by rattling about to three universities.

I wonder where I will live next. Must find a place. Christmas carols outside.

FRIDAY 18 DECEMBER 1959

The papers are telling me all about the success of Mikaere Rangi and his scholarship and cleverness and his bosses saying how good he'll be for the Shipping Business and Tourism . . .

SATURDAY 26 DECEMBER 1959

Dunno how I caught the Limited down to Wellington on Christmas Eve, finally moving the last things out of our flat, trying to finish off stuff at work, but the welfare problems dont stop just because it's Christmas, the band that had been playing carols in the street suddenly at the party in the court-room, playing St Louis Blues for us to slow-jive to; drinking a glass of cider with Arapeta, 'taua, taua'; somehow not being able to find Esther for the keys to the flat – Wystan found me and guided me, cidered, to her in a kind and gentlemanly manner; more dancing and packing, collapsing on to the Limited with thirty seconds to spare. Mikaere met the train in the middle of the night in the middle of the North Island! 'Merry Christmas'; Dad met me in Wellington, 'Merry Christmas' and then home to the smell of a Christmas tree and lots of letters and cards and nice to see all the family again. Gosh I've missed Andrew and Ross and we've done the dishes lots and sung 'Peggy Sue' and 'Blue Suede Shoes'.

❀

I STARTED 1960 BRIEFLY LIVING by myself in a flat (my diary says the rent was £7/10/0 per month) that used — I think — to be part of an Auckland brothel. The story may have been apocryphal: drunk voices echoed often from somewhere but I received no unexpected callers except the odd rat, and it was a great place for our ongoing parties, the girls from work waiting with fish and chips for the boys turning up with crates of DB Bitter and a guitar after the pubs closed at 6 p.m. and the bosses arriving in government cars. I had arranged to live with one of the girls from Maori Affairs, Mary Hume (whose father was a bank manager who believed healthy physical exercise was much more important than reading, so Mary used to sit reading under the dining-room table, hidden by a long tablecloth). But our Housing boss, Bert — who loved the parties — was nevertheless shocked that his workers should live with rats, and arranged that when Mary and I moved in together we should have one of the state flats in Greys Avenue, and my friend from Maori Welfare, Connie Smith, would be living upstairs in the same block with some of the other Māori women who didn't find it easy to get places to live . . . and I wanted to write about this, because it shocks me. Lately I had tea (fish and chips in an old car on an old wharf when he came off duty) with Police Constable Fred, or 'laughing Fred' as I used to call him when he worked at Maori Affairs and wheeled the Records Trolley around and laughed, and winked at me because of what we knew. Whose eyes are so dead, now that he's one of the Maori policemen. He told me that when he went to Police Training School they had to watch lots and lots of 'pornography' and violent things, night after night. Can that be true? Was he kidding? The Police? Why would they watch those things? Was he making it up? But god how he changed. Like his eyes died is all I can say, another expression I thought was just in books. But – the light went out. He used to make me laugh more than anyone I had ever met and he loved peeling potatoes! And now he 'has to get married' as we say, and the other night when we had those fish and chips in the car he cried in his policeman's uniform with his handcuffs tied to his belt because he cares for another Maori girl more. Poor everybody, and watch out for 'pornographized' cops.

When I did turn the magic age of twenty-one I was working in the Welfare Office as usual, but some of the boys in other parts of Maori Affairs came and collected me at 4.35 p.m. sharp when the pens went down, and took me and some of the other girls to the pub (the Lounge Bar, of course, where ladies could go if accompanied by a gentleman). But the barman wouldn't serve us because he didn't believe I was twenty-one, so finally I got all my birthday cards out of my bag to prove my age. My parents were very keen for me to have a 'proper' twenty-first birthday party in their house in Wellington . . . nice to see old friends, Mum and Dad did go to a lot of trouble: they are good to me (though Mum actually vacuumed while the guests were still there!).

In Auckland, even in our more respectable abode my new flatmate Mary and I could still hear drunks shouting in night streets and loud music echoed in from the city. And indeed sometimes music echoed out from our own windows when we had the same old parties: beer and fish and chips and a guitar after 6 p.m.

There was a strange, uneasy half-open door at the bottom of Greys Avenue; a friend and I blundered in one night and saw Chinese men in white clothes lying on bunks, calmly smoking strange pipes, and we blundered out again. It was an 'opium den', but we didn't know what an opium den was.

MAY 1960

Hardly ever write now. But I should at least have recorded – and how bizarre is this – Matt Te Hau and Brownie Puriri and Arapeta all had a meeting with me earlier in the year, to tell me (they treat me a bit like they own me sometimes) that I had to be a tutor at a Maori Language Adult Education Class because they were so short of teachers and there is some interest from people now in learning Maori. So: I am! Poor pupils getting me once a week, I don't think I'm that good at it, and they didn't really want me, at least half of them, they wanted 'a real Maori' and so those ones didn't come much. But a few have held on, still coming, still interested, still learning. But O Lucky Me, meeting Beth Ranapia.
Recently, on a train, I met that old first Auckland 'boyfriend' that I had that stupid 'affair' with, a surprise for both of us, we were slightly embarrassed and not sure what to say so we read together what Princess Margaret's butler said.

And against all the odds, there we were last night, me and Mikaere, he was in Auckland working, and we stayed up together until 3.30am – happier than we've been for a long time. I'm so glad. After that hurtful, terrible time, we became friends again, first by letters, carefully written. He thanked me for writing the first proper one. He wouldn't take me to the Capping Ball in Wellington – he is already 'involved' elsewhere – huh, so am I, a hundred times at least – so I supposed it couldn't be 'explained'.

So: the end of four years chasing all over the country for that BA ended when I was capped, in absentia, here in Auckland – the actual piece of paper a nothing to me after everything, but oh how much I – learnt.

Last night Mikaere's cautious barrier was down, we laughed together a lot, and remembered many things – I'd forgotten some of them. Odd that we should spend an evening and be almost happy, after all. He'll be leaving New Zealand soon.

XVI

MARIA DRONKE, WHO HAD BEEN so much of my life when I was younger, and who I'd always kept in touch with, asked if she could stay in our flat when she came to give a poetry recital in Auckland. I filled my bedroom with flowers for her because I knew how much she loved them. I remember — and wrote in my diary — that the first thing she did as she came into the room was quickly turn over a hand mirror so she couldn't see the glass. Theatrical lore: bad luck.

I of course went to the poetry reading, heard again the beautiful voice that I loved so much. She read New Zealand poetry as she always did, and T.S. Eliot as she always did, and I heard the old words: *'Time present and time past are both perhaps present in time future and time future contained in time past'*. I only found out much later that Maria had made a recording of *Four Quartets* from which these lines had come: T.S. Eliot himself had very much approved of her reading.

Before she left again she asked me about my life in Auckland and did not contain her huge disappointment when I told her. 'But — have you given up all acting, Barbie?' she said. 'Why aren't you acting again now that your studies are finished?' I didn't have any answer. She kissed me goodbye, still — I could feel it — disappointed in one of her special old pupils . . . I am so, so tired – and I find again and again that it is these moments when I see things in almost absolute clarity. My future for the first time is – myself. No Mikaere, no Win, no exams, no boy holding me in the night. No slum-living and madnesses. No mother to insist. No anyone. Just my own – weaknesses. Or strengths? I will do it. I WILL act again. But first – life's realities: the doctor says I – finally – must have my tonsils out now!

I had my tonsils out in Wellington, Mum 'insisted' — but I was glad and grateful she had: it didn't go as smoothly as expected. When it was at last over I had to do a lot of sitting and recuperating in my parents' house and looking out those windows over Wellington again. And I felt . . . unbelonging . . . in this city where things had changed forever. Win and Peter got married, went to London. As soon as I was more or less better, I got ready to go back to Auckland and whatever it might hold. And . . . Last night Mikaere and I met accidentally, I hadn't even told him I was here. In a coffee bar, very dark – first time we have ever been at the same place but not together. And that same tiredness, that makes me see things suddenly clearly. I was so conscious of him, his arm resting on my chair. And the way our eyes met when a man sang 'He Wawata': of course he was conscious too. And I knew that until the day I die part of me, however small, will belong to – what happened to us. That's all. Today he rang me and we talked for a long time with a kind of quiet intimacy. He leaves in a week. I suppose that is the last time we will ever talk to each other . . . Outside the big windows, the sun has gone, except for the tops of the hills in the distance.

XVII

. . . I WILL act again . . . I had written in my diary.

Maria Dronke, my special teacher, had been very surprised at — and disappointed in — me. I was one of her 'special' students, she knew how much I had wanted to be an actress. She didn't think such an ambition was a dream: she *was* an actress, she thought I had the talent to be one also and had spent a lot of time working hard with me. When she asked me that question, 'Have you given up acting?', I hadn't been on stage for four years. I had once spent a sort of sad couple of weeks working backstage for the annual university 'Extrav' show that was put on at the Wellington Opera House; I wasn't even on that stage I had once worked on as a schoolgirl: I was checking the props backstage — and I knew I was soon going to Dunedin.

And I had learned to think my hopes had just been dreams.

But her disappointment — and her words — had affected me. Maybe I was ready for them at last. As soon as I was recovered from the operation I was back at work in Auckland and had found myself acting work as well (unpaid of course, evenings and weekends) in an amateur arts company.

SUNDAY 25 SEPTEMBER 1960

I'M ACTING AGAIN.

Real, real happiness this morning, walking early in the beginning-summer sun to a rehearsal of 'Uncle Vanya'. I am acting again at last, I cant even begin to explain what it feels like to be back again at last. Playing Sonya, a wonderful part I can really do something with. Knowing that – something happens when the acting goes really well. I don't know what it is but – something happens.

Sonya says: 'Work. We must work.' Chekhov understands people's hearts. It's my job, through Sonya, to make people feel his understanding

I cant quite believe I'm writing the words: I'm acting again.

I LOVE IT.

XVIII

SUNDAY 9 OCTOBER 1960

God I love rehearsing 'Uncle Vanya'. I love this play. I love Chekhov.

Hard hard work. Magical work sometimes.

Ronnie Barker is the director, a strange short man with a thin black moustache who helps me draw Sonya out, but keep her in as well. Yes.

Learning my lines in spring sunshine.

Mary and I had dinner with some of the old Teachers' Training College guys, teachers now. October late sunshine, and the smell of roast mutton cooking in the old house some of them live in and school books to be marked, and one of the teachers, Bill Tawhai, telling us about his father. His father only went to primary school but nevertheless, while he was milking the cows on their small farm past Opotiki, near Te Kaha, he used to recite Shakespeare loudly, the kids could easily hear it outside the milking shed, because he – the father – thinks Maori oratory and Shakespeare are very alike. I do appreciate that connection.

And who persuaded Bill's parents to let him stay on in the sixth form, and go on to University and Teachers' Training College in Auckland? How amazingly co-incidental is this? My Maori teacher Beth Ranapia. Who used to teach down on the East Coast. How much so many people owe that amazing teacher! Beth Ranapia ought to have a statue!
An old man of 90 who is the landlord of the house shared the meal too. He has lovely very white hair, lots of it, and he said he has kept all his hair because he only ever uses cold water to wash it and no soap.
Bill, of the Shakesperean-cattle-milking father, speaks beautiful, beautiful Maori – spoke it at home as a kid, says he thinks and dreams in Maori. He's a nice man, I really like him – it was him who cooked the roast!

The East Coast? Their farm past Opotiki, near Te Kaha?
Te Kaha? Ummmm . . .
I hope not exactly exactly near the place we had that awful camping holiday with Auntie Ellie and Uncle Erling and the twins and Sally and I wanted to stay on in Maungatapu and sulked!? And I spat chewing gum on the road by the Te Kaha shop – on my sixteenth birthday I think. (I didn't mention that!)

XIX

SUNDAY 29 JANUARY 1961

Months pass. I don't really write any more.

'Uncle Vanya' so successful. God I loved doing it. And wont stop acting now.

I was in Wellington for Christmas. An afternoon with my wonderful Maria, she (and I) so glad I am acting; she talking about her 'university life', and brandy at tea-time, now she and dear John Dronke have gone to Europe for a while and Vanessa and Cath are on their way too. Win happy in London. Irv is getting married, which of course means our friendship cant go on the same. But it is a friendship that I've valued so much, and am grateful for, and he is too I know.

Mikaere writes from across the sea to say he has turned to the Moral Re-armament Church. He writes that he has forgiven my family.

My brother Ross was a schoolboy when he was caught up in the troubled past in our home. Many, many years later, and now a doctor, he one day attended a tangi and saw that Mikaere was one of the kaumātua standing at the meeting-house door greeting visitors. When Ross came to him in the line he put out his hand and said, 'We used to know one another. I'm Ross Ewing, Barbara's brother.'

Mikaere did not put out his hand. He silently looked straight through my brother as though he was not there, and turned to the next guest.

❀

AUGUST 1961

I used to keep a diary and now I don't. Months since I last wrote.
Win and Peter settled in London, Win expecting a baby.
I have left Maori Affairs (but still go to the parties in the courtroom of course!) All those old bossy kaumatua round the Maori Affairs Department put their heads together about me again as if they are in charge of me! and I'm now a Vocational Guidance Officer for Maori Girls for the Auckland and Northland region. (And an Actress.) And sometimes in my work I think of Violet Holder and hope I can – somehow – make a difference. But – oh it is very hard in the schools up North.

❀

. . . One of the women we know phoning me so triumphantly. I didn't realise Maori women had such a problem with us, as well as my mother. That was so stupid of me. So much I didn't understand.
But there are no secrets in Maori-land, so I knew about this anyway.
Mikaere has married his Maori girlfriend.

XX

WHEN I NEXT PICKED UP my pen again I was in my Vocational Guidance office. It was May 1962, months and months later. And I wrote and wrote and wrote in my diary, pages and pages, all on that one day. As if I was catching up with myself.

MAY 1962

Hello Diary.

Here I am.

At the moment I am rehearsing another play at night. But in the daytime here I am, a Maori Vocational Guidance Officer in the Education Department (writing this in the office), helping mostly Maori girls in Auckland and up north. I speak Maori quite fluently now and – I think – know and understand some of the girls a little bit. I have bought some pale pink glasses with plain glass in them, to look a bit older. In this job we drive up to the far north, to the schools up there, me and John Tapiata, who interviews all the boys. I love going up there, another world: native bush, same old manuka trees everywhere, small towns, the sea. And, autumn now, I still paddle at the Ninety-Mile beach as we go furthest north, to Houhora. Often stay in Awanui. And often at Kawakawa, where the railway line runs down the middle of the street, sitting on the verandah of the rickety old Kawakawa Hotel in the cold, 'Sad Movies' playing somewhere. Then talking to the girls about nursing and teaching ('I want to be a hairdresser,' they say), next morning at Motatau School.

Last visit up North I took with me my lines to learn for this play I am rehearsing!

And the last time I was in Wellington Mum was clearing out junk in the basement. She had tied string round all my old diaries and journals that I'd left when I moved to Auckland and, cross about something, she sort of shoved them at me, saying 'do what you like with them but I'm clearing them out of here'. Maybe she read them? But – I doubt it – too against her particular set of principles. Now what shall I do with them . . .?

The question arose because, as well as working as a Maori Vocational Guidance Officer I was supposed to be leaving the country.

At the end of 1961 I had just — suddenly — applied for, and won, a Government Drama Bursary for two years' study in London. I had been encouraged to do this by two very supportive people: Jack Tressider, the drama critic (and I think skiing reporter) on the *Auckland Star*, and Kenneth Poitevin, an amateur actor who had been in *Uncle Vanya* and was planning to go to London, where his family came from, and audition at a place I'd never heard of but which he described to me as 'the most famous acting school in the whole world': the Royal Academy of Dramatic Art . . . Seems queer, even now . . . and when I finished the interview and the audition (Tennessee Williams), it was so peculiar, I got that old feeling, of sort of sensing the room. I knew I'd won it, and all I thought was 'What have I done?'

But I kept *not* going to England, so that I think government officials finally got in touch, stating they would take the bursary away if I didn't send them my travel plans. I managed to put it off till September, helped by the fact I was rehearsing a play for the Auckland Festival. My friend from Carrington Hall in Dunedin, Lynley Orbell, was going to travel with me on the ship to London, the *Fairsea*, via Ceylon and Suez and Naples. Win and Peter were looking for a house to buy in London and if they found one I could rent a room from them. But . . . the idea of actually leaving N.Z. has been terrifying me. I cant – untangle myself.

So: I had — at last — chosen to change my life but was having a bit of trouble doing the changing. I liked the vocational work — but I was actually going to train as an actress. Now I was in another amateur production, the Grafton Theatre Company's production of Richard Beynon's *The Shifting Heart* for the 'FABULOUS FOURTEENTH AUCKLAND FESTIVAL', as it was advertised in the *New Zealand Herald*. The Fabulousness included much more prestigious performers than us, like Inia Te Wiata, the well-known bass-baritone who had become famous 'overseas', and Luisilla and His Spanish Dance Theatre who arrived on the ship the *Wanganella*.

The Shifting Heart is an Australian play about Italian immigrants and the difficulties and even violence they encountered in their new country. We played in the hall of St Andrew's Church in Symonds Street — the old church is still there but the church hall is now a car park. (At the same time as advertising the Fabulous Fourteenth Festival the same newspaper mentioned in an article some life-expectancy figures in New Zealand. Pākehā men: sixty-eight years. Māori men: fifty-four years. No mention of women.)

And so I had entered 'the theatre world': a world with which I was fairly unfamiliar despite all those Virgin Marys and school plays and Wellington Repertory schoolgirls. I didn't really know how to 'talk the talk' about productions and actors the way the others did. And I don't remember Maria Dronke ever using the phrase 'the theatre world'. There was no professional theatre in Auckland, but there were a number of amateur companies, just as in Wellington; and some of the actors in *The Shifting Heart* made some money, I think, in radio, and one had been in the New Zealand Players which was now defunct, but mainly they had to have other jobs as well, as I did — we all did it for love, not money. But I had popped up out of nowhere almost, and felt uneasy and out-of-place . . . and it's funny having coffee with the cast: I really feel un-belonging, a kind of weird stranger in the middle of their theatrical talk that I don't know how to do.

Obviously it was very quiet in the Vocational Guidance Office that May day in 1962, totally unlike the Maori Welfare Office. I went on and on writing:

> . . . I so miss Andrew and Ross, always glad when I see them, but not often enough. And will be going so far away from them so soon. Both left home quick. I'm so glad Ross has his heart's desire! he's in the Air Force, flying planes at last instead of trying to be one. Andrew, Christchurch engineering student, has a nice girlfriend, Gill, and will

probably be married very soon. And the 'older' sister? 23 years old and so many of my friends (and soon one of my brothers) married and settled and having babies, and I take off to the other side of the world, god I'm so glad Lynley is coming too on the ship, makes such a difference. And that I'll have somewhere to live in London.

No kids at home now. Once the boys had gone too Mum smashed down one of lounge walls and cancelled their bedroom and made the lounge bigger and put a piano in the space which she plays, occasionally. The few times I go home now she spoils me immensely and I really really do try not to be hard, to be a proper daughter.

But: she damaged me (and Mikaere and I damaged – and preserved – ourselves) – but she damaged Mikaere most of all and she still doesn't understand that. If she would accept any of my Maori friends now it would help her and me (even Ross says that aged 18 – an Air Force Pilot cadet!) – but she wont. No Maoris.

I don't miss Mikaere any more in the old way. But I still think of him sometimes, and what happened to us both. His letter about joining Moral Re-armament that time somehow made me want to cry – for him not for myself. MORAL-RE-ARMAMENT, what does that mean? It sounds like righteous guns.

I wrote in that very long entry on that autumn day that I couldn't 'untangle' myself. And — the only time ever in the diaries, I think — I admitted something, briefly. That I was on the whole not admitting or accepting.

That I, as well as Mikaere, had been damaged.

From so many years away, I see again the threads. As I read the very few entries of this time I am aware of something unspoken, mostly unwritten. Part numb, part reckless, I was making life-changing decisions, but casually, between parties, as if I was cleaning my teeth at the same time and didn't really care. The splinter of concrete. Splinters fester if they don't work their way out.

I might have settled into a serious, loving, long-term relationship: I couldn't.

> . . . I just cant seem to be able to 'settle down' like so many of – most of – my friends do. I became so fond of Bill, and we had some good times. He played Othello in a University production – HEROIC to play a big part like that out of the blue! – told of taking his copy to his home near Te Kaha and he and his Shakespeare-loving father making everyone pass the script around the kitchen table and play all the other parts, which helped him learn his lines! And he went to India, sent with some other boys by NZ Rotary, sent back proud photos of them with a dead tiger!
>
> But I – everything is my fault.
>
> I just – couldn't.
>
> I applied for the Bursary one day. I won it. I am going to London: Q.E.D. Bill said I am too selfish – because I chose the Bursary over him. We hardly see each other at all any more.
>
> I go to parties. I push the future away. And try not to think about anything.
>
> Ha. Just as I was writing that, Cherry Raymond from Broadcasting rang the office. She interviewed me for the Women's Session when I won the Bursary. She wants me

to audition for the part of a ten-year-old Maori boy for a programme she's doing called 'Hey Boy'.

That ludicrous casting. That's how it was, then.

SATURDAY 5 MAY 1962

4.15am. Coughing, but laughing. Just been to a party. This is so peculiar, reminds me of how it once was – look at me, no matter how late, writing at least something in my diary. This afternoon Jackie, from Maori Affairs, who has been living in our nice flat too, which makes it nicer, and I, went to the rugby at Eden Park: cheering crowds and cold. Then tonight we made tea and drank some cooking wine and laughed – she talks right out of a Jane Austen book: 'Now, my dear little lady, what opinions do you hold concerning this mauve gown I propose wearing this evening?' And then she and I went to a crowded party – lots of singing, and lots of beer and laughter and – as she calls it – 'inebriation'. 'I Fall to Pieces'. 'Tahi Nei Taru Kino'. Rehearsal later today so I better chuck this apple core out of the window and try and get some sleep. Yesterday I finished a whole long report for the Boss on Maori Vocational Guidance and I haven't learnt all my lines!

I was now a respectable civil servant by day, a rehearsing actress evenings and weekends — but still a party girl. And on Sunday mornings we would finally drag ourselves out of bed, put music on loud on our gramophone, and while Mary read the *Listener* Jackie and I would do the latest dance craze, 'the twist', in our night attire to wake ourselves up — then I had to go to a rehearsal for *The Shifting Heart*.

I also knew that as soon as the two-week run of the play was over I had to visit the girls in the schools up North — it would be for the last time — but I didn't give a thought for one moment to 'looking after myself'. As we got nearer to the opening of the play I got one of those familiar hacking coughs. I had already understood, from my small experience, about the amount of stamina acting in the theatre required, and I still had great trouble sleeping. What I hadn't yet learnt was the importance of training your stamina, supporting it with food and rest . . . umbrellas cross Queen Street outside the office window and the paper boy calls out the 'Star' and the traffic squelches past and time for me to go home and then go to the last rehearsals. This cough not good. I feel funny and then too warm, and then cough.

I was also at this very same time being stalked (we didn't know this word then) by a married man, another of my 'unsuitable' relationships. He had told me he was separated from his wife and sometimes even brought his three little boys to visit me; so when his wife — not separated at all — contacted me, and said the little boys had been told not to mention her at all when they saw me, I was so shocked and mortified that for weeks and weeks I had refused to even see him. He now wept and hid in the bushes by the block of flats, and followed me and, if I was picked up by a Vocational Guidance vehicle, put his face against the car window and banged on it. One of my flatmates said I had to see him: '. . . he might kill himself . . .' Finally his wife asked me to see him: '. . . he's a mess, I'm frightened he'll do something mad . . .' I saw him, and his wife, and his children, and we ate doughnuts, and his wife once told me . . . how she loved, when she was a little girl, watching the shadows of her ringlets dancing as she was playing . . . and the children waited for me at bus stops. (And so bizarre are narrative and plot and threads sometimes that I still see that family, and the children — and the grand-children — to this day.)

All that madness — and vocational reports, and visiting schools, and rehearsals, and parties — all going on at the same time.

TUESDAY 22 MAY 1962

Coughing a lot, same bloody illness as usual but the bloody tonsils operation was supposed to bloody fix this! Hot lemon juice and disprin for morning tea while teaching the Senior Vocational Guidance officers the new dance, the 'twist'. I've used Government Medical Supplies of cotton-wool that I took from the office (with the boss's approval!) to stuff the big Woolworths 36" bra to hide my skinniness and help me look pregnant for this play and had my dyed hair dyed brown to look Italian – it's now something the same colour as my eyebrows!

This (I did not know it) was only the first of many times I would have to stuff a big bra with cotton wool to enhance my small bosom — though this was the only time it was done to look pregnant. I could, indeed, write a whole chapter on false bosoms. Having being 'enhanced' with one in a Hammer Horror movie at the beginning of my career and becoming a minor cult heroine on account of this (no matter how often I publicly protested it was cotton wool), I was destined to be followed around by this appendage. It had another — large — triumph in a Granada TV series called *Brass*, and then in 2018 it, and I, suddenly appeared again on sale on Amazon in the form of tea towels, mugs, mouse mats, postcards, posters and fridge magnets — until the threat of legal action intervened.

The Glamorous Life: I am a fridge magnet.

FRIDAY 25 MAY 1962

Last two nights have collapsed into bed after rehearsal with special hot lemon drink and disprin. Have got a foul throat and cough, God knows how it will be for the opening tomorrow night. I look terrible. The set for 'The Shifting Heart' is terrific, oh I hope it goes well when it opens tomorrow night, and I don't cough. Ngaio Marsh came to a dress rehearsal last night – said she couldn't hear some because of the Italian-Australian accents. I wondered about that. We open tomorrow.

SATURDAY 26 MAY 1962

1.15am. The audience stamped!!! I think it went really well – I think it will be a success. And I think I was ok too. I met the Minister of Internal Affairs, Mr Gotz, afterwards and he seemed quite pleased he's given me the Bursary even though I'm taking a long time to go (!) Oh thank goodness. I feel such relief that it has opened well. I managed to control my cough by swigging at my bottle of cough mixture off-stage.

The Shifting Heart was so well reviewed (although the *Herald* reviewer said my 'voice didn't match up to her fiery temper') and so successful that the run was booked out and then extended for a further week, after a break of one week . . . but God that week off I cant have a rest, I must go on the trip up North to the schools there, that is the main part of my job and I must do it to see how those girls are getting on before I leave New Zealand. But what a fantastic success is what I should be writing, the audience really love this play. More stamping and extra curtain calls. If only I didn't feel so hot and sick.

SUNDAY 10 JUNE 1962

Sick.
Play now off for one week but I must must go north tomorrow. Mary has flu, maybe it's that, Jackie trying to look after us both but she isn't well either. I keep vomiting and very high temperature.

TUESDAY 12 JUNE 1962

Doctor came. Couldn't go north. Pneumonia.

My mother came to Auckland at once and dealt with doctors, TB enquiries, antibiotics, and made nourishing soups and meals: took total charge of the flat and its inhabitants for a week, as well as (I presume now) sleeping on a sofa. And when she left, she arranged for my eighteen-year-old brother Ross, who had some leave from the Air Force, to take her place. The extended run of *The Shifting Heart* began with someone else playing my part until I could get there — and the run was to be extended yet again . . . Doctor says I can now have little walks. Saw Bill this morning. He took me and Ross to Takapuna in a car he borrowed and we walked a bit on the wet sand in the grey morning and watched seagulls. Very peculiar, walking. I don't think Bill and I can feel much any more, too much went wrong. But I am glad it is sort of friendly, and it was really kind of him, hearing I'd been ill, to take us so we could walk by the sea . . . Oh if only I could just get to the theatre. But I cant.

But. With Ross there — making eggnogs and cooking steak and buying Winning Post chocolates, and making me laugh and showing off the latest, newest machine, a portable tape-recorder — I improved immeasurably. He was like a tonic, and back came that odd mad resilience that I had always been able to call on . . . now after two weeks at last at last at last I don't have a temperature so: I asked the doctor please please could I just try to do the play on Monday for the last week and if I fail will give it up completely. He knows the situation and wasn't very happy. Knows I keep sweating all the time but he sees how sensible Ross is and I kept saying I know I can do it and he finally said ok, try . . . Ross took me for another walk along the sand and the rocks at Castor Bay in the winter cold with three jerseys and a duffle coat, and he put his portable tape recorder on the sand, turned it on, and we did the twist to 'Ma, He's Making Eyes At Me'. And then we came home and had steak and chocolates and played Dinah Washington singing 'Where Are You?' and then he went through my part with me and I got puffed in the big emotional scenes, but I got through . . . Ross is wonderful . . . really I've made terrific progress – last Sunday I couldn't even get out of bed. I think I'm really quite a wiry person for all my skinniness . . . I rang the theatre and said I'd be there on Monday. I was.

MONDAY 25 JUNE 1962

About 7pm I sneezed and my nose started to bleed and visions of TB floated before my eyes. But I got there and everyone was pleased and it was ok – good in fact, though puffed, and the audience cheered. I feel SO relieved. The first thing I heard was that there is going to be a FURTHER extension – Mon, Tues, Wed of next week (with – wow – profits to be shared among the cast and back-stage crew! So I will be paid to act!) – but I feel so comforted that Sue, who has been standing-in, is around. She turned up tonight – I guess they weren't too sure – and I was so simply relieved to see her there. But I couldn't have done this without Ross. Twisting in the damp sand at Castor Bay got me moving and breathing properly again.

They have been so good at work – I also went in to see them today to apologise; now I've taken a few days unpaid leave – I just couldn't go back to both. That trip up North has been postponed for two weeks, hallelujah. I WILL see those girls once more.

MONDAY 2 JULY 1962

Ohhhhh. Ross has gone, and I'm back at work today. But I bought a cigarette lighter for him and ran home from work and cooked him steak for his lunch just before he left. He has been so marvellous. On Saturday night after the show he talked to me about the Air Force, and lots of the other men being older than him, and sex. And it's obviously a problem for him and I'm not sure of the right advice to give. I could be hypocritical and say all the expected conventional things but – I just cant do that somehow. I tried to say something useful that properly helps. I hope he will be happy. Once he gets past this lousy part-boy, part-man time. He's 18, still so young in many ways . . . I am so lucky to have a brother like him. I have also bought really nice presents for Mary and Jackie, to hell with money, because they have been so good to me through this long marathon. And I rang Mum too, to thank her. Tonight the audience stamped again and called 'Bravo!' 'I Fall to Pieces' on the radio. Ha. Indeed.

WEDNESDAY 4 JULY 1962

Sitting in a cold little room at Lynfield College in between interviews (writing my diary!), watching the cold sun melting the fog. Someone is sweeping the ashphalt, a violin is playing fairly uncertainly, and I can hear a typewriter. I just heard a teacher telling a girl off in such horrified tones and saying she'd tell her mother.

And then – tonight – I'll be on stage for the last performance. How bizarre.

I like this work. I like interviewing and seeing lots of different girls and noticing things about them. But in the city schools like this too many girls with angry eyes standing outside classrooms waiting to be told off. And voices of authority and some hatchet-faced Pakeha teachers. But oh no wonder so many of these Maori girls seem to want to leave these shiny new schools. Not like the schools up North. Ah, but 'the standard of education' everyone would say. And I see both sides now.

3.30am! – 'The Shifting Heart' had its absolutely absolutely last performance tonight. It was a good last show – then streamers, speeches and even press cameras – and pay! I like the smell of stage makeup and the dressing-room warming up as we arrive and the people – mostly. Apart from getting ill I found I 'settled' into the part after a while and got much better. But sad to do the play for the last time and horrible to walk on stage and see the set in pieces so quickly after the curtain came down. But – that's Show Business! AND schools up North next week!

XXI

AND INDEED THERE WE WERE, mid-winter, making the postponed visit to the schools right up near the top of New Zealand. School visits in the daytime, talking to visiting school inspectors one evening (and so cold that I was wearing in bed, I noted in my diary, jerseys, socks, spencer, singlet and my nightie). I had grown to love the North, driving along old roads, glimpses of sea through mānuka trees, cows huddling in fields, heavy rain now sometimes, and the window-wipers swishing back and forth. And still I was writing in my diary, almost like the old days.

TUESDAY 10 JULY 1962

Te Kao Maori District High School. 2pm. It seems so much the same. The hardest school I think, so far north and – away from things. Spent over an hour listening to the (Pakeha) Headmaster's troubles. I'm re-interviewing the girls I saw last time, but – truthfully – how much use am I being? – maybe not much here. A few I help, but not most of them. So many just – shrug when I ask about exams and suggest things. I think many of them just think they'll have kids soon so why bother. The sun is cold but it is sun.

Awanui Hotel. 11.45pm. When we'd finished our day at Te Kao we drove to Houhora and the hilarious 'Last Hotel in the North', where the cop phones first before he 'checks' after 6pm (!); dinner with John's friends then back here, driving erratically down thin dark winding roads and dead rabbits caught in the drunken headlights.

WEDNESDAY 11 JULY 1962

Taipa District High School. The (Pakeha) Headmaster has lent me his office to write up my notes. After assembly, kids run along the corridor to classrooms, that particular sound of kids running and shouting and laughing. I will miss all this. Some good girls here I hope I've helped, I'm making big amounts of notes on this trip so that I can write properly useful reports about each one for the next person. But – 'Hair-dresser' so many of them say. Should be more Maori teachers and headmasters – and Vocational Guidance Officers. And more books.

THURSDAY 12 JULY 1962

Kaeo District High School. I have just spent the most hilarious half hour. In the lunch hour the kids crowded into a classroom with half a dozen desks in the middle to prevent absolute shambles, to have dancing lessons (round and round the desks) for the school social next week. Heavy boys' boots crashing and clumping around, and giggling, and little boys dancing with big girls, and teachers making a couple of boys dance with me. Balling the Jack (?) – I didn't seem to know it! Kaeo is one of my favourite schools – it was the first one I came to – and by now I feel quite at home with the staff and the girls and have my lunch in the staffroom happily. I feel regretful that I wont be following things up, seeing how the girls are getting on. Already I notice a difference here: more maturity, less shyness with me. More ideas about what they might do. Maybe. But some teachers in the schools have said (to me) they'd rather talk to me than John about some of the Maori pupils because they don't have to be so – polite I think they mean – because he's a Maori – about things that they'd like to say about the Maori kids' lives here. Yes. But the trouble is they are all Pakeha teachers who say that. And I'm a Pakeha – and yes I do know what they mean and I understand it's a problem. But it's – in the end this cant be the way.

Midnight. Kawakawa Hotel. Motatau tomorrow and then back to Auckland. On the way down we stopped at Pahia and I watched the rough sea crashing and driftwood on the beach and it seems so – New Zealand somehow and – clot – I found I was crying. On to Kawakawa where Jim Pou from Maori Welfare and an artist-sculptor Arnold Wilson, were waiting for us in the bar – all immediately talking Maori nineteen to the dozen and me keeping up mostly: this funeral, that meeting, those people, that gossip, a few songs – this is how I learn still, the language. They ended up having a farewell mihi to me at one stage, Arnold and John and Jim Pou, 'Ahakoa he ma te kiri o te wahine nei, ko tana hinengaro he mea Maori.' White skin, Maori soul. (It isn't true, and I know it isn't true. But I know what they sort of mean. I learnt the language so I learnt other things.) And

> they went on to say I should, in fact I must, marry a Maori (ha) – and further comments that sound better in Maori! The main time I get lost in the Maori talk is when they're telling jokes in Maori talking faster and faster and drunk! – which always ends with terrific laughter and them bashing each other's shoulders.

My last day of interviewing young girls, trying to give them thoughts about, ideas for, their future was at Queen Victoria Maori Girls' School in Auckland. I felt I was just getting to know some of the girls there, and maybe getting through to some of them — and now I was at that school for the last time also. Perhaps they had learned something, at least, from me. I had learned from them. My very last interview before I was to go away across the sea to be an actress — which still felt like an odd dream — was spent learning a Māori song from one of the schoolgirls.

That night, for some reason, I dreamt of Mikaere.

After later studying and working in many places Mikaere Rangi returned home, totally involved forever in Māori matters, loved and respected among his people.

XXII

AND THEN SUDDENLY I WAS leaving in a month.

In my room in our Auckland flat I was surrounded by so many things. My books: I felt I had to take my New Zealand poetry books that I loved with me. And all my books of plays: Tennessee Williams, Chekhov, Ibsen, Shakespeare. My records: 'Rock Around the Clock', Elvis, 'Sad Movies', 'Crazy', Māori records — I had to take all that music with me. My photo albums: I had to have pictures of everybody. And the pile of old diaries. What should I do with them? I couldn't leave them here. My diary informs me I sat on my bed, surrounded by my life, and read C.P. Snow . . . who understands the machinations of the human mind so well. I would like to write as well as that. And how the physical scene is sometimes part of the moment (or the other way round). Auden said it too, as Maria explained with that red rose. And I recognise what they mean. When the moment is important one sort of – feels – the surroundings too . . .

The burglar I had met when I worked in the Maori Welfare Office who'd told me all about burgling, and I'd told him about extramural studying, had been back in prison for some time, and had enrolled at university — and was doing well. Sometimes on a Saturday afternoon I would take the bus to Mount Eden Prison and ask how it was going, talk about his studies. Now I had to go up there and say goodbye, though I knew that other friends would keep supporting him. (And I believe, very many years later, in between very many residences at Paremoremo Prison, and much help from a number of people — who sometimes found themselves unwittingly caught up in his escapades — he got his degree.) By the big door-gate as I left, a prison guard handed me one freesia and one gladioli — a goodbye present from the prison quarry: 'From your Māori friend,' said the Pākehā guard.

FRIDAY 24 AUGUST 1962

1.30am. The last party I'll ever go to at Maori Affairs – oh the stories those walls of the old courtroom with the shelves of old land records could tell! The best parties I've ever been to in my life were held in there! And dear Bert, the Housing boss, always insisting we mustn't report any bad behaviour to the police (strange people sometimes turned up, occasionally there was a purse stolen, or a fight) because then we'd get into trouble for using the Maori Land Court for parties!
John and I gave our speeches about Vocational Guidance for Maori pupils at the Careers Advisory Course today. Good. Then I had smallpox injection – cow's pus.

And then I got two somewhat seismic messages — on the same day.

MONDAY 27 AUGUST 1962

I've had a telegram from Lynley Orbell, she wont be coming on the 'Fairsea' and would I please cancel her berth. She is getting married.

So: I'll be going to England by myself after all.

And: a letter from Win to say, they haven't been able to find a house in London.

So: I wont be able to stay with them after all.

Jazz is pouring out of Vincent Street, loud.

A last party in the Auckland flat where we sang the old party songs together one more time; both my brothers arrived (and slept on the floor afterwards, surrounded by very many empty brown bottles). Shouts for Ross to sing his famous number 'Speedy Gonzales' (The Fastest Mouse in All Mexico)! Finally Ross absolutely insisted on accompanying Jackie and me to buy more fish and chips for everybody. We each held one of his arms, but he nevertheless tripped somewhat drunkenly and fell gently to the pavement from whence one of his funny voices (I think it was a line from Joe E. Brown in the film *Showboat*) echoed out into Karangahape Road: 'Now, look here, I think I'd better sit this one out!' And finally, nearly morning, we waved goodbye to the drunken government cars weaving down Greys Avenue.

And not many hours later I said goodbye to Andrew and Ross also — but not before Ross played us some of our somewhat raucous singing on his portable tape-recorder. We always thought we sang so beautifully!

But I felt — it was like panic when we said goodbye. And, oddly, I saw Andrew felt it too.

THURSDAY 6 SEPTEMBER 1962

Nearer. A letter from Win about her baby daughter, Jane. A jersey from Mum. Tickets. Labels for the boat. Bill and I met in a coffee shop. He told me (what I already knew ages ago of course, the kumara-vine is much more efficient than the grape-vine) that he is engaged to a Maori school teacher. I am glad anyway that we met and talked and said goodbye in a proper, friendly(ish) way. Then I walked home, my stiletto heels clicking past the poor men wanting a woman to pick up, wind blowing my hair everywhere. Raining.

What I wanted always was security and freedom. Cant be done.

Met Wystan Curnow for lunch. He is now father of ten week old Nathaniel.

FRIDAY 7 SEPTEMBER 1962

Left Vocational Guidance today. Desk cleared out. Last reports about the girls, and my recommendations as a Maori Vocational Guidance Officer, finished.

A visit to say goodbye to my grandmother, over eighty now, in Timaru. Conscious — and I was right — that I might never see her again. Cold feet in her little oven again as we used to, and she told me she would like me to be married one day, and she was sorry I had had such a difficult time 'and he had such a nice face', and I wrote in my diary how sad it was that her husband had died so young, when my father was fifteen, and what a wonderful young girl she must have been . . . she'd had her hair set, and she's very quiet if we go out anywhere, I think she misses quite a lot because she is going deaf but at home she is hilarious

– a real hard case, and makes me laugh. I've never thought of this before – maybe it is, after all through her that Dad and Ross have the same, very particular and funny, sense of humour . . . Again I wrote that if I grew old I would like to be like her — and I was still totally unaware of her story.

And now I *am* old, and she is here, young: she hangs on my wall in a beautiful oval colour-tinted photograph in a gilt frame, wearing an Edwardian gown: the Mayor's Lady. And now I do know her story: her husband the Mayor, Head of the Lodge, whisked away by his Masonic brothers, leaving her with three children and a shop and shame. And I remember that old lady who laughed at herself and her flutters on the horses and put her feet in the oven to keep warm, and her outside lavatory.

But of course I suddenly realise now.

My wish, if I grew old, came true. All those fragile fears that haunted my young life countered over and over again by that small, surprising, mad, determined resilience that I could always somehow find, deep down inside myself.

And — after all — that sense of humour.

My grandmother.

IF I *HAD* EVER WRITTEN any sort of formal autobiography (and if I'd burnt my diaries instead of reading them) it would have been very different from this.

It would — of course — have been less truthful.

And certainly less personal.

It would have been much more sophisticated, more glamorous: glitzier, the usual. I would have written (self-depreciatingly: I am a New Zealander after all) of my very lucky life as an actress, as a writer, all the books I have written, all those famous people I met, worked with, the wonderful parts I was lucky enough to play, the horror films, the huge stage roles, the leads in the TV series — all that stuff. And I certainly would not have investigated my younger self.

And so I would never have understood how the story — connects.

In my diaries I several times quote T.S. Eliot who says that time present and time past are both perhaps present in time future. And time future is contained in time past. What else have I been writing about here than that? I am sure now, when I consider the lives of others as well as my own, that there is more than the straight narrative to a life: its progression and its joys and its sorrows and its years. There are also the threads, *if we can find them.* That — ghostly sometimes — are weaving themselves through the narrative. Telling the real story.

The twenty-first-century historian-philosopher Yuval Noah Harari suggests the possibility that intelligent algorithms we humans have created may well make emotional intelligence obsolete: that these intelligent algorithms will learn, by the use of data, to know us better than we know ourselves. I'm glad I got here with my particular 'data' before an algorithm.

I know very well now that without facing up to the diaries I would have 'drawn myself' differently. My 'phantom' autobiography would have been, I guess, the picture of myself, and the past, that I had settled on, that I presented publicly. Even believed.

Sod's Law. I opened the diaries.

FRIDAY 14 SEPTEMBER 1962

11pm Wellington. I sat in the big front room of my parents' house all day. I heard unfamiliar familiar sounds: that grand-daughter clock chiming that we used to have in our old house. And Dad mowing the lawn. Sounds of another life. Cocoa in bed.

SUNDAY 16 SEPTEMBER 1962

Thank goodness the very last party is over, my parents' farewell party last night which Mum insisted they should arrange. Seemed ok. Finished up rather nicely with a few young ones twisting madly and drinking whisky that Dad was dispensing! BUT in the middle of it all Andrew turned up from Christchurch. He'd rung about 6pm to say goodbye, it was hard. He said goodbye – then he just jumped on a plane and flew up from Christchurch! And when everyone had gone, last ones before midnight (of course), he and I went and had coffee at the Mexicali Coffee shop – what a dive – and we talked and it was easier than we'd ever been before. We talked about everything and Gill and him getting married and I am so glad they will be happy and – just everything about our lives. He's nearly a chemical engineer already! If he hadn't come we mightn't have got this close – now it will always be all right. I'm so, so glad. Before we went to bed we tried to play (we can neither of us play) 'This Is a Lovely Way to Spend an Evening' on Mum's new piano, and laughed. He's gone now.

Before I left Wellington for the last time I had lunch with my old English teacher from college, Molly Gambrill, and thanked her.

She had taught me a great deal. My Māori teacher, Beth Ranapia, her red lipstick brightly applied, hugged me by the cable car, knowing — better than many — my story and I thanked her for all her knowledge and support. And I said goodbye to Irv, the married man now, who had been such a good friend to me. Maria Dronke, back from across the world, and I, on my way there, had brandy together, she so pleased about how my life had turned round at last; she of course was well on her way to achieving her degree in German and English Literature. And I thanked her. She had taught me so much, and had set me on my path.

And before I caught the night train I went up on the cable car and looked over the city of my youth one more time . . . Wellington doesn't hurt me now in that physical way, there's just – a shadow.

WEDNESDAY 19 SEPTEMBER 1962

Back in Auckland it seems strange, as though, really, I am already gone.

And I have said goodbye to my parents. Oh I hope they will be safely in their house looking over the city when I get back. It's – terrible to have to think of anything bad, illness, death. Anything.

But – Ohhh I have no idea what to say to my mother and we can never – be close until I find a way; maybe I have waited too long and will regret my – my hardness, my uselessness. But . . . I simply don't know what to say to her.

After my father died in his small rented flat in 1980, Mum sold the house with the huge windows and went to live in a little house in a retirement village where, she told me firmly, she spent 'some of the happiest days of my life'. She came to visit her overseas children, just as Dad had, and after seeing me carry a bag of washing to a London laundrette *insisted* on obtaining a washer-dryer for me, though I *insisted* I didn't want or need one.

And finally — narrative, plot or simply irony — Mum started for the first time in her life to keep a diary. Mostly about medical matters and meeting friends for afternoon tea. But also about the only woman in Lenin's revolutionary cabinet, Alexandra Kollontai, the woman who first said 'the personal is political'. My brother Andrew and my mother both lent me money when I set up, in London, the first production of the one-woman play I had written about her. I was therefore able to pay everyone who worked on the show, long before I was later invited to perform the play in other countries and we got paid for our work — and I could pay Mum and Andrew back.

And during what turned out to be my last phone call to Mum, my partner in London told her he had just seen me kissing the aforementioned washer-dryer because outside it was raining so hard, and Mum laughed.

But right up until she died in 1989 my mother and I never spoke of — the past.

THURSDAY 20 SEPTEMBER 1962

Trying to pack and trying to prepare my script for 'Hey Boy!' The voice of a ten-year-old Maori boy, how mad, my last New Zealand employment.

Memories – and suitcases – everywhere. Saw Bill one more time. We drove down to the wharf and watched the lights out there. But there isn't anything to say and at last I just – cried. Which I haven't done at all; he put his arms around me and held me gently till I stopped. That was real kindness. Neither of us had anything to say at all. God, I'm so pathetic, I should be excited; my tears are all about need and insecurity and fear of the future and being in Wellington listening to the old clock and not knowing what to say to Mum, and Dad mowing the lawn.

Bill spoke a lot of Maori as he went – only parts of which I understood. Sort of to himself, he was still sort of chanting as he left.

And I suppose – maybe I wont hear the Maori language any more when I go . . .

SUNDAY 23 SEPTEMBER 1962

12.30am. Everything still fantastically unorganised so I hardly ever go to bed. Mostly it's difficult because I have to move everything out of this flat and have nowhere really to come back to. Surrounded by suitcases and a big wooden tea-chest and a rubbish bin.

TUESDAY 25 SEPTEMBER 1962

Midday. How good to sit down and find some peace to write just for a moment. Fancy finding it here in a Dentist's waiting room! It's been so odd, these last days, writing again like I used to – everything is just one large panic, cases everywhere, and the tea-chest, all have to be down on the wharf this afternoon and aren't, clothes, books, diaries. And the heart.

WEDNESDAY 26 SEPTEMBER 1962

The ship's departure was delayed but I was still one of the very last passengers on board – the gangway had been taken down, I was late because we had one last party and sang. I went up the crew's gangway.

From the deck, I saw huge ropes being thrown up from the wharves, felt the engine throbbing through the deck-planks.

As the big ship slowly moved away into the night 'Now Is the Hour' faded, faces blurred in the lights on the wharf, arms still raised in farewell. The hundreds of coloured paper streamers, still attaching for a moment, grew taut. Then the streamers broke.

And then they fluttered downwards, and the dark distance widened.

ACKNOWLEDGEMENTS

THANK YOU TO EVERYONE at Massey University Press who has been involved with the publication of this book.

One Minute Crying Time could not have been written without the involvement of a number of people who appear in its pages — named or un-named — and I am very grateful to them for discussions and memories.

Nor could it have been written without some of the extraordinary New Zealand women who are involved in publishing, most of whom I have been lucky enough to work with over the years since I began writing professionally. They have, in their different ways, advised, criticised, encouraged, admonished and supported me during the writing of this book — through sometimes very difficult times. To Robyn Bargh, Karen Ferns, Nicola Hill, Nicola Legat, Joan Mackenzie and Bridget Williams — although only I am responsible for the final telling of this story, thank you. I know how lucky I am.

I have also been greatly helped to check facts and photos — and memories — by Nick Bollinger, Anna Bowbyes, Warren Butterworth, Murray Edmond, Virginia Edmond, Martin Edmond, Mira and Neil Forrest, Aroha Harris, Anthony Hewlett, Julie Hill, Robin Marlar, Jane Parkin and Gary Wilson.

And, as always, my thanks to my agent Mic Cheetham, and to the computing experts Ben Campbell, Dick Drinkrow and Tim Maki, who have always answered with patience my panicked SOS calls for emergency technical advice.

ABOUT THE AUTHOR

BARBARA EWING is a New Zealand-born actress, novelist and playwright. She completed a BA in New Zealand, majoring in English and Māori, and worked in the Department of Maori Affairs and as a Maori Vocational Guidance Officer. She went to London on a government-awarded bursary and was accepted into the Royal Academy of Dramatic Art. After graduating with the 1965 Gold Medal she went on to become a well-known television, film and stage actress. She has also written nine successful novels, and has been published in twelve languages. She regularly returns home to New Zealand.

MASSEY
UNIVERSITY
PRESS

First published in 2020 by Massey University Press
Private Bag 102904, North Shore Mail Centre
Auckland 0745, New Zealand
www.masseypress.ac.nz

Design by Kate Barraclough
Cover illustration: *Dahlias in Jar* by Pamela Wolfe, reproduced courtesy of the artist and ARTIS Gallery

The following extracts have been reproduced with permission:
Pages 13–14, 50: Kazuo Ishiguro, *My Twentieth Century Evening and Other Small Breakthroughs*, published by Faber & Faber, 2017
Page 15: Ruth Dallas, 'Photographs of Pioneer Women', from *Country Road and Other Poems 1947–52*, published by Caxton Press, 1953
Page 83: Allen Curnow, 'Wild Iron', from *Allen Curnow: Collected Poems*, published by Auckland University Press, 2017. Copyright Tim Curnow
Pages 235, 295: T.S. Eliot, *Four Quartets*, published by Faber & Faber, 1943

A catalogue record for this book is available from the National Library of New Zealand

Printed and bound in China by Everbest Investment Ltd

ISBN: 978-0-9951229-5-6
eISBN: 978-0-9951095-0-6